ACE YOUR MIDTERMS & FINALS

PRINCIPLES OF ECONOMICS

Other books in the Ace Your Midterms and Finals Series include:

Ace Your Midterms and Finals: Introduction to Psychology

Ace Your Midterms and Finals: U.S. History

Ace Your Midterms and Finals: Fundamentals of Mathematics

Ace Your Midterms and Finals: Introduction to Physics

Ace Your Midterms and Finals: Introduction to Biology

ACE YOUR MIDTERMS & FINALS

PRINCIPLES OF ECONOMICS

ALAN AXELROD, PH.D.

McGraw-Hill

New York   San Francisco   Washington, D.C.   Auckland   Bogotá
Caracas   Lisbon   London   Madrid   Mexico City   Milan
Montreal   New Delhi   San Juan   Singapore
Sydney   Tokyo   Toronto

Library of Congress Cataloging-in-Publication Data

Axelrod, Alan
    Ace your midterms and finals: principles of economics / Alan
Axelrod.
       p.   cm. — (Ace your midterms and finals series)
    Includes bibliographical references and index.
    ISBN 0-07-007006-7
    1. Economics—Examinations—Study guides. 2. Economics—
Examinations, questions, etc. I. Title. II. Series.
HB74.6.A94 1999
330'.076—dc21
                                           99-17542
                                             CIP

McGraw-Hill

A Division of The McGraw·Hill Companies

1 2 3 4 5 6 7 8 9 0 DOC/DOC 9 0 4 3 2 1 0 9

ISBN 0-07-007006-7

*The sponsoring editor for this book was Barbara Gilson, the editing
supervisor was Paul R. Sobel, and the production supervisor was
Modestine Cameron. It was set in Minion by Carol Norton for The Ian
Samuel Group, Inc.*

Printed and bound by R. R. Donnelley & Sons Company.

McGraw-Hill books are available at special quantity discounts to use
as premiums and sales promotions, or for use in corporate training
sessions. For more information, please write to the Director of Special
Sales, McGraw-Hill, 11 West 19th Street, New York, NY 10011. Or
contact your local bookstore.

 This book is printed on recycled, acid-free paper containing
a minimum of 50% recycled, de-inked fiber.

CONTENTS

CONTENTS

HOW TO USE THIS BOOK

YOU KNOW THE DRILL. ON THE FIRST DAY IN A SURVEY, INTRODUCTORY OR "CORE" course, the professor talks about grading and, saying something about the value of the course in a program of "liberal education," declares that what he or she wants from her students is original thought and creativity and, above all, he or she does not "teach for" the midterm and final.

Nevertheless, the course certainly *includes* one or two midterms and a final, and these account for a very large part of the course grade. Maybe the professor can with a straight face disclaim *teaching for* these exams, but few students would deny *learning for* them.

True, you know that the purpose of an introductory course is to gain a useful familiarity with a certain field, not just to prepare for and do well on two or three exams. Yet the exams *are* a big part of the course, and, whatever you learn or fail to learn in the course, your performance as a whole is judged in large measure by your performance on these exams.

So the cold truth is this: More than anything else, curriculum core courses *are* focused on the midterm and final exams.

Now, traditional study guides are outlines that attempt a bird's-eye view of a given course. But *Ace Your Midterms and Finals: Principles of Economics* breaks with this tradition by viewing course content through the magnifying lens of ultimate accountability: the course exams. The heart and soul of this book consists of eleven midterms and chapters containing finals prepared by *real* instructors, teaching assistants, and professors for *real* students in *real* schools.

Where did we get these exams? Straight from the professors and instructors themselves.

◆ All exams are real and have been used in real courses.

◆ All exams include critical "how-to" tips and advice from the creators and graders of the exams.

◆ All exams include actual answers.

Let's talk about those answers for a minute. In most cases, the answers are actual student responses to the exam. In some cases, however, the instructors and professors have created "model" or "ideal" answers. Usually, the answers included are A-level responses. Sometimes, however, they are not perfect (because they are real). In all cases, you'll find full commentary by the instructors, who point out what works (and why) and what could use improvement (and why—as well as how to improve it).

This book also contains more than the exams themselves.

◆ In Part One, "Preparing Yourself," you'll find how-to guidance on what economics professors look for, how to think like an economist, how to study more effectively, and how to gain the performance edge when you take an exam.

◆ Part Two, "Study Guide," presents a quick-and-easy overview of the content of typical surveys of microeconomics and macroeconomics. It clues you in on what to expect in these courses.

◆ Part Three, "Midterms and Finals," give the exams themselves, grouped by college or university.

◆ In Part Four, "For Your Reference," you'll find a handy glossary of key terms in economics and a brief list of recommended reading.

What This Book *Is Not*

Ace Your Midterms and Finals: Principles of Economics offers a lot of help to see you through to success in this important course. But (as you'll discover when you read Part One) the book *cannot* take the place of

◆ Doing the assigned reading

◆ Keeping up with your work and study

◆ Attending class

◆ Taking good lecture notes

◆ Thinking about and discussing the topics and issues raised in class and in your books

Ace Your Midterms and Finals: Principles of Economics is not a substitute for the course itself!

What This Book *Is*

Look, it's both cynical and silly to invest your time, brainpower, and money in a college course just so that you can ace a couple of exams. If you get A's on the midterm and final, but you come away from the course having learned nothing, you've failed.

We don't want you to be cynical or silly. The purpose of introductory, survey, or "core" courses is to give you a panoramic view of the knowledge landscape of a particular field. The primary goal of the college experience is for you to acquire more than tunnel intelligence. It is to enable you to approach whatever field or profession or work you decide to specialize in from the richest, broadest perspective possible. College is education, not just vocational training.

We don't want you to "study for the exam." The idea is to study for "the rest of your life." You are buying knowledge with your time, your brains, and your money. It's an expensive and valuable commodity. Don't leave it behind you in the classroom at the end of the semester. Take it with you.

But even the starriest-eyed idealist can't deny that midterms and finals are a big part of intro courses and that even if your ambitions lie well beyond these exams (which they should!), performing well on them is necessary if you are to realize those loftier ambitions.

Don't, however, think of midterms and finals as hurdles—obstacles— that you must clear in order to realize your ambitions and attain your goals. The exams are there. They're real. They're facts of college life. You might as well make the most of them.

Use the exams to help you focus your study more effectively.

Most people make the mistake of confusing *goals* with objectives. Goals are the big targets, the ultimate prizes in life. Objectives are the smaller, intermediate steps that have to be taken to reach those goals.

Success on midterms and finals is an objective. It is an important, sometimes intimidating, but really quite doable step toward achieving your goals. Studying for—working toward—the midterm or final is *not* a bad thing, as long as you keep in mind the difference between objectives and goals. In fact, fixing your eye on the upcoming exam will help you to study more effectively. It gives you a more urgent purpose. It also gives you something specific to set your sights on.

And this book will help you study for your exams more effectively. By letting you see how knowledge may be applied—immediately and directly—to exams, it will help you acquire that knowledge more quickly, thoroughly, and certainly. Studying these exams will help you to focus your study in order to achieve success on the exams—that is, to help you attain the objectives that build toward your goals.

—*Alan Axelrod*

CONTRIBUTORS

William P. Albrecht, *Professor of Economics, University of Iowa (Chap. 25)*

David Augustin, *Instructor in Economics, Loyola University of Chicago (Chap. 27)*

Scott William Fausti, *Associate Professor of Economics, South Dakota State University (Chap. 29)*

Robert M. Feinberg, *Professor of Economics, American University (Chap. 19)*

Constantin Ogloblin, *Teaching Fellow in Economics, Kent State University (Chap. 26)*

Charles F. Revier, *Associate Professor of Economics, Colorado State University (Chap. 22)*

Esther-Mirjam Sent, *Assistant Professor of Economics, University of Notre Dame (Chap. 28)*

Yesim Subasim, *Graduate Teaching Assistant in Economics, Clemson University (Chap. 21)*

Beck Taylor, *Assistant Professor of Economics, Baylor University (Chap. 20)*

William E. Whitesell, *Mary B. and Henry P. Stager Professor of Economics, Franklin and Marshall College (Chap. 23)*

Willard E. Witte, *Associate Professor of Economics, Indiana University (Chap. 24)*

ABOUT THE AUTHOR

Alan Axelrod, Ph.D., is the author of many books, including *Booklist* Editor's Choice *Art of the Golden West, The Penguin Dictionary of American Folklore,* and *The Macmillan Dictionary of Military Biography.* He lives in Atlanta, Georgia.

PART ONE

PREPARING YOURSELF

CHAPTER 1

PRINCIPLES OF ECONOMICS: WHAT THE PROFESSORS LOOK FOR

ECONOMICS HAS BEEN CALLED THE "DISMAL SCIENCE." THE ORIGIN OF THIS UNWELcome nickname is the grim, hard, "dismal" nature of the realities with which economics grapples, beginning with the notion of scarcity as the basic condition of human existence. However, a significant number of students find economics a dismal science for other reasons.

They hate it. And they dread it.

They take only whatever econ courses are necessary to satisfy a core requirement or the requirements of a business or other major. They take the courses like so many bitter pills.

> My primary objectives in teaching introductory microeconomics are to get students to understand some key concepts of microeconomics at the intuitive level, to appreciate the application of microeconomics to real problems, and to gain an understanding of the way in which economists think about the world.
>
> —Robert M. Feinberg, professor, American University

Let's face it. Economics *is* a demanding discipline. For many students, the course work does not, in fact, come easily. But why should this be so? After all, for the most part, economics deals with familiar things, issues and activities that affect our lives every day, that affect our individual welfare, that affect our individual prospects for future wealth, and that affect our collective welfare and prospects as a nation. We're *all* interested in these issues. (Doubtless one of the reasons you and your family have chosen to allocate some portion of your "scarce resources" to a college education is precisely to maximize prospects for future wealth.)

So why do so many students face econ courses with trepidation at best and quaking dread at worst?

There are at least three reasons.

1. **Economics is an eclectic discipline.** This means that it draws on many skills and many allied disciplines. It borrows from history, from politics, from public policy, from international affairs, from mathematics, from statistics, from psychology, and from the sciences and social sciences generally. It also persistently straddles the "academic world" of theories and abstract concepts and the "real world" of business, banking, and government. Just when you finally get comfortable manipulating the algebraic of some economic concept, you are asked to understand the impact of the Sherman Act or how commercial paper functions as a money instrument or how deregulation of the long-distance telephone carriers has affected the communications industry.

2. **Economics is a cumulatively rigorous discipline.** That is, its principles, assumptions, and procedures interlock and depend on one another. If your attention lapses or you fail to make the effort to grasp concept A fully, your understanding of concept B will then be flawed, and by the time you get to concept C, you'll probably be lost. Economics is a discipline that is difficult or impossible to "pick up in the middle." You've got to be present at the start and highly attentive at each step of the way.

3. **Economics requires a willingness to think in economic terms.** What trips up many beginning economics students is the very fact that this discipline engages the real world—*their* world. So many of the fundamental assumptions of economics seem to grow from or even duplicate common sense, that it is all too easy to fall back on common sense. Yet as soon as you stop questioning commonsense assumptions, as soon as you take them for granted, you will find your path diverging sharply from that of the economist. Studying economics does not require you to abandon your intuitive understanding of the world and your commonsense notions about how individual, national, and world economies work, but it does require you to *question* these assumptions and not take them for granted. Usually, you'll be best off if you understand and accept that economics looks at the real world and attempts to reduce some part of its dynamics to a model, a simplification. Once you accept this modeling approach, you can work *within* the model, deriving your assumptions and conclusions from how the model works, rather than from what you may believe about the "real world."

> I have observed that economics is a hard subject for most students. Generally, interpreting the graphs—of which there are many in this course—is a big problem. I advise students to attend lectures and participate in class discussions. The best time to learn is *in the classroom*. It is unlikely that a student who has not understood in class will go home, read the book or go over notes, and then clearly understand the subject. It is in the best interest of the student to read the assigned chapters from the book before coming to the lecture. Never be ashamed to ask questions in the classroom."
>
> —Yesim Subasim, graduate teaching assistant, Clemson University

But it is also a mistake to focus exclusively on models and numbers and graphs and formulas. Remember that the purpose of all of this modeling is, ultimately, to explain some aspect of the economy. Through such explanations, you can more

The methods of economic inquiry are perhaps best described as "eclectic," meaning that they are drawn from many sources and selected according to their usefulness to the subject matter. Economists borrow from all the social sciences in order to theorize about human behavior. They borrow from mathematics in order to express theories concisely. And, finally, they borrow from statistics in order to make inferences from real-world data about hypotheses suggested by economic theory.

Economists are interested in understanding human behavior not only for its own sake, but also because of the policy implications of this knowledge. How can we know what to expect from changes resulting from public policy or business decisions unless we understand why people behave the way they do?

As in other scientific disciplines, theory in economics is an abstraction, or simplification, of innumerable complex relationships in the real world. When thinking about some aspects of behavior, economists will build a model that attempts to explain the behavior under examination. The elements of the model are derived from economic theory. Economists study the model to see what hypotheses, or predictions, are suggested by the model. These can then be checked against real-world data.

Economists clearly believe that they can make a significant contribution to the discussion and resolution of many important social issues. It is hoped that by the time you finish this course, you will agree with this belief."

—Esther-Mirjam Sent, assistant professor, University of Notre Dame

effectively manage your financial life, and you can more effectively participate in the management of a business or a government. Economics can indeed seem dead and dismal if you lose sight of its intimate and direct connection with issues of individual and collective wealth and well-being. It is one thing to look at curves plotted on a graph and point to a "recessionary gap," but quite another to see that the recessionary gap means lost jobs, and that if the gap becomes sufficiently large, it may mean a depression, which may perhaps lead to profound and enduring privation, suffering, revolution, and war. This is the way the world works and has worked throughout history. Economics seeks to understand the dynamics behind the forces that both sustain our well-being and threaten it.

People who work with numbers, statistics, and numerically based correlations are typically written off as bean counters, drudges without imagination—individuals who would feel quite at home in a dismal science. The fact is that possessing and developing a strong imagination is of great value in studying economics. Working with models requires imagination. Questioning and inquiring into basic economic processes, which most of us take for granted, likewise requires a combination of lively curiosity and active imagination. Connecting what the models tell you with the processes at work in the real world calls for an ample imagination.

Perhaps the economic habit of thought that requires the most imagination is learning to see any individual economic fact or any particular economic transaction as part of a dynamic system rather than an isolated event. As the economist looks at the world, nothing occurs in a vacuum. A change in one "variable" results from a change in another and has an impact on that variable and any number of other variables. Economics attempts to describe *systems*, not just isolated events, yet it also tries to show how the workings of an entire system are embodied in any particular event. Income, for example, is not just something a worker gets for doing a job. It is a function of production, and it also represents the potential to consume, which, in turn, represents the potential for income. Most economic concepts are systematic and circular, with actions, reactions, and feedback all to be accounted for. Imagination will not only help you to see this "big picture," even as you struggle with a particular concept, graph, or equation, but also enable you to transform the models of economics into ideas of considerable elegance and even beauty.

Imagination applied to what you learn in the classroom and from your texts will also allow you to apply your growing understanding of the economic view of reality to your daily reality. This ranges from deciding how to allocate your "scarce resources" over the next week or month or semester to interpreting what you read or hear of the daily news. It will help you to make informed choices as a consumer, and also as a citizen and a voter.

Helpful Habits

Don't hang up your imagination at the classroom door. It will certainly make your introduction to economics easier, more meaningful, and more fun. But if economics doesn't have to be a *dismal* science, well, it's not all fun and games, either. Studying economics does require memorizing certain concepts and principles.

◆ You'll need to become familiar and comfortable with certain fundamental relationships expressed as equations and graphs.

◆ You'll need to ensure that you understand each step before moving onto the next. This can be difficult. The temptation to skip over hard material is a natural temptation, but if you yield to it, you will inevitably get lost. Failure to understand is cumulative. "A chain is only as strong as its weakest link," goes the old saying. It is up to you to ensure that each link in your understanding of economics is as strong as you can make it before moving on to the next.

◆ You'll need to take in and commit to memory a substantial new vocabulary.

> Success in the course requires reading the textbook carefully *before* lectures, with pencil in hand to sketch the key relationships discussed. The student should use all homework assignments and Study Guide problems as opportunities to practice *using* and *applying* the analytical apparatus to understand real-world phenomena. It is also important to attend class and participate actively in all lectures and class discussions.
> —Charles F. Revier, associate professor, Colorado State University

This last point is critical. Economists use a special, precisely defined vocabulary, so that economics is rife with specialized jargon. Not only do you need to acquire and understand this vocabulary, so that you become comfortable with interpreting it and using it yourself, you need to avoid the many pitfalls presented by the fact that this specialized vocabulary often resembles everyday speech, but that, more often than not, such resemblances are misleading. For example, we all know what *income* is, right? It's the salary you get paid for doing a job. It's the money you get for selling something you own. And so on. As used by economists, however, *income* may be defined simply as the highest level of sustainable consumption. Or take the phrase *marginal benefit*. Hearing this in casual conversation, you might conclude that the subject under discussion is some slight or unimportant advantage derived from some activity. To an economist, however, *marginal benefit* is the increase in total benefit created by the addition of one more unit of input or output.

> You need to learn to think about the issues raised using the framework of economics, not your common sense, or your own personal opinions.
> You must work at learning this material. It isn't enough to simply read through the notes and textbook. You need to be able to apply the material.
> —Willard E. Witte, associate professor, Indiana University

And so it goes. Acquire the habit of learning the specialized vocabulary of economics and distinguishing that vocabulary from everyday speech. Be certain to use the terms you learn and use them appropriately.

Beyond Brute Memory

Beyond this affirmation of the importance of learning concepts and memorizing basic equations, graphs, and terms, be aware that most economics instructors take pains to advise that memorization, necessary as it is, is much less important than applying original thought to an understanding of the relationships among the various principles, equations, graphs, and terms you learn.

The study of economics, then, is not primarily a matter of memory—though memory is important—it is a matter of analysis and critical thinking.

Analysis requires gathering and examining the facts of a particular economic issue and drawing conclusions about the relationships among the facts, especially cause-and-effect relationships. Economics instructors generally expect you attain two broad goals:

1. To master a body of economic knowledge—the fundamental concepts, equations, graphs, and terms
2. To analyze the relationships among these elements, to apply them to specific situations, and to draw conclusions about the *significance* of the operation of these elements

Reaching the first goal requires reading assigned texts and attending classes and lectures. Reaching the second goal requires the following:

1. Developing critical reading and listening skills
2. Developing analytical thinking skills
3. Developing discussion and oral presentation skills
4. Developing problem-solving skills
5. Developing analytical writing skills

You can see from this list that while your professor certainly expects you to read assigned material and to pay attention in class, she or he expects even more that you will not simply "absorb" material, but will develop at least five important skills. That economics requires more than hitting the books and taking lecture notes comes as a shock to some students. They *expect* to be required to develop special skills in art classes, say, or in physical education and sports electives. But in economics? "This isn't even my major!"

Well, take a good look at that list of skills. You should be pleased

I state the objective of the course in my syllabus: 'Economics is the science of allocation of scarce resources among unlimited wants. Our objective in this course is to learn to think in a manner consistent with the existence of scarcity.' Further, my own objective is to teach the students an understanding of the decision-making process of the economic agents in the economy: the individual buyer, the individual seller, and the government.

"A student who has taken this course will have an idea about the economic environment around him or her. He or she will be able to apply the material of this course to the real world. I believe that economics is a way of looking at and thinking about life—and it is an efficient way of doing so; therefore, by taking this course, students will acquire a way of thinking that will be useful in their business and personal lives."

—Yesim Subasim, graduate teaching assistant, Clemson University

Students should develop an ability to apply the mainstream macroeconomic models to understand the causes, consequences, and cures for unemployment, inflation, slow growth, and exchange rate fluctuations; to assess the likely impact of government policy actions on macroeconomic performance; and to predict the consequences of various disturbances. In general, they should work toward an appreciation of and a facility with the economic way of thinking."

—Charles F. Revier, associate professor, Colorado State University that an introductory economics course presents an opportunity to do much more than memorize facts and figures. Success in the course requires developing and honing that list of skills—and the application of these skills is hardly limited to the academic study of economics. Regardless of your educational and vocational plans, how could you fail to benefit from an ability to see issues clearly and reduce them to essential elements (problem-solving skills)? a facility for understanding and evaluating information (critical reading and listening skills)? an ability to do something productive with information gathered analytical thinking skills)? and to present information clearly, persuasively, and effectively (discussion and oral presentation skills and analytical writing skills)?

In short, most of what your econ professor expects from you involves developing the skills of a good student—not a passive absorber of information, but an active, thinking *student* of information. These skills will help you in all your course work and, even more important, are essential to any reasonably high-level job in the "real world" beyond college.

> "I try to encourage my students to think 'outside the box,' to look at their own lives and the decisions they make in the context of the basic economic principles I teach them, and to analyze issues and events occurring at the local, state, national, and global level. I want them to see the importance of identifying the economic forces that produce the issues and events that affect them, and then to think about the consequences of these events for their own lives and how they should adjust their behavior or plans, given a particular change in the economic environment around them."
>
> —Scott William Fausti, associate professor, South Dakota State University

Matters of Opinion

Engaged actively, critically, and analytically, the facts of economics really do come to life for the simple reason that they are seen as real, as issues that affect our lives and shape the destiny of our nation, our world, and ourselves. That's great news for the beginning economics student. However, economics courses do present certain pitfalls.

The most common trap into which students fall is mistaking opinion for analysis. You will find your professor or discussion section-leader repeatedly asking you "what you think" about a certain current event or set of data. By all means, respond. And however you have formed your opinion, you are certainly entitled to it.

But will expressing that opinion earn you points in a university economics class?

Probably not—unless you transform that opinion into *analysis*. This requires supporting your opinion with principles and assumptions learned in class or from your reading.

Many students in discussion sections of introductory economics courses become frustrated because the instructor repeatedly asks, "What do you think?" only to shoot down an opinion because it lacks supporting facts, principles, or evidence. You can avoid this frustration by understanding that when you are asked "what you think," you

> My primary aim in this course is to help students attain a basic understanding of the 'economic way of thinking,' improve their ability to reason and think critically, and critically dissect economic information presented in the popular media. The course requires students to develop high-level synthesis skills, which enable them to take concepts and definitions and apply them to solve unfamiliar problems. They must also learn the language of economics and be able to use theoretical models to explain real world observations.
>
> I advise students to attend class regularly, read the text before the lecture, complete homework in a timely and conscientious way, and spend approximately ten hours per week studying economics, including class time.
>
> —Beck Taylor, assistant professor, Baylor University

You must learn (memorize) certain basic relationships (for example, those relating to the National Income and Product Accounts), but you also need to understand the logic of these relationships.

—Willard E. Witte, associate professor, Indiana University

How should you study economics? Not! Instead, you should practice. Active learning is the only way to learn the material. Do not waste valuable hours trying to remember masses of material. Do not become overwhelmed by the details. Instead, concentrate on the overall structure. The text has literally thousands of important details but only a dozen or so major themes.

Esther-Mirjam Sent, assistant professor, University of Notre Dame

Instructors in disciplines that make extensive use of numerical and graphical expressions—math, chemistry, economics, and the like—advise students to translate such expressions into words: to *read* equations and graphs. Not only is this an effective means of fully understanding the meaning of a mathematical or graphical expression, it is also an effective way of communicating that meaning to others—and, in a class paper or essay-exam response, an effective way of communicating to your instructor that you fully understand the expression at issue.

are being asked for an interpretation of fact rather than a mere opinion. Interpretation of fact involves developing the skills listed a moment ago.

Let's consider those skills briefly.

Perhaps you've seen one of those demonstrations that are common in psych courses, pre-law classes, or introductory criminal justice courses. The instructor is lecturing as usual at the front of the class. Suddenly, someone rushes into the classroom, does and says something outrageous, then promptly exits. After the tumult dies down, the professor turns to the class and asks the students to jot down answers to a set of questions about what they have just witnessed: What was the intruder wearing? What was the intruder's gender? How tall? Fat? Thin? What, exactly, did the intruder say? And so on. Invariably, these witnesses will return an array of different and often contradictory answers to these questions. If there are thirty witnesses, there are bound to be thirty quite distinct responses. One person will express certainty that the intruder was a man. Another says that she was a woman—dressed in a red sweater. No, says another, it was a pink blouse. Actually, it was a bright red scarf with a white shirt. And so on.

Turn on the television, open a newspaper, or talk to a friend, and you will be exposed to a variety of statements about the economy. Doubtless, you'll find great variation among perspectives. Your instructor will expect you to develop some skill in evaluating these perspectives critically. Know your sources and consider their motives, motivations, and level of information. Your instructor expects you to question what you read and hear, not to take it at face value.

We've all had the discouraging experience of plowing through a book, reading every word, closing the cover, and then realizing that we have comprehended absolutely none of it. Finishing all reading assignments in a timely manner is important, but doing so is of little value if you fail to think about what you've read.

Now, the phrase "think about" is pretty vague and abstract. Let's be more specific about what you should do with what you've read. Connect one fact, one event, one principle, one mathematical or graphical expression to another. Maybe you know the definition of supply and demand. But just what does this fundamental economic relationship imply in a particular problem under consideration?

Reading and listening critically and thinking analytically are important skills, but they're pretty lonely. The products of critical analysis are intended to be shared. Besides, until you communicate your observations, thoughts, and conclusions, your instructor has no way to evaluate your performance and progress in the course. For this reason, your instructor expects you to develop skills in discussing issues and presenting arguments.

Class discussion is a balancing act. It is, unfortunately, the rare class or discussion section in which all students participate. Typically, the majority hang back and take notes while the instructor chats with a vocal minority. Your instructor expects you to participate in class discussion. Usually, the more you participate, the better. But let's pay attention to the word *usually*. It's all too easy to fall in love with the sound of your own voice. Don't monopolize the discussion. Listen to the interpretations of others. Also, practice courtesy. Don't patronize, mock, or put anyone down for a remark that is made. Learn to focus your arguments on other arguments, not on personalities. Instead of saying, "Joe, you're just wrong about the New Deal," ask a question about the subject: "Well, Joe, what about the cost of the New Deal programs?" The object of class discussion is not to win an argument, but to explore all sides of an issue. Keep the issues in the foreground, and keep personalities out of the picture completely.

As for solving problems and exercises in economics, do not be satisfied with memorizing rote solutions and merely going through the motions of getting to the answer. Your objective should be less to *arrive* at an answer than to understand the *process* of arriving at that answer. Without an understanding of the process, the answer has little significance. Problem solving is more a skill than a set of acquired abstract rules. As with any skill, the most effective way of acquiring facility with problem solving is to practice.

◆ Work any practice problems you are given.

◆ Work the problems in your textbook or workbook.

◆ Make up problems of your own.

This last activity is especially useful for really digging into the workings of the process at the heart of any problem.

You expect to be required to work numerically based problems in an econ course, but you may be surprised (perhaps unpleasantly) to find essays as part of the course work and essay questions on midterm and final exams. A growing number of introductory economics courses include essays, perhaps in the form of class papers or in the form of examinations.

Now, writing comes hard for many students, and the very phrase

> Primary course objectives are to help students learn the key principles of microeconomics, develop the economic way of thinking, and apply the power of economic analysis to real-world situations in order to be able to reach informed conclusions and make decisions.
>
> The student should try to understand key concepts rather than memorize definitions, focus on learning how to use the tools of economic analysis, and make sure he or she can read and understand graphs, which help to visualize many important economic relationships. Moreover, the student should do as many end-of-chapter and study-guide problems as possible. The proverb "Practice makes perfect" is very true regarding studying economics.
>
> —Constantin Ogloblin, teaching fellow, Kent State University

> You need to understand that many terms are used in economics in specific ways that differ from their vernacular use. You must pay careful attention to the definition of the terms used.
>
> —Willard E. Witte, associate professor, Indiana University

> True/false exam answers are graded for all steps in the reasoning process to stress understanding instead of memorization. Essay questions encourage students to apply economic models. Don't fall behind; don't memorize; apply the learned material whenever possible; focus on intuition and reasoning.
>
> —Esther-Mirjam Sent, assistant professor, University of Notre Dame

> I am most interested in having students develop the capability to approach questions from an economic point of view; for example, thinking in terms of opportunity cost, cost vs. benefits, and cause and effect (within a systematic framework). I am less interested in a demonstration of knowledge of specific details.
>
> —Willard E. Witte, associate professor, Indiana University

"analytical writing"—which is what an economics professor expects from you—can be intimidating. Good analytical writing requires thorough familiarity with your subject, a willingness to find and use the right words, and an ability to organize your ideas. These three elements require dedication and hard work; however, there are some shortcuts you should take advantage of.

First, when you are responding to essay questions in an exam or other assignment, look at the question carefully. What exactly does it ask? Is it made up of a number of component questions (subquestions)? In what order do these occur? Look at the question, and try to use it to structure your essay response. That is, if the question asks you to discuss points 1, 2, 3, and 4, structure your essay in that order. If it asks for 2, 4, 3, and 1, try to respond accordingly, answering 2, 4, 3, and 1 rather than 1, 2, 3, and 4.

Next, be sure your response uses the appropriate terms appropriately.

Finally, most economics essays and essay-exam responses combine narrative explanation with illustration in the form of equations or graphs. Coordinate these elements closely. Be certain your equation or graph illustrates what you say, and use what you say to interpret the equation or graph.

> "For a class of twenty-five honors students, the course objectives are that, by the end of the term, students will be able to:
>
> a. Explain the causes of the key macroeconomic concerns—unemployment, inflation, economic growth, and exchange rate fluctuations—and assess their consequences for society.
>
> b. Understand both the prospects for and the limitations of government macroeconomic policy.
>
> c. Conduct their own analyses of the likely effects of specific macroeconomic disturbances or policy actions.
>
> d. Watch the macroeconomic news items in the media with both greater interest and greater understanding.
>
> e. Follow both current and future political debates over economic policy with an ability to separate the sense from the nonsense, and to vote accordingly.
>
> Examination questions are intended specifically to test the ability to apply macroeconomic models for the purposes described above.
>
> —Charles F. Revier, associate professor, Colorado State University

The Challenge

The study of economics is challenging, and, make no mistake, you are expected to master a good many facts and concepts, but, even more important, you are also expected to make those facts and concepts sufficiently your own so that you can apply them to real-world economic issues.

How do you make complex facts and concepts "your own"?

Many people read themselves to sleep at night. Curl up with a good book, read a few pages, nod off. Well, reading is one of life's great pleasures, and it can be most soothing. The object of reading your economics texts and reviewing your lecture notes, however, is not sleep. Get out of the habit of reading passively, of the soothing (all *too* soothing) habit of merely taking in words. Instead, learn to read aggressively. Take notes. Underline important passages. Work problems for yourself, and summarize each chapter in your own words.

In your own words. That's important. One of the most effective ways of learning is to rephrase material in your own words. Take the words in, then revolve them in your mind and imagination, so that you can express them in language that you are comfortable with and that is meaningful to you.

Does all this sound a bit overwhelming?

Well, there is an upside to an introductory economics course, too. While the study of economics calls for many skills, the subject also appeals to interests that come naturally to you.

Whatever else economics consists of, it speaks directly to your present and future wealth and welfare, to the many economic choices you must make, ranging from how to finance a car to how to choose a career to what political candidates you should support. Ultimately, your understanding of economics may mean the difference between your being involved in a business that falters or one that succeeds. While you develop the challenging skills the study of economics requires, be sure not to let go of the real-world urgency and excitement of what the field is really all about.

> Even if you are taking this course just because it's required, try to get interested in economics, study it as though you really want to learn it and to use it in your everyday life, not just to pass the exams; think of this course as an intellectual adventure. Also remember: "Anything worth doing is worth doing well." Aim high and you'll hit the target.
>
> —Constantin Ogloblin, teaching fellow, Kent State University

CHAPTER 2

KEYS TO SUCCESSFUL STUDY

THIS CHAPTER OUTLINES SKILLS THAT ARE INDISPENSABLE TO SUCCESSFUL STUDY, with special emphasis on skills that are important to the study of economics.

But let's not start thinking about economics just yet. Let's just start thinking. After all, isn't that what college and college courses are all about?

Well, not quite. Think about it.

For the ancient Greeks of Plato's day, about 428 to 348 B.C., "higher education" really *was* all about thinking. Through dialogue, back and forth, the teacher and his student *thought* about economics, mathematics, physics, the nature of reality—whatever. Perhaps the teacher evaluated the quality of his student's thought, but there is no evidence that Plato graded exams, let alone assigned the student a final grade for the course.

That was a long time ago. Times have changed.

"Don't Study for the Grade!"

Today, you get graded. All the time, and on everything you do.

Now, most of the professors, instructors, and teaching assistants from whom you take your courses will tell you that the "real value" of the course is its contribution to your "liberal education." A professor may even solemnly protest that she does *not* "teach for" the midterm and final. Nevertheless, the introductory, survey, and core courses almost always *include* at least one midterm and a final, and these almost always account for a very large part of the course grade. Even if the professor can with a straight face disclaim *teaching for* these exams, few students would deny *learning for* them.

The truth is this: More than anything else, most curriculum core courses are focused on the midterm and final exams.

"Grades Aren't Important"

Let's keep thinking.

You and, most likely, your family are investing a great deal of time and cash and sweat in your college education. It would be pretty silly if the payoff of all those resources were a letter grade and a numerical GPA. Ultimately, of course, the payoff is knowledge, a feeling of achievement, an intellectually and spiritually enriched life—*and* preparation for a satisfying and (you probably hope) financially rewarding career.

But the fact is that if you don't perform well on midterms and finals, your path to all these forms of enrichment will be blocked. And the fact *also* is that your performance is measured by grades. Sure, almost any reason you can think of for investing in college is more important than amassing a collection of A's and B's, but those stupid little letters are part of what it takes to get you to those other, far more important goals.

"Don't Study *for* the Exam"

Most professors hate exams and hate grades. They believe that making students pass tests and then evaluating their performance with a number or letter makes the whole process of education seem pretty trivial. Those professors who tell you that they "don't teach for the exam" may also advise you not to "study for the exam." That's not exactly what they mean. They want you to study, but to study in order to learn, not in order to pass the exam.

This is well-meaning advice, and it's true that if you study *for* the exam, intending to ace it, then promptly forget everything you've "learned," you are making a pretty bad mistake. Yet those same professors are part of a system that demands exams and grades, and if you don't study for and *for* the exam, the chances are very good that you won't make the grade and you won't achieve the higher goals that you, your family, *and your professors* want for you.

Lose-Lose or Win-Win? Your Choice

When it comes to studying, especially in your introductory-level courses, you have some choices to make. You can decide that grades are stupid, not study, and perform poorly on the exams. You can try not to study for the exams, concentrating instead on "higher goals," perform poorly on the exams, and never have the opportunity to reach those higher goals. You can study *for* the exams, ace them all, then flush the information from your memory bank, collect your A or B for the course, and move on without having learned a thing. These are all lose-lose scenarios, in which no one—neither you nor your teacher (nor your family, for that matter)—gets what he, she, or they really want.

Or you can go the win-win route.

We've used the words *goal* and *goals* several times. For an army general, winning the war is the goal, but to achieve this goal, he must first accomplish certain *objectives*, such as winning battle number one, number two, number three, and so on. Objectives are intermediate goals or steps toward an ultimate goal.

Now, put exams in perspective. Performing well on an exam need not be an alternative to achieving higher goals. It should be an objective necessary to achieving those higher goals.

The win-win scenario goes like this: Use the fact of the exams as a way of focusing your study for the course. Focus on the exams as immediate objectives, crucial to achieving your ultimate goals. *Do* study for the exam, but not *for* the exam. *Don't* mistake the battle for the war, the objective for the goal; but *do* realize that you must attain the objectives in order to achieve the goal.

And *that*, ladies and gentlemen, is the purpose of this book:

◆ To help you ace the midterm and final exams in introductory-level economics courses . . .

◆ . . . without forgetting everything you learned after you've aced them.

This guide will help you *use* the exams to master the course material. This guide will help you make the grade—and actually learn something in the process.

Focus

How many times have you read a book word for word, finished it, and closed the cover—only to realize that you've learned almost nothing from it? Unfortunately, this is something we all experience. It's not that the material is too difficult or that it's over our heads. It's that we mistake reading for studying.

For many of us, reading is a passive process. We scan page after page, the words go in, and, alas, the words seem to go out. The time, of course, goes by. We've *read* the book, but we've *retained* all too little.

Studying certainly involves reading, but reading and studying aren't one and the same activity. Or we might put it this way: studying is intensely focused reading.

How do you *focus* reading?

Begin by setting objectives. Now, saying that your objective in reading a certain number of chapters in a textbook or reading your lecture notes is to "learn the material" is not very useful. It is an obvious but vague goal rather than a well-defined objective.

Why not let the approaching exam determine your objective?

"I will read and retain the stuff in chapters 10 through 20 because that's what's going to be on the exam, and I want to ace the exam."

Now you at least have an objective. Accomplish this *objective*, and you will be on your way to achieving the *goal* of learning the material.

◆ An *objective* is an immediate target. A *goal* is for the long term.

Concentrate

To move from passive reading to active study requires, first of all, concentration. Setting up objectives (immediate targets) rather than looking toward goals (long-term targets) makes it much easier for you to concentrate. Few of us can (or would) put our personal lives "on hold" for four years of college, several years of graduate school, and X years in the working world in order to concentrate on achieving a *goal*. But just about anyone can discipline himself or herself to set aside distractions for the time it takes to achieve the *objective* of studying for an exam.

Step 1. Find a quiet place to work.

Step 2. Clear your mind. Push everything aside for the few hours each day that you spend studying.

Step 3. Don't daydream—now. Daydreaming, letting your imagination wander, is actually essential to real learning. But right now you have a specific objective to attain. This is not the time for daydreaming.

Step 4. Deal with your worries. Those pressing matters that you can do something about *right now*, take care of. Those you can't do anything about, push aside for now.

Step 5. Don't worry about the exam. Take the exam seriously, but don't fret. Instead of worrying about the prospect of failure, use your time to eliminate failure as an option.

Plan

Let's go back to that general who knows the difference between objectives and goals. Chances are that he or she also knows that you'd better not march off to battle without a plan. Remember, you don't want to *read*. You want to *study*. This requires focusing your work with a plan.

The first item to plan is your time.

Step 1. Dedicate a notebook or organizer-type date book to the purpose of recording your scheduling information.

Step 2. Record the following:
  a. Class times
  b. Assignment due dates

    c. Exam dates

    d. Extracurricular commitments

    e. Study time

Step 3. Inventory your various tasks. What do you have to do today, this week, this month, this semester?

Step 4. Prioritize your tasks. Everybody seems to be grading you. Now's *your* chance to grade the things they give you to do. Label high-priority tasks "A," middle-priority tasks "B," and lower-priority tasks "C." Not only will this help you decide which things to do first, it will also aid you in deciding how much time to allot to each task.

> **TIP:** If you are in doubt about what tasks should be assigned the highest priority, it is generally best to allot the most time to the most complex and difficult tasks and to get these done first.

Step 5. Enter your tasks in your scheduling notebook, putting them in an appropriate order and assigning a duration to each that accords with its priority.

Step 6. Check off items as you complete them.

Step 7. Keep your scheduling book up to date. Reschedule whatever you do not complete.

Step 8. Don't be passive. Actively monitor your progress toward your objectives.

Step 9. Don't be passive. Arrange and rearrange your schedule to get the most time when you need it most.

Packing Your Time

Once you have found as much time as you can, pack it as tightly as you can.

Step 1. Assemble your study materials. Be sure you have all necessary textbooks and notes on hand. If you need access to library reference materials, study in the library. If you need access to reference materials on the Internet, make sure you're at a computer.

Step 2. Eliminate or reduce distractions.

Step 3. Become an efficient reader and note taker.

An Efficient Reader

Step 3 requires further discussion. Let's begin with the way you read.

Nothing has greater impact on the effectiveness of your studying than the speed and comprehension with which you read. If this statement prompts you to throw up your hands and wail, "I'm just not a fast reader," don't despair. You can learn to read faster and more efficiently.

Consider taking a "speed reading" course. Take one that your university offers or endorses. Most of the techniques taught in the major reading programs actually do work. Alternatively, do it yourself.

Step 1. When you sit down to read, try consciously to force your eyes to move across the page faster than normal.

Step 2. Always keep your eyes moving. Don't linger on any word.

Step 3. Take in as many words at a time as possible. Most slow readers aren't slow-witted. They've just been taught to read word by word. Fast and efficient readers, in contrast, have learned to read by taking in groups of words. Practice taking in blocks of words.

Step 4. Build on your skills. Each day, push yourself a little harder. Move your eyes across the page faster. Take in more words with each glance.

Step 5. Resist the strong temptation to fall back into your old habits. Keep pushing.

When you review material, consider skimming rather than reading. Hit the high points, lingering at places that give you trouble and skipping over the stuff you already know cold.

> **TIP:** Are you a—ugh!—*vocalizer*? A vocalizer is a reader who, during "silent" reading, either mouths the words or says them mentally. Vocalizing greatly slows reading, often reduces comprehension, and is just plain tiring. Work to overcome this habit—except when you are trying to memorize some specific piece of information. Many people do find it helpful to say over a sentence or two in order to memorize its content. Just bear in mind that this does not work for more than a sentence or paragraph of material.

An Interactive Reader

Early in this chapter we contrasted passive reading with active studying. A highly effective way to make the leap from passivity to activity is to become an *interactive* reader.

Step 1. Read with a pencil in your hand.

Step 2. Use your pencil to underline key concepts. Do this consistently. (That is, *always* read with a pencil in your hand.) Don't waste your time with a ruler; underscore freehand.

Step 3. Underline *only* the key concepts. If everything seems important to you, then up the ante and underline only the absolutely *most* important passages.

Step 4. If you prefer to highlight material with a transparent marker (a Hi-Liter, for example), fine. But you'll still need a pencil or pen nearby. Carry on a dialogue with your books by writing condensed notes in the margin.

> **TIP:** The physical act of underlining actually helps you memorize material more effectively—though no one is quite sure why. Furthermore, underlining makes skimming for review more efficient and effective.

Step 5. Put difficult concepts into your own words—right in the margin of the book. This is a great aid to understanding and memorization.

Step 6. Link one concept to another. If you read something that makes you think of something else related to it, make a note. The connection is almost certainly a valuable one.

Step 7. Comment on what you read.

TIP: Some students are reluctant to write in their textbooks because it reduces resale value. True enough. But is an extra five dollars at the end of the semester worth it if you don't get the most out of your multi-thousand-dollar and multi-hundred-hour investment in the course?

Taking Notes

The techniques of underlining, highlighting, paraphrasing, linking, and commenting on textbook material can also be applied to your classroom and lecture notes.

Of course, this assumes that you have taken notes. There are some students who claim that it is easier for them to listen to a lecture if they *avoid* taking notes. For a small minority, this may be true; but the vast majority of students find that having taken notes is essential when it comes time to study for midterms and finals. This does not mean that you should be a stenographer or court reporter, taking down each and every word. To the extent that it is possible for you to do so, absorb the lecture in your mind, then jot down major points, preferably in loose outline form.

Become sensitive to the major points of the lecture. Some lecturers will come right out and tell you, "The following three points are key." That's your cue to write them down. Other cues include the following:

TIP: No one can tell you just how much to write, but bear this in mind: Most lecturers read from notes rather than fully composed scripts. Four double-spaced typewritten or word-processed pages (about a thousand words *in note form*) represent sufficient note material for an hour-long lecture. Ideally, you might aim at producing about 75 percent of this word count in the notes you take—perhaps 750 words during an hour-long lecture.

◆ **Repetition.** If the lecturer repeats a point, write it down.

◆ **Excitement.** If the lecturer's voice picks up, if his or her face becomes suddenly animated, if, in other words, it is apparent that the material at this point is of particular interest to the speaker, your pencil should be in motion.

◆ **Verbal cues.** In addition to such verbal elbows in the ribs as "This is important," most lecturers underscore transitions from one topic to another with phrases such as "Moving on to . . ." or "Next, we will . . ." or the like. This is your signal to write a new heading.

◆ **Slowing down.** If the lecturer gives deliberate verbal weight to a word, phrase, or passage, make a note of it.

◆ **Visual aids.** If the lecturer writes something on a blackboard or overhead projector or in a computer-generated presentation, make a note.

Filtering Notes

Some students take neat notes in outline form. Others take sprawling, scrawled notes that are almost impossible to read. Most students can profit from *filtering* the notes they take. This most emphatically does *not* mean rewriting or retyping your notes. This is a waste of time. Instead, underscore the most important points, filtering out the excess. If you have taken notes on a notebook or laptop computer, consider arranging the notes in clear outline form. If you have handwritten notes, however, it probably isn't worth the time it takes to create a neat outline. Spend that time underlining or highlighting the most important concepts.

Build Your Memory

Just as a variety of speed-reading courses are available, so a number of memory-improvement courses, audiotapes, and books are on the market. It might be worth your while to scope some of these out, especially if you are planning to go into a field that requires the memorization of a lot of facts. In the meantime, here are some suggestions for building your memory:

◆ Be aware that most so-called memory problems are really learning problems. You "forget" things because you never learned them in the first place. This is usually a result of passive reading or passive attendance at lectures—the familiar in-one-ear-and-out-the-other syndrome.

> **TIP:** Before you tote your laptop or notebook computer to class, make certain that the instructor approves of such note-taking devices in the classroom. Most lecturers have no problem with them, but some find the tap-tap-tapping of maybe more than a hundred students distracting.

◆ Memorization is made easier by two seemingly opposite processes. First, we tend to remember information for which we have a context. Students in old-fashioned economics classes quite rightly grouse about having to remember "a bunch of numbers and formulas." Why is this so hard? Because such things are too often taught (or learned) out of context, as a meaningless list rather than as part of an interrelated system of thought.

◆ Second, memorization is often made easier if we break down complex material into a set of key phrases or words. You may find it easier to memorize the key points relating to inflation and unemployment than to memorize a narrative description of these two phenomena.

◆ It follows, then, that the best way to build your memory where a certain subject is concerned is to try to understand information in context. Get the "big picture."

◆ It also follows that, even if you have the big picture, you may want to break down key concepts into a few key words or phrases.

How We Forget

It is always better to keep up with your class work and studying than to fall behind and desperately struggle to catch up. This said, it is nevertheless true that most forgetting occurs within the first few days of exposure to new material. That is, if you "learn" one hundred facts about subject A on December 1, you may forget twenty of those facts by December 5 and another ten by December 10, but on March 1 you may still remember fifty facts. The curve of your forgetting tends to flatten. You may eventually forget all the facts, but you will forget fewer and fewer each week.

Now, what does this mean to you?

It means that you need to review material you learned earlier in the course. You cannot depend on having mastered it two, three, four, or more weeks earlier.

Should you bring a tape recorder to class? The short answer is, probably not. To begin with, some instructors object to having their lectures recorded. Even more important, however, is the tendency to complacency that a tape recorder creates. You may feel that you don't have to listen very carefully to the "live" lecture, since you're getting it all on tape. This is a mistake, since the live presentation is bound to make a greater impression on you, your mind, and your memory than a recorded replay.

The Virtues of Cramming

Ask any college instructor about last-minute cramming for an exam, and you'll almost certainly get a knee-jerk condemnation of the practice. But maybe it's time to think beyond that knee jerk.

Let's get one thing absolutely straight: You cannot expect to pack a semester's worth of studying into a single all-nighter. It just isn't going to work. However, cramming can be a valuable *supplement* to a semester of conscientious studying.

◆ You forget the most within the first few days of studying. (Or have you forgotten?) Well, if you cram the night before the exam, those "first few days" won't fall between your studying and the exam, will they?

◆ Cramming creates a sense of urgency. It brings you face to face and toe to toe with your objective. Urgency concentrates the mind.

◆ Assuming that you aren't totally exhausted, material that you study within a few hours of going to bed at night is more readily retained than material studied earlier in the day.

Burning the midnight oil may not be such a bad idea.

Cramming Cautions

Then again, staying up late before a big exam may not be such a hot idea, either. Don't do it if you have an early-morning exam. And don't transform cramming into an all-nighter. You almost certainly need *some* sleep to perform competently on tomorrow's exam.

Remember, too, that while cramming creates a sense of urgency, which may stimulate and energize your study efforts, it may also create a feeling of panic, and panic is never helpful.

TIP: Memorization is important, make no mistake. However, it is usually overrated. Virtually all of the teaching assistants and professors who have contributed to this book counsel students to think rather than merely memorize. When grading exams, most economics professors look for evidence of thought—of a thoughtful grasp of broad and basic concepts—rather than a regurgitation of facts memorized in rote fashion.

Cramming is not a substitute for diligent study throughout the semester. But just because you *have* studied diligently, don't shun cramming as a *supplement* to regular study, a valuable means of refreshing the mind and memory.

Polly Want a Cracker?

We've been talking a lot about memory and memorization. It's an important subject and, for just about any course of study, an important skill. Some subjects—economics included—are more fact- and memory-intensive than others. However, beware of relying too much on simple, brute memory. Try to assess what the professor really wants: students who demonstrate on exams that they have absorbed the facts he or she and the textbooks have dished out, or students who demonstrate such skills as critical thinking, synthesis, analysis, imagination, and so on. Depending on the professor's personal style and the kind of exam he or she gives (predominantly essay vs. predominantly multiple choice, for example), you may actually be penalized for parroting lectures. ("I know what *I* think. I want to know what *you* think.")

Use This Book (and Get Old Exams)

One way to judge what the professor values and expects is to pay careful attention in class. Is discussion invited? Or does the course go by the book and by the lecture? Also valuable are previous exams. Many professors keep these on file and allow students to browse through them freely. Fraternities, sororities, and both formal and informal study groups sometimes maintain such files, too. These days, previous exams may even be posted on the university department's World Wide Web site.

Of course, you are holding in your hand a book chock full of sample and model midterm and final exams. Read them. Study them. And let them focus your study and review of the course.

Study Groups: The Pro and the Con

In the old days (whenever that was), it was believed that teachers *taught* and students *learned*. More recently, educators have begun to wonder whether it is possible to *teach* at all. A student, they say, *learns* by teaching him- or herself. The so-called teacher (who might better be called a "learning facilitator") helps the student teach him- or herself.

Well, maybe this is all a matter of semantics. Is there really a difference between *teaching* and *facilitating learning*? Or between *learning* and *teaching oneself*? The more important point is that the focus in education has turned from the teacher to the student, and students, in turn, have often responded by organizing study groups, in which they help one another study and learn.

These can be very useful:

◆ In the so-called real world (that is, the world after college), most problems are solved by teams rather than by individuals.

◆ Many people come to an understanding of a subject through dialogue and question and answer.

◆ Studying in a group (or even with one partner) makes it possible to drill and quiz one another.

TIP: Many memory experts suggest that you try to put the key terms you identify into some sort of sentence, then memorize the sentence. Others suggest creating an acronym out of the initials of the key words or concepts. No one who lived through the Watergate scandal in the 1970s can forget that President Nixon's political campaign was run by CREEP (Committee to RE-Elect the President), and even non-science majors remember how biologists traditionally classify living things by memorizing a sentence such as this: *Ken Put Candy On Fred's Green Sofa* (kingdom, phylum, class, order, family, genus, species).

TIP: Any full-time college student studies several subjects each semester. This makes you vulnerable to interference—the possibility that learning material in one subject will interfere with learning material in another subject. Interference is usually at its worst when you are studying two similar or related subjects. If possible, arrange your study time so that work on similar subjects is separated by work on an unrelated one.

◆ In a group, complex subjects can be broken up and divided among members of the group. Each member becomes a "specialist" on some aspect of the subject, then shares his or her knowledge with the others.

◆ Studying in a group may improve concentration.

◆ Studying in a group may reduce anxiety.

However, study groups are not without their problems:

◆ All too often, study groups become social gatherings, full of distraction (however pleasant) rather than study. This is the greatest pitfall of a study group.

◆ All members of the group must be highly motivated to study. If they are not, the group will become a distraction rather than an aid to study, and it is also likely that friction will develop among the members, some of whom will feel burdened by "freeloaders."

◆ The members of the study group must be committed not only to study but to one another. Study groups fall apart—bitterly—if members, out of a sense of competition, begin to withhold information from one another. This *must* be a Three Musketeers deal—all for one and one for all—or it is worse than useless.

TIP: If you hate cramming, don't do it. It's not for you, and it will probably only raise your anxiety level. Get some sleep instead.

◆ The group may promote excellence—or it may agree on mediocrity. If the latter occurs, the group will become destructive.

In summary, study groups tend to bring out the members' best as well as worst study habits. It takes individual and collective discipline to remain focused on the task at hand, to remain committed and helpful to one another, to insist that everyone shoulders a fair share, and to insist on excellence of achievement as the only acceptable standard—or, at least, the only valid reason for continuing the study group.

CHAPTER 3

SECRETS OF SUCCESSFUL TEST TAKING

S OMETIMES IT SEEMS THAT THE DIFFERENCE BETWEEN ACADEMIC SUCCESS AND something less than success is not smarts versus nonsmarts or even study versus nonstudy, but simply whether or not a person is "good at taking tests." That phrase—"good at taking tests"—was probably first heard back when the University of Bologna opened for business late in the eleventh century. The problem with phrases like this is that while they are true enough, they are not very helpful.

Fact: Some people *are* and some people *are not* "good at taking tests."

So what? Even if successful test taking doesn't come easily or naturally to you, you can improve your test taking skills. Now, if you happen to have a knack for taking tests, well, congratulations! But that won't help you much if you neglect the kind of preparation discussed in the previous chapter.

Why Failure?

In analyzing performance on most tasks, it is generally better to begin by asking what you can do to succeed. But in the case of taking tests, success is largely a matter of avoiding failure. So let's begin there.

When the celebrated bank robber Willy "the Actor" Sutton was caught, a reporter asked him why he robbed banks. "Because that's where the money is," the handcuffed thief replied. At least one answer to the question of why some students perform poorly on exams is just as simple: "Because they don't know the answers."

There is no "magic bullet" in test taking. But the closest thing to one is *knowing the course material cold.* Pay attention, keep up with reading and other assignments, attend class, listen in class, take effective notes—in short, follow the recommendations of the previous chapter—and you will have taken the most important step toward exam success.

Yet have you ever gotten your graded exam back, with disappointing results, read it over, and found question after question that you realize you *could* have answered correctly?

"I *knew* that!" you exclaim, smacking yourself in the forehead.

What happened? You really *did* prepare. You really *did* know the material. What happened?

Anxiety—Good and Bad

The great American philosopher and psychologist William James (1842-1910) once advised his Harvard students that an "ounce of good nervous tone in an examination is worth many pounds of . . . study." By "good nervous tone" James meant something very like anxiety. You *should not* expect to feel relaxed just before or during an exam. Anxiety is natural.

Anxiety is natural because it is helpful. "Good nervous tone," alert senses, sharpened perception, and adrenalin-fueled readiness for action are *natural* and *healthy* responses to demanding or threatening situations. We are animals, and these are reactions we share with other animals. The mongoose that relaxes when it confronts a cobra is a dead mongoose. The student who takes it easy during the microeconomics final . . . Well, the point is neither to fight anxiety nor to fear it. Accept it, and even welcome it as an ally. Unlike our hominid ancestors of distant prehistory, we no longer need the biological equipment of anxiety to help us fight or fly from the snapping saber teeth of some animal of prey, but every day we do face challenges to our success. Midterms and finals are just such challenges, and the anxiety they provoke is real, natural, and unavoidable. It may even help us excel.

What good can anxiety do?

◆ Anxiety can focus our concentration. It can keep the mind from wandering. This makes thought easier, faster, and, often, more acute and effective.

◆ Anxiety can energize us. We've all heard stories about a 105-pound mother who is able to lift the wreckage of an automobile to free her trapped child. This isn't fantasy. It really happens. And just as adrenalin can provide the strength we need when we need it most, it can enhance our ability to think under pressure.

◆ Anxiety moves us along. We work faster than when we are relaxed. This is valu-

TIP: Most midterm and final exams really *are* representative of the course. If you have mastered the course material, you will almost certainly be prepared to perform well on the examination. Very few instructors purposely create deceptive exams or trick questions, or even questions that require you to think beyond the course. Most instructors are interested in creating exams that help you and them evaluate your level of understanding of the course material. Think of the exams as natural, logical features of the course, not as sadistic assignments designed to trip you up. Remember, your success on an examination is also a measure of the instructor's success in presenting complex information. Very few teachers can—or want to—build careers on trying to fail their students.

able, since, for most midterms and finals, limited time is part of the test.

◆ Anxiety prompts us to take risks. We've all been in classes in which the instructor has a terrible time trying to get students to speak and discuss and venture an opinion. "Come on, come on," the poor prof protests. "This is like pulling teeth!" Yet, when exam time comes, all heads are bent over bluebooks or notebook computers, and the answers—*some* kind of answers—are flowing forth, or at least grinding out. Why? Because the anxiety of the exam situation overpowers the inertia that keeps most of us silent most of the time. We take the risks we have to take. We answer the questions.

◆ Anxiety can make us more creative. This is related to risk taking. "Necessity," the old saying goes, "is the mother of invention." Phrased another way: We do what we have to do. Under pressure, many students find themselves taking fresh and creative approaches to problems.

So don't shun anxiety. But, unfortunately, the scoop on anxiety isn't all good news, either.

Anxiety evolved as a mechanism of *physical* survival. Biologists and psychologists talk of the "fight or flight" response. Anxiety prepares a threatened animal either to fight the threat or to flee from it. The action is physical and, typically, very short term. In our "civilized" age, however, the threats are generally less physical than *intellectual* and *emotional*, and they tend to be of longer duration than a physical fight or a physical flight. This means that the anxiety mechanism does not always work to enhance our chances for "survival"—in this case, our chances of surviving the course by performing well on exams. Some of us are better than others at adapting the *physical* benefits of anxiety to the *intellectual* and *emotional* challenges of an exam. Some of us, unfortunately, are unable to benefit from anxiety, and for still others of us, anxiety is downright harmful. Here are some of the negative effects anxiety may have on exam performance:

◆ Anxiety can make it difficult to concentrate. True, anxiety focuses concentration. But if it focuses concentration on the anxious feelings themselves, you will have less focus left over for the exam. Similarly, anxiety may cause you to focus unduly on the perceived consequences of failure.

◆ Anxiety causes carelessness. If anxiety can prompt you to take creative risks, it can also cause you to rush through material and, therefore, to make careless mistakes or simply to fail to think through a problem or question.

◆ Anxiety distorts focus. Anxiety may impede your judgment, causing you to give disproportionate weight to relatively unimportant matters. For example, you may become fixated on solving a lesser problem at the expense of a more important one. This is related to the next point.

TIP: Exam question are battles in a war. No general expects to win every battle. Accept your losses and move on. Dwell on your losses, and you will continue to lose.

◆ Anxiety may distort your perception of time. You may think you have more or less of it than you really do. The result may be too much time spent on a minor question at the expense of a major one.

◆ Anxiety tends to be cumulative. Many test takers have trouble with a question early in the exam, then devote the rest of the exam to worrying about it instead of concentrating on the rest of the exam.

◆ Anxiety drains energy. For a short period of time, anxiety can be energizing and invigorating. But if anxiety becomes chronic, it begins to tire you out. You do not perform as well.

◆ Anxiety can keep you from getting the rest you need. If it is generally unwise to stay up all night *studying* for an exam, how much less wise is it to stay up uselessly *worrying* about one?

How can you combat anxiety?

TIP: More serious stimulant drugs ("speed," "uppers") are *never* a good idea. They are both illegal and dangerous (possibly even deadly), and, for that matter, their effect on exam performance is unpredictable. The chances are that they will impede your performance rather than aid it (although you may erroneously *feel* that you are doing well). Also avoid over-the-counter stimulants. These are caffeine pills and will probably increase your anxiety rather than improve your performance.

Step 1: Don't fight it. Accept it. Remember that anxiety is a natural response to a stressful situation. Remember, too, that some degree of anxiety aids performance. Try to learn to accept anxiety and *use* it. Let it sharpen your wits and stoke the fires of your creativity.

Step 2: Don't worry about how you feel. Focus on the task. Usually, you will feel better once you overcome the initial jitters and inertia. William James, who lauded "good nervous tone," also once observed that we do not run because we are frightened; rather, we are frightened because we run. If you concentrate on your fear and act as if you are afraid, you will become even more fearful.

Step 3: Prepare for the exam. Do whatever you must do to master the material. Build confidence in your understanding of the course, and your anxiety should be reduced.

Step 4: Get a good night's sleep before the exam.

Step 5: Avoid coffee and other stimulants. Caffeine tends to increase anxiety. (However, if you are a caffeine fiend, don't pick the day or two before a big exam to kick the habit. You will suffer withdrawal symptoms.)

Step 6: Try to get fresh air shortly before the exam. This is especially valuable if you have been cooped up for a long period of time studying. Take a walk. Get a look at the wider world for a few minutes.

Have a Plan, Make a Plan

A large component of destructive anxiety—probably the largest—is fear of the unknown. Reduce anxiety by taking steps to reduce the component of the unknown.

Step 1: To repeat, do whatever is necessary to master the material on which you will be examined.

Step 2: Use the exams in this book to familiarize yourself with the kinds of exams you are likely to encounter.

Step 3: If possible, examine old exams actually given in the course.

Let's pause here before going on to Step 4. Just reading over the exams in this book or leafing through exams formerly given in the course will not help you much. Instead,

♦ Analyze the types of questions asked. Are they essay or objective questions? (We'll discuss these shortly.) Do they call for regurgitation of memorized material, or are they more "think"-oriented, requiring significant initiative to answer?

♦ Don't just predict which questions you could and could not answer. Try actually answering some of the questions.

♦ If you are looking at sample exams with answers, evaluate the answers. How would you grade them? What would you do better?

♦ Don't just stand there, *do* something. If your analysis of the sample exams or old exams reveals areas in which you are weak, address those weaknesses.

> **TIP:** Don't make the mistake of devoting all your time to trying to make last-minute repairs to weak spots ("I've got one hour to read that textbook I should have been reading all along!") and ignoring your strengths. Develop your strengths. With any luck at all, the exam will give you an opportunity to show yourself at your best—not just trip you up at your worst. Be as prepared as you can be, but remember, there is nothing wrong with excelling in a particular area. Play to your strengths, not your weaknesses.

An effective way to reduce the unknown is to create a plan for confronting it. Let's go on to Step 4.

Step 4: Make a plan. Begin *before* the exam. Decide what areas you need to study hardest. Based on your textbook notes and—especially—on your lecture notes, try to anticipate what kinds of questions will be asked. Work up answers or sketches of answers for these.

Step 5: Make sure you've done the simple things. The night before your exam, make certain that you have whatever equipment you'll need. If you will be allowed to use reference materials, bring them. If you are permitted to write on a laptop or notebook computer, make certain your batteries are fully charged. If you are writing the exam longhand, make certain you have pens, pencils, paper. Bring a watch.

Step 6: Expect a shock. The first sight of the exam usually packs a jolt. At first sight, questions may draw a blank from you. Questions you were sure would appear on

TIP: When you study for an exam, it is usually best to assign a high priority to the most complex and difficult issues, devote ample time to these, and master them first. When you *take* an exam, however, and you are under time pressure, tackle first what you can most readily and thoroughly answer, then go on to more doubtful tasks. Your professor will be more favorably impressed by good or correct answers than by failed attempts to answer questions that you find difficult.

the exam will be absent, and some you never expected will be staring you in the face. Don't panic. *Everybody* feels this way.

Step 7: Write nothing yet. Read through the exam thoroughly. Be certain that you (a) understand any instructions and (b) understand the questions.

Step 8: If you are given a choice of which questions to answer, choose them now. Unless the questions vary in the point value assigned to them, choose those that you feel most confident about answering. Don't challenge yourself.

Alternative Step 8: If you are required to answer all the questions, identify those about which you feel most confident. Answer these first.

Step 9: After you have surveyed the exam, create a "time budget": Note—jot down—how much time you should give to each question.

Step 10: Reread the question before you begin to write. Then plan your answer.

Plan Your Answer

Perhaps you have heard a teacher or professor say about the exam he or she has just handed out: "The answers are in the questions." This kind of remark is more helpful than it may at first seem.

Begin by looking for the key words in the question. These are the verbs that tell you what to do. Typical examples of these are

- *Compare*
- *Contrast*
- *Criticize*
- *Define*
- *Describe*
- *Discuss*
- *Evaluate*
- *Explain*
- *Illustrate*
- *Interpret*
- *Justify*
- *Outline*
- *Relate*
- *Review*
- *State*
- *Summarize*
- *Trace*

You will find these key words primarily in essay rather than objective or short-answer questions, so we will have much more to say about them in Chapter 5, which is devoted to answering the essay exam. But be aware that the following key words are often found in short-answer questions:

- To *define* something is to state the precise meaning of the word, phrase, or concept. Be succinct and clear.

- To *illustrate* is to provide a specific, concrete example.

- To *outline* is to provide the main features or general principles of a subject. This need not be in paragraph or essay form. Often, outline format is expected.

- To *state* is much like to define, although a statement may be even briefer and usually involves delivering up something that has been committed to memory.

- To *summarize* is to state briefly—in sentence form— the major points of an argument or position or concept, the principal features of an event, or the main events of a period.

As has just been mentioned, advice on answering essay examinations is the subject of Chapter 5. For the moment, just be aware that you will want to budget time for creating a scratch outline of your essay answer.

Approaching the Short-Answer Test

While the value of planning is more or less obvious in the case of essay exams, you will also find it valuable in "objective," multiple-choice, or other short-answer exams. These are of two major kinds:

1. **Recall exams** include questions that call for a single short answer (usually there is a single "correct" answer) and fill-in-the-blank questions, in which you are asked to supply missing information in a statement or sentence.

2. **Recognition exams** include multiple-choice tests, true-false tests, and matching tests (match one from column A with one from column B).

If the exam is a long one and time is short, invest a few minutes in surveying the questions, so that you can be certain to answer those you are confident of, even if they come near the end of the exam.

Be prepared to answer multiple-choice questions through a process of elimination, if necessary. Usually, even if you are uncertain of the one *correct* answer among a choice of five, you will be able to eliminate one, two, or three answers that you know are *incorrect*. This at least increases your odds of giving a correct response.

Unless your instructor has specifically informed you that he or she is penalizing guesses (actually taking away points for incorrect responses versus awarding zero points to unanswered questions), do guess the answers even to those questions that leave you in the dark.

Plan your responses to true/false questions carefully. Look for telltale qualifying words, such as *all, always, never, no, none,* or *in all cases.* Questions with such absolute qualifiers often require an answer of *false,* since relatively few general statements are *always* either true or false. Conversely, questions containing such qualifiers as *sometimes, usually, often* and the like are frequently answered correctly with a response of *true.*

A final word on guessing: *First guess, best guess.* Statistical evidence consistently shows that a first guess is more likely to be right than a later one. Obviously, if you have responded one way to a question and then the correct answer suddenly dawns on you, do change your response. But if you can only guess, go with your first or "gut" response.

Take Your Time

Yes, yes, yes, this is easier said than done. But the point is this:

◆ Plan your time.

◆ Work efficiently, but not in a panic.

◆ Make certain that your responses are legible.

◆ Take time to spell correctly. Even if an instructor does not consciously deduct points for misspelling, such basic errors will negatively influence her evaluation of the exam.

◆ Take time to check your mathematical work. Are the formulas correct? Did you calculate correctly?

◆ Take time to check your graphical work. Economics exams often involve drawing and/or labeling graphs. Make sure your drawings are legible, and make doubly sure that you have labeled all points, intersections, and axes correctly. The instructors who have contributed to this book repeatedly observe careless errors of labeling. Points are lost for this.

◆ If a short answer is called for, make it short. Don't ramble.

◆ Use *all* the time allowed. The instructor will not be impressed by a demonstration that you have finished early. If you have extra time, reread the exam. Look for careless errors. Do not, however, heap new guesses on top of old ones; where you have guessed, stick with your first guess.

Essay Exams: Read On

Many Econ 101 students are shocked and dismayed to find that they are expected to answer essay exam questions.

"*Essays!* That's for English and history. Economics is about numbers, not words!"

While it is true that many economics instructors give multiple-choice, fill-in-the-blank, and numerical or graphical problem-solving questions exclusively, many also include essay questions. Some introductory-level exams even consist *entirely* of essay questions. And, in other cases, questions call for "mini-essays"—short narrative explanations of economic principles and applications and solutions to problems.

Economists are more than number crunchers—and a growing number of instructors want you to learn that fact firsthand. Therefore, please continue to the next chapter for advice on preparing for and writing effective essay responses.

CHAPTER 4

THINKING LIKE AN ECONOMIST: KEYS TO WORKING THROUGH ISSUES AND PROBLEMS IN ECONOMICS

Y ESIM SUBASIM, A GRADUATE TEACHING ASSISTANT IN ECONOMICS AT CLEMSON
University, lays it on the line: "I have observed that economics is a hard subject for most students." Yet the discipline of economics is quite easy to define.
It takes as its most basic assumption that resources are always "scarce." That
is, there is never enough of anything (goods, money, and so on) to supply
everyone with everything they need or want. Economics then draws from this a
single crucial conclusion: Because resources are scarce, people must make choices
(trade-offs) among them. If you see economics as essentially a *descriptive* behavioral
science, you may then define it as the study of how people allocate their scarce
resources. If you see it as more *prescriptive* than descriptive, you may define it as the
study of how society may *efficiently* allocate scarce resources.

Well, if this is the work of an economist, it would seem to be quite easy to "think
like an economist." Why? Because economics, as just defined, is nothing more than
common sense applied to everyday decisions concerning such areas as work, production, spending, saving, and investment.

Unfortunately, appearances are deceiving. While it is true that economists study
and consult "common sense," they do so in a highly organized, disciplined way. And,
even more important, they often find that they must depart from what common sense
suggests. For example, common sense might suggest that saving is always good for the
economy. After all, "a penny saved is a penny earned!" It's just plain common sense.

Yet, if too many people save rather than buy, producers of goods suffer. If they save
rather than make financial investments, producers also suffer. When this happens,

the economy enters a slump, wages are lowered, and jobs are lost. By and by, less money is available for saving—precisely because people have been saving too much!

Economics is rife with scenarios like this—situations that seem to fly in the face of common sense.

So the first big step you need to take toward thinking like an economist is not to *abandon* common sense, but not to let yourself be a slave to it either. You must think *beyond* it—just as, say, Columbus did when he refused to believe that he would sail off the edge of a world that common sense told him was clearly and obviously flat.

Model It

How do you make this leap beyond common sense?

Economists begin by creating *economic models*: simple, usually scaled-down representations of complex, large-scale real-world situations. A model is a way of identifying, defining, and organizing all one's assumptions, so that nothing is taken for granted.

◆ Models identify the variables in the economic situation under consideration.

◆ Models are used to study the range of possible interactions and cause-and-effect relationships among these variables.

◆ By cutting through the haze of complexity, models provide insight into the real world.

◆ Models may also provide a kind of experimental platform on which various solutions to economic problems can be tested.

Watch Your Language

Just as you must get used to sometimes looking at the world through models rather than directly, so you should become accustomed to talking about the world using the specialized language of economics.

Economics has a vocabulary all its own. Essential to success in economics courses is learning the vocabulary and then using it *precisely*. This requires memorization, but it also requires care and thought. Many beginning economics students run into difficulty because much of the specialized vocabulary of economics overlaps the common vocabulary of everyday speech. For example, when an economist speaks of *investment*, she means the purchase of machinery or equipment to make production possible. Thus, a widget maker will invest in a new machine tool to make widgets more efficiently. When a noneconomist speaks of *investment*, he usually means putting money in the stock market. (Economists call this *financial investment*, not simply *investment*.) Worse, noneconomists tend to lump personal financial investment with savings and oppose these to money that is spent on mortgage payments, car payments, consumer goods, and so on. As economists see the world, however, savings are *very* different from financial investment.

You don't have to become paranoid or paralyzed in the way you use the language of economics. Just make certain that you understand each new term you encounter. Whether you think of economics as a descriptive or a prescriptive study, the first step in the study of any economic problem or situation is *description*, and economics provides an ample and precisely defined vocabulary to facilitate such description. The specialized terms of economics are the *tools* of the discipline. To work with economics, even at the introductory level, you must have a sound knowledge of the basic tools. It's pretty hard to drive a nail with a screwdriver. Pick up the hammer instead. It's pretty hard to describe an economic scenario if you apply a word like *investment* when you really mean *savings*.

Let Us Assume

Take a walk. Or hop in the car and take a drive. Look around you. The evidence of economic activity is everywhere. In fact, it is dazzling in its complexity.

Think about that word *dazzling*. If you are dazzled, you cannot see clearly.

How do you regain clear vision?

You figure out a way to filter out some of the elements that confuse, confound, and dazzle you. If you're out in the dazzling sunlight, maybe you just put on a pair of sunglasses. If you're out in the dazzling economy, you can (as we have seen) create a smaller-scale, simplified model in order to reduce the confusion, and you can also make certain *simplifying assumptions*.

Assumptions are tools used to focus attention on only the relevant details. Assumptions isolate the most important aspects of a situation or problem. To think like an economist, make yourself familiar with the following assumptions.

Other Things Being Equal

As you study the sample exams in this book, you will frequently encounter the Latin phrase *ceteris paribus*. It means "other things being equal," and it is an assumption that allows the economist to study one relationship at a time. For example, let's say you are asked a question about how the wage of widget makers might affect the supply of widgets. Now, the fact is that many things may affect the supply of widgets, but if you are asked to focus exclusively on the relationship between wages and widget supply, you have license to apply the *ceteris paribus* assumption: "*Ceteris paribus*, a rise in the wage of widget makers will . . ." In other words, "Other things being equal, a rise in the wage of widget makers will produce such and such an effect on the supply of widgets."

Many economics problems, especially in introductory courses, rest on the *ceteris paribus* assumption. Without it, you could spend the entire semester working on the very first problem you are asked to solve—and *still* not arrive at an answer.

Rationality

Economists are not psychologists, but, like psychologists, they make certain assumptions about human (and corporate) behavior. For example, it is certainly possible that an individual somewhere under some set of circumstances might purposely throw his money away. Such irrational behavior would interest a psychologist, but it is of no interest to an economist. The economist assumes that individuals and firms make *rational* economic decisions. This does not mean that they necessarily make the right decisions, or the shrewdest, or the best. But they make decisions they *believe* will be to their benefit. As the economist sees it, individuals don't set out to waste their money. They set out to allocate their scarce resources efficiently. Similarly, no firm *tries* to go broke. It is assumed that a firm behaves in a way that it believes will maximize profits or minimize costs.

In short, to think like an economist, you must assume that, where economic choices are concerned, individuals and firms behave rationally.

Technological Assumptions

Much of economics requires thinking in terms of inputs and outputs. As you learn in Physics 101, matter and energy are neither created nor lost—they are simply transformed. You get no output without input, and without the promise of output, you will get no input.

You will frequently encounter stated technological assumptions, assumptions about how inputs are converted into outputs. In economics, the most familiar technological assumption is the law of diminishing returns. It states that as more and more units of input (usually labor) are brought to bear in the production of some output, the amount of additional output produced by each additional unit of input will become smaller and smaller.

NOTE: In stating the law of diminishing returns, we really ought to begin with the phrase *ceteris paribus*, since factors other than input might well influence output.

The Long and the Short of It

Some of the most important economic assumptions concern time or, more precisely, time frame. Economic processes are dynamic: They occur in time, and they change over time.

Sometimes, specific time spans are part of an economic problem, but, often, you will be asked to think in terms of two broad categories: *short run* and *long run*.

We have implied that the language of economics is very precise. But how precise can such apparently vague phrases as "short run" and "long run" be? Just how short is short? How long is long?

Well, you were warned. The specialized language of economics often overlaps everyday language, and that overlap can be misleading. For economists, *short run* and *long run* don't refer to specific time *spans* at all, they refer to the number of variables that are allowed to change within the period of analysis.

◆ "In the long run," *all* variables are subject to change.

◆ "In the short run," at least one variable is not allowed to change.

Thinking in terms of the long and short run allows one to assess the impact of whatever variables are allowed to change—and *only* the impact of those variables.

Seeing the Forest

Everyone is familiar with the expression concerning failure to see the forest for the trees. If you focus too intensely on details, you'll miss the big picture. Economists sometimes have to work with the very specific products and problems of particular industries, but, more often than not, it is useful to lump specific items of a similar nature into a single category. These categories are sometimes called *aggregates*. Important aggregate categories include the following:

◆ **Consumers:** Any individuals who make purchases or who consume goods.

◆ **Financial intermediaries:** Banks and other financial institutions.

◆ **Government:** May be federal, state, or local.

◆ **Land:** Encompasses the physical setting on which production takes place as well as land as a natural resource. Farm land is land that produces food. As economists see things, iron ore is also land, used to produce steel.

◆ **Capital:** Used by itself, machinery and buildings used in production. *Financial* capital refers to money assets held by a firm.

◆ **Labor:** Any and all human work required to produce an output product. This might be physical or intellectual work.

◆ **Entrepreneurial ability:** A general term for the input of skill with which all the factors of production are organized and managed.

◆ **Factor payments:** Amounts given to the *factors* of production in return for their contribution to producing output. Factors may be workers (labor), who are paid *wages*. But factors also include land (which is paid for by *rent*—even if the "land" is owned, the costs associated with ownership are referred to as rent); capital (which is paid for by *interest*); and entrepreneurs (the managers or owners of a business, who are paid by *profits*).

Thinking Graphically

Economists use special terminology precisely and they are always careful to define their assumptions, but they live and breathe graphs. If you are not accustomed to interpreting and creating graphical representations of numerical relationships, you need to devote time to practice with graphs. You need to become comfortable with them.

Even a crash course in graphical representation is beyond the scope of this book.

The lesson to learn now is to *study* the graphs you will encounter throughout any economics course. By study, we mean *interpret*: think about the meaning of what you are seeing. The best way to go about this is to look at a graph and try to explain *in words* the relationships illustrated. This is not something you learn to do all at once. It takes practice—just as reading words on a page or notes on a musical score takes practice. There is nothing about C-A-T that *looks* like a cat, but, with practice, we learn to see a cat when we read *cat*. The same principle applies when working with graphs.

Equations

If there is one thing that makes some students more queasy than the prospect of working with graphs, it's the idea of working with equations. Actually, equations and graphs are interrelated, and just about any relationship that can be graphed can also be expressed as an equation. However, if only two variables are involved, a graphical representation of a relationship is usually easier to grasp than the same relationship expressed as an equation. When more and more variables are added, however, graphs become quite complex and even bewildering. When this happens, they lose their power as effective communicators of meaning. Equations then become the easier way of understanding relationships among variables.

In lectures and in your textbooks, you will encounter a vocabulary of economic equations that is just as essential as the verbal vocabulary we have already discussed. Just as you must make an effort to understand each specialized term in economics, you should work on understanding each basic equation. These are the building blocks and basic tools of the course.

TIP: Resist the temptation to skip over the graphs you find in your textbook. Devote at least as much attention to these as you do to the words on the page. An ability to work with graphs easily is essential to the successful study of economics. It is a skill that can be acquired with practice.

At the introductory level, most economic equations tend to be straightforward linear equations—that is, they are equations expressing relationships that can be graphed as straight lines. A linear equation might be used, for instance, to express the relationship between an individual's income and her expenditures. In introductory courses, you are less likely to encounter many nonlinear equations. Nonlinear relationships—relationships between variables that cannot be expressed as a straight line, but require a curve—are usually presented graphically in introductory- level courses.

Be There

Economics is a complex subject. It has to be, because it deals with some of the most complex realities of society. It is also an *eclectic* subject; that is, it borrows from various fields and disciplines, including the behavioral sciences, mathematics, and statistics. Yet economics is also an *orderly* discipline. It rests on clearly stated assumptions. It has clearly stated objectives and goals.

The key to successfully studying a subject that is complex, eclectic, and orderly is to proceed step by step, and to make certain that you understand each step before you move on to the next. Learn the vocabulary *well*. Understand the basic set of economic assumptions *well*. Learn to work with graphs and equations *well*.

◆ Don't skip over material.

◆ Don't just start reading words without taking the time and making the effort to understand them.

◆ Don't just glance at the graphs you encounter. Interpret them by translating what you see into words.

◆ Ditto for equations. Don't look at equations as abstract math problems. *Read* them. Translate them into words.

Be there. When you study your textbook, *study* it. Practice the concepts you read about. Economics is as much a set of skills as it is an intellectual pursuit. Acquiring and developing any skill requires active practice, not just passive reading.

Be there in class. Don't skip classes. Attend lectures. Take notes. Ask questions. Most instructors believe that *most learning takes place in the classroom*. This means actively listening to lectures, actively participating in class discussions, and—very important—asking questions *as they occur to you*. If you don't understand something in a lecture, ask about it as soon as possible. This is by far the most effective way of learning.

More Than a Set of Problems

Let's go back to that forest and trees cliché. Resist falling into the trap of thinking about economics as a series of problems to be solved or exercises to be worked on. These are elements of the course, to be sure. But keep in mind that the purpose of economics is not to create interesting graphs or complicated equations or to translate financial transactions into a package of specialized jargon. The purpose of economics is to understand key aspects of human and social behavior, with the ultimate goal of improving our lives.

"But I'm not going to be an economist. I won't be in a position to determine the nation's economic policy. What do I look like, Alan Greenspan?"

Okay. Maybe you won't ever be an economic adviser to presidents or the head of the Federal Reserve. But the fact is that with every vote you cast and with every personal economic decision—financial investment and purchase—you make, you will play a role in determining economic policy. Learning to see such choices clearly is to make better, more effective choices that may well improve your life and even the lives of your fellow citizens.

CHAPTER 5

THE ESSAY EXAM: WRITING MORE EFFECTIVE RESPONSES

WHILE MOST EXAMS IN INTRODUCTORY-LEVEL ECON COURSES INCLUDE MULTIPLE-choice and fill-in-the-blanks segments, many include (and a significant number emphasize) essay questions. Some exams include short-answer essays—questions requiring a paragraph or two in response—as well as longer essays, which may consume several pages of an exam "blue book."

Downside and Up

Griping is of little value at the outset of any enterprise, including an economics course that requires facility not only with numbers and graphs, but also with words. Nevertheless, griping is human and natural, so we'd better get it out of the way.

Essay exams have the following distinct disadvantages:

1. They are intimidating. Even experienced, professional writers may get a shudder when they sit down to a blank page. Where do you begin? Worse, where do you go once you've begun?

2. Essay questions generally require deeper and broader knowledge of a subject than multiple-choice questions do.

3. Essay exams are time-consuming to take. It may be difficult to budget your time effectively.

4. Essay exams test not only your knowledge of course material, but also your language and writing skills. This may seem like an unfair demand.

5. Essay questions may contain a significant element of subjectivity. Often, the

issues are gray rather than black and white. Not only does subjectivity enter into your response, it also plays a role in the instructor's evaluation of the response. An instructor may respond to the skill of the presentation (or lack of such skill) as much as she does to the substance of the answer.

In fairness, essay exams are almost as demanding for the instructor as they are for the students. They are much more difficult and time-consuming to grade than "objective" tests are. The instructor who uses essay exams is demonstrating a genuine commitment to his students and his subject.

So there's the downside. But each of these negatives has a corresponding positive—if you know how to find and exploit it. Look:

1. True, your blue book may be blank, but your mind doesn't have to be. First, there are effective ways to prepare for the questions on an essay exam—and we'll talk about these shortly. Second, take a good, long, careful look at the question. It should give you plenty to get you started. Get into the habit of using the terms, parts, and structure of the question as a kind of framework on which you construct the terms, parts, and structure of your answer.

2. If essay questions usually require deeper and broader knowledge of a subject than multiple-choice questions do, they also offer a deeper and broader stage on which you can play out your understanding of the course material. When you respond to short-answer and multiple-choice questions, you are limited by the instructor's rules: true or false; a, b, c, or d. It's a kind of binary situation. Either you know the correct answer or you don't—and if you don't, you lose. In responding to an essay question, you certainly need to address the question in all its parts (don't stray, don't evade, don't get off the track), but you have much more control. You can focus on the areas you know most about. You can play to your strengths and minimize your weaknesses.

3. Essay exams are time-consuming to take. That's a fact. And your instructor knows it. He takes into account the pressure of limited time and the fact that you are writing a single draft when he evaluates the essay. This generally prompts him to overlook a lot of sins of omission and even outright errors. Time pressure actually *reduces* your instructor's expectations.

4. If essay exams test not only your knowledge of course material, but also your language and writing skills, it behooves you to polish those skills. Good writing will earn extra points. It's that simple. You may not know more about economics than the person sitting next to you, but if you write more effectively, you will earn a higher grade. An added bonus: The more clearly and effectively you can express yourself, the better your own understanding of the material you are writing about will be. Effective writing not only communicates knowledge to others, it helps you to communicate with yourself.

5. Essay questions contain a significant element of subjectivity, it is true, and this can give you that much more "room" to be right. Create a skillful presentation, and you are likely to be evaluated positively, even if you miss some issues.

Study and Preparation

Even if they deny it, most instructors tend to "teach for the midterm and final." More accurately put, they construct exams that genuinely reflect the course content, including the particular themes and topics that are emphasized. Do instructors ask "trick questions"? Rarely. Do they deliberately try to mislead you, hiding exam material in the background of the course, as if it were an Easter egg? Almost never. The fact is that instructors want you to succeed. Good test performance tells them that they have gotten through to you. The more students who do well, the more successful an instructor feels. This being the case, be certain to take careful lecture notes. Make a good set of general notes, but also listen selectively for

> **TIP:** Some instructors prepare examinations well ahead of time, but most write them up shortly before they are given. Usually, the instructor will review her notes in preparation for writing an exam. This makes it even more likely that well-emphasized subjects and issues will appear on the exam.

◆ Points that stand out

◆ Points that are repeated

◆ Points preceded by such statements as "Now, this is important," "This is a major issue," and the like.

Assume that any point, theme, or topic that is given special emphasis will appear as an exam topic. The more emphasis it is given, the more likely it is to appear as an essay exam question.

Typically, course lectures mesh with textbook assignments, additional assigned outside reading, and perhaps class handouts. Take notes on all of these sources. Handouts are usually especially important. Assume that handout material will figure in some way on any exam.

> **TIP:** Do not confine your preparation to your notes. If past course exams are available for your review, review them. Use them as practice tests. Of course, you should also make use of the exams in this book. These days, many instructors post past exams on a special web site devoted to the course.

Avoid passivity. Ask the instructor to talk about the scope of the exam. Also seek out students who have taken the course before. Ask them about the exam. Many instructors have favorite themes or concerns that get repeated from year to year.

You Are Not Alone

You needn't face the exam alone. Group study is often a highly effective way of preparing for essay exams. Indeed, many instructors encourage students to form study groups. This is because group discussion tends to bring out major themes and issues—the meat and potatoes of essay exams—rather than mere facts, which are the focus of short-answer or multiple-choice exams.

Don't make the mistake of allowing the study group to dissolve into a social hour. Consider focusing the discussion by having each member of the group make up a sample essay question. Use these as the topic of discussion.

Limited Possibilities

Let's assume you're not musically inclined. Now, look at the score of, say, the Beethoven *Moonlight Sonata.* All those notes! All those chords! How does anyone ever learn how to read so much simultaneous information, much less translate it into sound on a keyboard?

PITFALL: By all means, examine tests from previous semesters, but don't make the mistake of assuming that these will simply be repeated this semester. Most instructors change their tests from year to year. Examine past tests to get an idea of the type and scope of questions asked, not to learn the specific questions.

Well, it requires study, hard work, and practice—and inborn musical talent helps, too. But it really isn't as hard as it appears to the unmusical. While theoretically there are an infinite number of ways in which musical notes can be combined and deployed, in actual practice, the possibilities are, in fact, limited. Most chord and note sequences occur in recognizable groups and patterns. Just as, when you read a book, you don't spell out individual words or struggle to recognize individual letters, but instead more or less unconsciously interpret familiar linguistic patterns and phrases, so a musician processes the notes he sees.

Now, you may think that the range of possible questions on an essay exam is virtually infinite, but like the notes of a musical score or the words on a novel's page, the range is limited—and this is true regardless of the subject.

There are a limited number of questions that can be asked about any theme, subject, or topic. Furthermore, each question is controlled by a key word. Knowing those key words—and understanding their meaning—will help you to prepare adequately for the exam. Here they are:

Analyze Literally, take apart. Break down a subject into its component parts and discuss how they relate to one another.

Compare Identify similarities and differences between (or among) two (or more) things. End by drawing some conclusion from these similarities and differences.

Contrast Set two (or more) things in opposition in order to bring out the differences between (or among) them. Again, draw some conclusion from these differences.

Criticize Make a judgment on the merits of a position, theory, opinion, or interpretation concerning some subject. Support your judgment with a discussion of relevant evidence.

Defend Give one side of an argument and offer reasons for your opinion.

Define   State as precisely as possible the meaning of some word, phrase, or concept. Develop the definition in detail.

Describe   Give a detailed account of something. Where historical subjects are concerned, this account will typically be chronological.

Evaluate   Appraise something, rendering a judgment as to its truth, usefulness, worth, or validity. Support your evaluation with relevant factual evidence.

Explain   Clarify something and provide reasons for it.

Identify   Define or characterize names, terms, places, or events.

Illustrate   Provide an effective example of some stated point, principle, or concept.

Outline   Show the main features of some event, concept, idea, political movement, and so on. Omit the details. Often, such an answer will be in outline rather than narrative form.

Pros and cons   A more specialized form of *evaluate*. List and discuss the positives and negatives about a certain position, idea, event, movement, and so on.

One or more of these intellectual operations are basic to just about any essay. Look for these key words in an essay question.

Many of these operations focus on just two elements:

◆ Cause
◆ Effect

Indeed, most economics essay questions deal with causes and effects. Be prepared in advance to work with both elements.

Test Time: The Problem of Inertia

If you've just finished an exam in Physics 101, maybe you recall what Sir Isaac Newton had to say about inertia—the tendency of a body in motion to remain in motion and a body at rest to remain at rest. Sitting down to an essay question on exam day, many students are confronted by their own personal form of inertia. You look at the question. And look at it. And look at it some more, hoping, perhaps, that the letters will magically rearrange themselves on the page to yield up the answer.

The bad news, of course, is that they will do no such thing. But the good news is that the germ of the answer is, in fact, in the question. How do you overcome essay test inertia—that paralyzing difficulty in getting started? Just read the question. *Really* read the question.

TIP: You can use the operations and elements just discussed to focus your study notes. For example, instead of listing a bunch of unrelated facts about demand, why not focus your notes in terms of causes and effects, and also *trace* changes in demand to their causes? You might then study demand by *outlining* the factors that influence it, such as consumer income, prices of substitutes, prices of complements, population of buyers, and tastes.

In fact, don't worry about writing just now. Sit down and read *all* the questions before you begin to write anything.

Here's why:

◆ If you are given a choice of which questions to answer (say two out of three), you want to be sure that you answer the ones you know best.

◆ Questions are sometimes related. You want to get an idea of just how they are related to one another, so that you don't "waste" too much of your answer on one question to the neglect of another.

◆ You need to assess your time needs. Are there some questions that will require more time than others?

◆ You want to make certain that you answer the questions you are confident about first. Given a limited amount of time, be certain that you get to your best shots first and complete them before attending to the questions you're less confident about.

Before you begin to write, be absolutely certain that you understand each question completely. Read each question actively, aggressively, with pencil in hand:

TIP: People who give a lot of speeches are fond of offering this formula for a successful speech—"Tell them what you are going to say. Say it. Then tell them what you said." You might keep this in mind when you are answering an essay question, although you should elaborate on the formula a bit:

1. State your subject or thesis.
2. Briefly state how you will discuss it (A, B, C, D—or maybe C, A, B, D).
3. Answer the question.
4. Concisely summarize your answer.
5. Draw any additional conclusions as to significance, ramifications, etc.

◆ Identify and underline key words, including those listed above as basic operations and elements.

◆ Be certain to do what the key words ask. For example, don't just *define* when you are asked to *explain*.

◆ If a question is complex, consisting of several subquestions, make certain you understand and answer all parts of the question.

Generally, you should let the question provide the basic structure for your response. If a question consists of subquestions A, B, C, and D, begin by answering A, then answer B, C, and D. If you have a *very good* reason for changing the order of your response, be certain to explain it. For example, you might begin: "Because C is essential to understanding A, B, and D, I will begin by discussing C, then proceed to A, B, and D."

Finally, answer the question—and *only* the question. Make certain that you address all parts of the question, but don't go beyond what the question asks—unless, after you have thoroughly addressed each aspect of the question, you feel it is important to bring in additional issues. If you do so, tell your reader what you are doing, so that he won't think you've misunderstood the question and are simply going off on a tangent.

To Outline or Not to Outline
Sometimes, pulling out ideas in response to an essay question is difficult, halting,

and laborious. Sometimes, however, you are flooded with ideas. Either situation can make inertia more powerful and, at worst, bring on mental paralysis or, at the very least, cause you to write a poorly organized essay. To prevent these outcomes, apportion your time so that you spend about half of the exam period planning and outlining your response.

Now, an essay exam outline does not have to be a formal outline with major and minor headings. A simple list may be sufficient. Just make a map of your answer, setting down the main points that need to be covered. This will have three effects:

1. It will help ensure that you do not leave out something important.
2. It will help you organize the logic of your response.
3. It will reduce your anxiety.

The first two points are obvious. The last is less obvious, but no less important. Without an outline, you may fear that you will forget something important or get lost in your response. Get the main points out of your head and onto paper quickly, and you won't have to worry about forgetting anything or getting lost.

Structure Strategy

Make the structure of your essay exam response as clear and obvious as possible. Begin with a thesis statement, a statement or listing of the main idea you will support and develop in the body of the essay.

Where do you get your thesis statement?

The first place to look is the question: "What is the purpose of antitrust laws? Give two examples to illustrate how antitrust can achieve this purpose. Discuss at least one criticism of U.S. antitrust law."

There's the question. Begin by getting to the point: "The purpose of antitrust laws is to keep markets reasonably competitive in order to avoid the loss in consumer welfare that comes from monopoly prices."

This thesis statement should naturally lead you to explain how you intend to support it: "One example is Section 1 of the Sherman Act, which outlaws restraints of trade such as price fixing." And so on.

In general, make the thesis statement as simple and as direct as possible. State your thesis. Present your plan for supporting your thesis. Here, the question even supplies the plan. It asks you to support your thesis with examples, so you begin by stating, "One example . . ."

Follow your plan in the body of the essay:

I. The purpose of antitrust laws is to keep markets reasonably competitive in order to avoid the loss in consumer welfare that comes from monopoly prices.

II. Example 1
   A. One way it serves the purpose expressed in I

    B. Another way it serves the purpose

    C. Maybe yet another way

III. Example 2

    A. One way it serves the purpose expressed in I

    B. Another way it serves the purpose

    C. Maybe yet another way

IV. Criticism of the law (asked for in the question)

    A. Relate to example 1

    B. Relate to example 2

V. Conclusion: Antitrust laws are effective/ineffective.

The K.I.S.S. Formula

Can you really get ahead by giving your professor a K.I.S.S.? Well, sort of. This acronym stands for *Keep It Simple, Stupid.*

Now, let's get something straight. This does not mean that you should overly simplify complex ideas or issues, let alone avoid them. But it does mean that you should structure your presentation of ideas in as simple a form *as possible.* This means:

- ◆ Be concise.
- ◆ Be direct.
- ◆ Start the essay with a thesis statement.
- ◆ Start each paragraph with a topic sentence announcing the subject of the paragraph.
- ◆ Try to make a single major point in each paragraph.
- ◆ When you move on to a new point or new idea, start a new paragraph. Answers to essay exams usually have short paragraphs—certainly shorter than what you'd write in a term paper, for example.
- ◆ Draw a definite conclusion

Specify, Always Specify

Wherever possible, avoid abstraction. In place of vague generalizations, make very specific points that use specific examples. Examples are important in any essay response, and they are especially important in economics essays.

Signposts

Develop a repertoire of verbal signposts. One of the most effective signposts is enumeration. For example, instead of saying "Several factors contributed to the Great

Depression," write "Five major factors contributed to the Great Depression." Then go on to list and discuss all five factors.

Enumeration accomplishes three things:

1. It creates the impression that you are in control of the information.

2. It creates an impression of precision and completeness.

3. It sets up an expectation in the reader, who is satisfied when that expectation is fulfilled. You promise five items. You deliver five items. The reader is impressed.

Other signposts include words and phrases such as:

To begin with, . . .
First ,. . .
Next ,. . .
Therefore, . . .
If . . ., then
Because . . .
The result of . . .
. . . caused by . . .
However, . . .
Except for . . .
Including . . .
For example, . . .
Although . . .
Since . . .
Consequently, . . .
Finally, . . .
In conclusion, . . .

> **TIP:** The language of economics is very precise. Make certain that you use it correctly. For example, in everyday speech, we might use the word *demand* and the phrase *quantity demanded* fairly interchangeably. To an economist, however, these are two very different things; in some situations, the *quantity demanded* of a good might change without a change in the *demand*.

Use these to get your reader from one point to the next, to make clear exceptions, and to point your reader toward your conclusions.

A Few Words on Words

Take the time to choose your words carefully. This does not mean trying to impress the instructor with big words or fancy words, but rather trying to find the right words, the words that most precisely say what you mean.

◆ Use the language of economics. Identify and become comfortable with the specialized terms used in lectures and textbooks. Understand them thoroughly. Use them appropriately in writing the exam essays.

◆ Avoid slang. Slang not only is imprecise but creates a poor impression.

TIP: Try to budget time to reread and proofread your essay. Catch and correct errors of usage, grammar, and spelling.

◆ Prefer strong nouns and verbs to adjectives and adverbs. This will help you to be more precise: "A recession is a definite decline in GNP" is a far weaker statement than "A recession is a decline in GNP that lasts for at least two quarters."

◆ Express yourself in a direct manner. Don't load up sentences with unnecessary words. Try to make each word count. Use the active voice instead of the passive voice: "The CPI measures the cost of a market basket of consumer goods" is a much stronger sentence than "A market basket of consumer goods is measured by the CPI."

◆ Avoid unnecessary qualifying phrases and waffling words, such as "it has been said" or "I think" or "it seems to me" or "it seems likely that." Make direct statements.

◆ Avoid padding and repetition: "The PPI is a wholesale measure, in contrast to a retail measure, and it measures a basket of wholesale goods bought by producers, on a wholesale basis, early in the production of goods."

◆ Avoid errors of usage, grammar, and spelling. If you have trouble in these areas, work on them. Such errors undercut your credibility.

Neatness Counts

Take enough time to write legibly. Make your work as easy to read as possible. If the instructor has to struggle to decipher your handwriting, she will easily lose the thread of your discussion, and your grade is likely to suffer as a result.

Recycle!

When the graded exam comes back to you, resist the temptation either to pat yourself on the back or to kick yourself in the backside. Instead, carefully read the examiner's comments. Learn from them. Schedule a conference to discuss the exam—*not* with the goal of getting your grade changed, but with the goal of identifying those areas that can use improvement.

TIP: Many economics essays are illustrated by graphs or charts. These must also be legible, with all features clearly—and correctly—labeled. Slow down. Take enough time to be neat.

When you have a conference, try not to respond defensively. Invite frank feedback. Don't get offended or upset. Instead, look for patterns. Does the instructor say that you simply failed to answer the question adequately? That you didn't answer all parts of the question? That you answered vaguely? That you punctuated poorly? That you didn't use enough examples? Diagnose areas that need improvement, even as you identify your strengths. Your ultimate goal is to avoid repeating errors while working to duplicate your successes.

PART TWO

STUDY GUIDE

CHAPTER 6

INTRODUCTION TO ECONOMICS: THE MAJOR TOPICS

"**W**ITHOUT SCARCITY," OBSERVES ROBERT M. FEINBERG, PROFESSOR OF ECONOMICS at American University, "economics ceases to be an interesting subject for study." Scarcity is the bedrock on which economics rests, a core truth of the human condition. The desire and ability to consume are potentially boundless, but the resources available are always limited—that is, scarce. Because of scarcity, individuals, firms, governments, and societies all make choices about allocating resources. Consumption requires sacrifice, trade-offs. Allocation—just what sacrifices people choose to make in order to acquire certain goods—involves determining the value of goods (the term *goods* includes all output products, including services).

In society, prices—a price system—have evolved as a means of allocating scarce resources. The price system allows individuals and firms to determine what goods they can afford and in what quantities, depending on available income. The price system is an expression of the interrelationship between the products available and the desire and ability to possess them.

Production Possibilities Frontier

Obviously, the wants, needs, and desires of a population consisting of thousands or millions are complex and varied. How can they be meaningfully studied?

Economists reduce this most basic economic situation to a model, which is represented in what is usually the very first graph presented in any introductory economics text or course. Called the production possibilities curve or production possibilities frontier (PPF), it is a graphical representation of the maximum outputs that can be produced with available inputs. The modeling simplification is this: Economists assume that all goods can be placed into two major categories, whose levels are measured along the two axes of the graph. The graph therefore shows the cost of acquiring more of one good in terms of the other, based, of course, on the economy's capacity to produce both categories of goods.

Opportunity Cost

The amount of one good that must be sacrificed in order to acquire more of the other good is called *opportunity* cost, another very basic economic concept.

Supply and Demand

In addition to the PPF model, the essential model of supply and demand represents the eternal dilemma posed by scarcity and choice.

Supply is the ability of producers to furnish goods at various prices.

Demand is the desire of individuals and firms to consume goods at various prices (*goods* includes any output product, including services).

The interaction between the supply of and demand for a given good determines its price and the quantity of the good produced and sold.

Specific areas of an economics course are generally devoted to issues of supply, demand, and the interrelationships between the two. As complex as economics is, it can be broken down into the study of these three broad areas.

> **TIP:** Early in your economics course, you are likely to see "guns" and "butter," generally graphed along the X and Y axes of the PPF, used as the most basic categories of goods. This dramatically reflects a dilemma basic to most societies: how to allocate resources between defense/war and basic sustenance. Economics can all too easily become a dry, abstract subject—mere numbers, graphs, jargon, and equations. It is helpful to get down to earth as often as possible by thinking in real-world terms: not just Good X versus Good Y, but guns versus butter. This demonstrates the high stakes of any economic system. Untold numbers of governments have risen and fallen over the issue of guns versus butter.

Marginal Considerations

We have repeatedly underscored the importance of understanding each term or concept before moving onto the next. In common use, the adjective *marginal* is virtually synonymous with *unimportant*. For economists, however, the concept of the margin and marginality is of crucial importance.

As we have seen, economics is often the study of choices, or decisions to allocate scarce resources to producing butter, thereby sacrificing a certain quantity of guns, or to producing guns, thereby forgoing some butter. The concept of the margin is the economist's tool for studying the mechanism of choice.

◆ **Marginal utility** is the additional utility (or satisfaction) that a consumer gets from consuming one more unit of a good. (Remember, consuming that additional unit requires additional sacrifice of scarce resources. Thus marginal utility is a measure of willingness to sacrifice to a certain degree.)

◆ **Marginal cost** is the additional cost to a firm of increasing production by one more unit of output. (Will that additional unit result in profit that will justify the additional cost? Or will it sink the firm?)

◆ **Marginal revenue** is the additional revenue a firm will receive if it sells one more unit of output.

◆ **Marginal physical product** is the additional output a firm can produce if it uses one more unit of input.

The Micro and Macro Views

While a few colleges and universities offer "Introduction to Economics" courses, the vast majority divide their introductory offerings into two broad courses: microeconomics and macroeconomics. Typically, microeconomics is regarded as somewhat more basic than macroeconomics.

TIP: The *aggregate* concept is important in economics. While it is most important in macroeconomics, it also figures in microeconomics, which must often consider such factors as *market demand* and *market supply*, both aggregate concepts, even when focusing on the situation of the individual consumer and producer.

Microeconomics studies the factors determining the relative prices of goods and inputs in terms of individual producers and consumers. Macroeconomics studies the overall economy, including such collective issues as the business cycle, inflation, and unemployment.

Microeconomics

First and foremost, microeconomics is concerned with the choices individual consumers make in allocating their income on goods. Second, microeconomics studies how individuals determine how much labor (or other resource endowments, such as capital or land) they sell to firms in exchange for income.

If microeconomics studies consumers, it also studies suppliers: firms. Microeconomics studies how firms should efficiently use inputs to produce output at the greatest profit and the lowest costs. Based on production costs and the prices at which goods will sell in the market, firms must decide how much output to produce. Microeconomics studies this, as well as the interaction of individuals and firms—an interaction that determines, among other things, prices.

The material surveyed in Chapters 7 through 13 is an overview of what is usually included in introductory microeconomics courses.

Macroeconomics

Whereas microeconomics studies individual consumers and firms, macroeconomics deals with *aggregates*—broad groupings of consumers, producers, investors, and government.

Macroeconomics studies such broad, large-scale social-economic issues as economic growth, unemployment, and inflation. These are dimensions of the overall, collective state of the economy. Macroeconomics is concerned not only with the consumers and firms (both considered collectively) but with government, which plays a key role in the overall economy through monetary and fiscal policies.

The material surveyed in Chapters 14 through 18 is an overview of what is usually included in introductory microeconomics courses.

Road Map

Remember, this book is a guide to help you use midterms and finals, inevitable facts of college life, to focus your study of economics. It is not a comprehensive introduction to economics, and it is certainly not a substitute for reading your textbooks, attending lectures, and actively participating in class discussion. This chapter and the others in Part Two of this book should serve you as a road map, pointing out the main features you will encounter on your trip through the course. We have already inventoried the most basic assumptions and principles of economics. Here are the major themes and topics that are built on these assumptions and principles and that are reflected in the next 12 chapters.

PPF and Supply and Demand
- PPF
- Supply and demand
- Market equilibrium
- Elasticity
- Elastic and inelastic demand
- Causes of demand elasticity
- Price elasticity of supply
- Income elasticity of demand

The Role of Consumer Choice
- The main assumptions: rationality and utility
- Working with the utility concept
- Law of diminishing marginal utility
- Utility maximization
- Substitution
- Market demand curve

The Role of the Producer
- Time frames
- Measuring output
- Law of diminishing returns
- Returns to scale
- Costs

• Fixed costs
• Variable costs
• Total costs
• Marginal cost
• What happens in the long run?

Models of Competition
• The model of perfect competition
• Profit maximization in perfect competition
• Shutdown
• Imperfect competition
• Monopoly
• Monopolistic competition
• Oligopoly
• Collusion
• Price leadership model
• Kinked-demand model
• Demand and MR curves under oligopoly
• A special case: price discrimination

How Businesses Are Built, Financed, and Regulated
• How businesses are organized
• Individual proprietorship
• Partnership
• Corporation
• Government regulation
• Safety and the environment
• Monopoly regulation

Labor
• Supply and demand
• Issues of demand
• Issues of supply
• Monopsony
• The role of labor unions
• Why has union membership declined?
• Discrimination and segregation
• Dual-labor-market model
• Human-capital model
• More models of discrimination

The Real World: Public Goods and Externalities
- Special problems posed by public goods
- External economies and diseconomies
- Pollution costs-—and benefits
- The Coase theorem: an alternative to government regulation

Macroeconomic Overview
- The tripartite economy and the circular flow
- The business cycle
- Unemployment and full employment
- Okun's law
- Government's role
- Inflation
- Measuring economic activity
- Calculating GNP
- Other measures of national income
- Price indexes
- Measuring the money supply
- Unemployment measures

The Basic Macro Model
- Aggregate demand
- Consumption
- Saving
- Investment
- Government spending
- Aggregate expenditure
- Equilibrium of output and income
- The multiplier effect: the role of investment
- Foreign trade

Fiscal and Monetary Policy
- Aspects of fiscal policy
- Multiplier effects
- Money
- Financial instruments, institutions, and markets
- The banking system
- The Role of the Federal Reserve
- The Federal Reserve and monetary policy

• Monetary policy and inflation

The Full Macro Model
  • Equilibrium
  • The role of labor
  • The Phillips curve
  • Stagflation
  • Deficit spending or balanced budget?

International Trade and Other Issues in Macroeconomics
  • Why trade?
  • Should trade be free?
  • Should trade be restricted?
  • Accounting for international trade
  • Policies to correct payment imbalances
  • Other macroeconomic issues
  • The classical model
  • Keynesianism
  • Monetarism
  • Supply-side economics

CHAPTER 7

PPF AND SUPPLY AND DEMAND

EARLY IN ANY ECONOMICS COURSE, YOU WILL BE INTRODUCED TO THE CONCEPTS OF THE production possibility frontier (PPF) and supply and demand. We have introduced both in the previous chapter.

PPF

Because the PPF graph is so basic to economics, let's look at one:

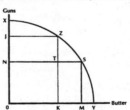

The PPF is an example of economic modeling—simplification—at its most extreme. It assumes that the society produces only two goods (or categories of goods). In beginning courses, these two goods are often identified as guns and butter. The basic idea is that consumption of one good requires a sacrifice of the other, and the PPF illustrates this trade-off graphically.

Note that guns is graphed on the X axis and butter on the Y axis. Resources are *by definition and by the nature of things* scarce, so that there are limits to the amount of guns and butter that can be produced together using these resources. The PPF curve shows the different combinations of guns and butter that will *most efficiently* use the scarce resources. A resource used to produce guns, cannot then be used to produce butter, and vice versa.

Here's how the graph works: At point *X*, all resources are devoted to producing quantity *X* (the maximum quantity) of guns—and no butter. At point *Y*, all resources are used to produce butter, without leaving any for guns. Between these extremes, some guns and some butter are produced. At the point marked *Z*, for example, amount *J* of guns is produced, and amount *K* of butter is produced.

Why is the PPF curved? Because it illustrates that some of society's resources are better at producing one of the goods than the other. As we move away from point *X* or *Y* toward the middle of the curve, we can produce more of one good in return for sacrificing relatively little of the other. At points nearest the middle of the curve (*Z* or *S*, for example), resources that are better at producing one of the goods can more readily specialize. In contrast, points closer to *X* and *Y* require more of one good to be given up in order to produce a given quantity of the other.

The PPF is used to map *efficiency*, *inefficiency*, and *unattainability*.

Points that are actually on the PPF curve are referred to as *technically efficient*, because, in exchange for a given quantity of one good, the maximum possible amount of the other can be produced. Contrast any point *inside* the PPF. At point *T*, for example, quantity 0*N* of guns is produced in return for sacrificing quantity 0*K* of butter, but at point *Z*, quantity 0*J* of guns is produced in exchange for the same quantity, 0*K*, of butter. That's *NJ* more guns!

While points along the PPF are more efficient than points within the PPF, points outside the PPF are neither efficient nor inefficient, but simply unattainable. The society has insufficient resources to produce quantities at points beyond the PPF.

TIP: PPF is a fundamental graph, but you can't tell from it alone what the *allocatively efficient point* (the most efficient point) is. That requires using the PPF in conjunction with another graph, called the social indifference curve.

Supply and Demand

The concepts of supply and demand are as fundamental to economics as the PPF. Think of supply and demand as two sides of an equation at the heart of any society in which the economy is not entirely dictated by government authority.

Supply: Firms decide what, how, and how much to produce. Demand: Households (in economics, *households* are the basic consuming unit) decide what and how much to consume. All economic activities that determine how society allocates its scarce resources depend on supply and demand. When the forces of supply and demand are balanced, *market equilibrium* results, which means that quantity demanded and quantity supplied are the same, at the same price. Equilibrium in a given market is rare and fleeting, but as soon as either supply or demand changes, the economic forces that tend to create equilibrium come into play. Supply and demand are dynamic and tend toward an equilibrium, which is often upset.

Demand

Demand is the willingness of consumers to buy various amounts of a given product at various prices. Beware of commonsense assumptions here! Demand does not directly reflect what households want or need, it reflects what they are willing and able to pay for. The sum of demand of all households is called *market demand*.

Demand is governed by the *law of demand*, which states that quantity demanded will be low at high prices and high at low prices. This law may be illustrated by a *demand curve*, a straight line that slopes downward, from left to right (i.e., negatively), reflecting high demand at low prices and low demand at high prices.

While *demand* is an expression in the market of consumers' willingness to buy various quantities of product at various prices, *quantity demanded* is the actual amount of a good that will be purchased in the market at a given price. It is quantity demanded, not demand, that is graphed against price on the demand curve.

Supply

As demand is one side of the fundamental economics equation, supply is the other side. It is the expression in the market of the cumulative willingness of all firms to produce various amounts of product at various prices.

Market supply is the aggregate quantity of a good that all firms that produce that good (not all firms produce every product) will make available at all possible prices. The amount produced depends on the market price firms can get for the good.

The *law of supply* is a mirror image of the law of demand: Quantity supplied will be low at low prices and high at high prices. The law of supply may be illustrated by a *supply curve*, which usually slopes upward from left to right (i.e., positively), reflecting low quantity supplied at low prices and high quantity supplied at high prices.

As with the distinction between *demand* and *quantity demanded*, it is the *quantity supplied*, not the *supply*, that is graphed on the supply curve.

> **The negative demand curve applies to so-called *normal goods*. A minority of goods, called *Giffen goods*, do not "obey" the law of demand. Their demand curve slopes the wrong way, with quantity demanded rising with higher prices. A prestige wristwatch—a Rolex, say—is an example of a Giffen good; it is desirable precisely because it is expensive and is perceived as conferring some valuable level of prestige on its owner.**

Market Equilibrium

Market equilibrium is a balance between supply and demand; it occurs at the price at which quantity supplied and quantity demanded are equal. This can best be seen in a graph:

The line *SS* is the supply curve, and the line *DD* is the demand curve. Axis *P* represents price, and *Q* represents quantity supplied (for the supply curve) or quantity demanded (for the demand curve). Only at point *E* are the quantities supplied and demanded equal at the same price. This is market equilibrium.

In the real world, markets may or may not reach equilibrium and, in any case, seldom remain in equilibrium for long. Demand or quantity demanded may rise or fall for a variety of reasons, and the same is true of supply or quantity supplied. Even apart from this, firms may change pricing policies. All of these factors will create disequilibrium; however, as soon as disequilibrium is created, market forces will act to restore equilibrium. This is a basic property of an unregulated economy—that is, an economy that is not totally controlled by government authority.

Economists concentrate much attention on the causes of disequilibrium and the dynamics through which equilibrium is restored.

Shifts (also called changes) in demand are changes in the position of the demand curve, which may move outward (if market demand increases) or inward (if market demand decreases). Such shifts may be produced by

◆ Changes in consumer income.

◆ Changes in consumer tastes.

◆ Changes in the price of a *substitute good*—a good that can be substituted for the good in question. For example, the demand for butter may shift outward if the price of margarine (a substitute good) rises.

Shifts in supply are changes in the position of the supply curve; like changes in demand, they can be either outward (if market supply increases) or inward (if market supply decreases). Such shifts can be caused by

◆ Changes in factor prices. *Factor prices* are the prices of the various things firms use to produce the good in question.

◆ Change in the number of firms in the industry. More firms in an industry will increase the supply; fewer will decrease it.

◆ Change in the way an industry is structured. For example, an industry may consist of many small firms, then develop into an industry dominated by a few large firms. This change in structure may alter supply.

◆ Technological change: New ways of producing a good may dramatically affect supply.

TIP: Be careful to distinguish between a *shift in demand* and a *shift in quantity demanded*. When demand shifts, the market demand curve moves to a new position (outward or inward). A change in quantity demanded can occur on the *same* demand curve if the supply curve shifts.

Elasticity

So far, the concepts and assumptions presented as fundamental to economics have been quite straightforward. Rather more difficult is the concept of elasticity, the ratio of the percent change in one variable to the percent change in another. You are likely to be introduced to three types of elasticity:

1. **Price elasticity of demand** describes how quantity demanded responds to changes in price.

2. **Price elasticity of supply** describes how quantity supplied responds to changes in market price.

3. **Income elasticity of demand** is a measure of how quantity demanded responds when consumer income changes.

Questions of elasticity require a level of comfort with algebra. The equation that is basic to issues of elasticity is

$$E_{XY} = \%\Delta X / \%\Delta Y$$

where E is elasticity, X and Y are the variables in question, and Δ is the mathematical symbol for "change in."

Elastic and Inelastic Demand

When demand is elastic, percent changes in quantity demanded are greater than percent changes in price, so that when price falls, total revenue (the total sum spent on the good in the market, TR) increases. When price rises, total revenue decreases. When demand is inelastic, the reverse of this situation is true.

Causes of Demand Elasticity

Demand elasticity is determined by four factors:

> **TIP:** As with the terms *shift in demand* and *change in quantity demanded,* be careful to distinguish between *shift in supply* and *change in quantity supplied.* A shift in supply occurs only when the supply curve moves inward or outward. A change in the quantity supplied may occur on the same supply curve if the demand curve shifts.

1. **Substitutability.** A good with many substitutes has a more elastic demand than one with fewer substitutes.

2. **Importance**. By "importance," economists mean importance relative to the consumer's budget. Demand for goods that represent a small portion of a consumer's budget is usually inelastic; that is, consumers give little thought to the price of such goods. They are very concerned, however, about changes in the price of goods that represent a significant portion of their budget; therefore, demand for such goods tends to be quite elastic.

3. **Adjustment time.** Demand tends to be more elastic in proportion to the amount of time consumers have to adjust to price changes. Given time, consumers can find substitute products or alter their habits of consumption.

4. **Necessity of the good.** Goods perceived as necessities tend to have relatively inelastic demand. A diabetic whose life depends on insulin will not buy less insulin, let alone stop buying insulin, because its price increases. In contrast,

goods perceived as luxuries are subject to more demand elasticity.

Price Elasticity of Supply

Price elasticity of supply is a measure of how quantity supplied responds to changes in demand. In the long run (given sufficient time for various market adjustments to be made), supply tends to be elastic. In the short run, however, supply tends to be inelastic, because firms cannot always adjust production quickly. In a minority of situations, supply is *perfectly inelastic;* that is, supply cannot change at all, regardless of price. Goods that are by their nature absolutely limited in supply—the works of Rembrandt, or Corvette Stingrays (vintage collectible cars that are no longer man-ufactured)—are subject to inelastic supply. Inelastic supply also applies when we look at the *immediate run* for the production of some goods—a span of time so brief that a firm cannot possibly adjust production. In the case of some very elabo-rate or expensive goods—a major factory, for example—the so-called immediate run may represent a significant span of time. It may take months or years to build new facilities required in order to increase production.

Income Elasticity of Demand

Quantity demanded of a good often responds to consumer income. Usually, this income elasticity of demand is positive; that is, the greater the income of the con-sumer, the greater the quantity demanded of the good. Such a good is described as a *normal good.* In the case of *inferior goods,* however, income elasticity of demand is negative; that is, as consumer income increases, quantity demanded of the inferior good falls. A butcher shop in a gentrifying neighborhood—a neighborhood for-merly populated by people of modest means and now experiencing an influx of wealthier individuals—will probably experience a decrease in quantity demanded of hamburger and an increase in quantity demanded of top sirloin steak.

CHAPTER 8

THE ROLE OF CONSUMER CHOICE

FOR MANY BEGINNING ECONOMICS STUDENTS, THE PROMISE OF FINDING THE KEYS TO how consumers make choices is an exciting one. After all, isn't this what business is all about? Determining what will sell, then going about creating that product? Of course, the subject is also a daunting one. How can one possibly reduce to a handful of formulas the variety of desires, tastes, and aspirations that motivate human behavior?

Yet that is precisely what economics does—and, once again, it does it by beginning with certain simplifying assumptions about how individuals assess available alternatives to attain desired objectives.

The Main Assumptions: Rationality and Utility

Economists assume first that consumers behave rationally. Once again, we must exercise caution: We must understand the term *rational* as an economist understands it, not as it may be understood in everyday usage. It may be impossible to convince your Aunt Ida that purchasing a two-dollar bottle of spring water is a "rational" decision when perfectly good tap water is available at an extremely small fraction of that price. Uncle Fred may find your desire for a $40,000 automobile highly *irrational* when adequate transportation can be found for a quarter of that price.

To economists, however, *rational* is not synonymous with wise, prudent, frugal, or shrewd, but simply means that, in making purchasing decisions, people attempt to maximize their satisfaction from consumption. That is, they attempt to purchase the best combination of goods they can, given their income. Expressed another way, consumers attempt to *maximize utility*, subject, as always, to scarcity of resources, which may be called budget constraint.

Working with the Utility Concept

For the economist, *utility* is the satisfaction derived from consumption of goods. The economist assumes that consumers can measure the utility they get from various combinations of goods (often called *market baskets*) and can thereby make rational decisions about how to allocate their incomes in order to maximize utility.

Economists often attempt to measure utility objectively .

◆ **Cardinal utility** assigns a satisfaction unit (called a *util*) to utility. This form of measurement uses cardinal numbers and attempts to measure utility in absolute terms.

◆ **Ordinal utility** attempts to measure utility in relative terms by ranking level of satisfaction. One can ask consumers if they like product A more than product B, or one can determine if more of product A than of product B is consumed.

◆ **Total utility** is the total satisfaction derived from all goods purchased by a consumer. For a particular good, it is also possible to speak of the total utility derived from all the units consumed of that good.

◆ **Marginal utility** of a good is the additional utility a consumer receives from consuming one more unit of the good.

Law of Diminishing Marginal Utility

A crucial element in the economist's view of consumer behavior is the law of diminishing marginal utility, which states that, for a normal good, marginal utility diminishes as consumption of the good is increased. Hungry? That first hot dog tastes awfully good. Its marginal utility (MU) is high. Have another. Because you're not as hungry, the MU of the second hot dog is lower. For a third, it's lower still, and (unless you are very hungry indeed) MU is probably insufficient to motivate the purchase of a fourth hot dog.

TIP: Rationality and utility are assumptions. We all know that consumers do not always make the best purchasing decisions. The economist merely assumes that they always try to make the best decisions and that they don't set out (irrationally) to make the wrong decisions. For purposes of interpreting economic models, assume that the best decisions are made—that utility is maximized.

Utility Maximization

As always, scarcity prevails. Consumers have limited incomes with which to buy goods; therefore, they seek to maximize utility—to derive the greatest utility possible from their purchases.

The principle of utility maximization holds that consumers attempt to buy the combination of goods that yields the greatest possible total utility. The consumer's object is to allocate income so that the marginal utility per dollar spent is the same for all goods consumed. If the consumer finds that she is deriving more utility from spending on good X than from spending on good Y, she will purchase more of good X until its marginal utility diminishes to the point where the marginal utility of X (MU_X) is the same as that of Y (MU_Y). At this point, there will be no more switching between goods X and Y: *Total utility* has been maximized. This can be expressed by the equation $MU_X/P_X = MU_Y/P_Y$, where MU is marginal utility and P is price.

Another expression, MU_X/MU_Y, is the *marginal rate of substitution* (MRS), the ratio at which consumers are willing to trade between a given pair of goods at the margin. If, for example, a consumer will trade 4 of good X for 1 of good Y, good X has 4 times the utility of good Y: $MRS_{XY} = 4$. Starting with this basic expression, it becomes possible to calculate trade-offs at various prices between pairs of goods.

Substitution

Questions of marginal utility and marginal rate of substitution bear directly on the choices consumers make. The *income effect* measures the change in a household's effective income due to a price change in a good, while the *substitution effect* measures the change in consumption of a good due to a change in its price.

Note that households are considered *price takers* (not *price makers*). That is, the individual consumer cannot sufficiently influence the demand for a good to change ("make") its price, but must take whatever price is set. As far as the individual consumer is concerned, market supply is perfectly elastic, and price will remain unchanged no matter how much or how little of a good that consumer chooses to buy. But the utility-maximizing consumer will buy more of a good only if its price falls, so that the consumer's demand curve for a good is always downward sloping.

The sum of all individual consumers' demand is the *market demand*. At a given price, each consumer is willing to buy a certain amount of a good. The total of these amounts is the quantity demanded at that given price.

But consumers don't merely choose to allocate limited income to a certain good. Most goods have substitute goods.

◆ **Close substitutes:** The consumer can distinguish a difference between close substitutes and may consume some of each, but a change in the price of one will lead to changes in the consumption of all. If the price of good X rises, consumers will buy less of good X and more of close substitute good Y. If the price of X falls, they will buy more of X and less of Y.

◆ **Perfect substitutes:** Consumers can distinguish no difference between these goods; therefore, the only determinant of choice is price. They will consume only the cheapest.

Another important choice relationship is between *complementary goods*—that is, goods that are commonly consumed together. Computers and computer software are examples of *complementary goods*. So are cream cheese and bagels or shoes and socks.

If the price of complement A falls, consumption of it and also of complement B will rise. If bagels become cheaper, people will buy more bagels and more cream cheese.

Market Demand Curve

The horizontal summation of the individual consumers' demand curves is the *market demand curve*. It plots the price of a good on the vertical axis and quantity demanded on the horizontal axis. Points along the curve show the relationship between quantities demanded and price.

The market demand curve introduces yet another aspect of the role of consumer choice in economics. The law of diminishing marginal utility says that consumers are (in effect) willing to pay more for the first unit of a good than for succeeding units. Thus a market demand curve may indicate that consumers are willing to pay $10 for the first unit, $9 for the second, and $8 for the third. If the market price for this good is established at $8, there is a $2 difference between what consumers are willing to pay for the first unit and what they actually pay. There is a $1 difference between what consumers are willing to pay for the second unit and what they actually pay. There is no difference between these prices for the third unit.

With regard to the first unit, there is a *consumer surplus* of $2. With regard to the second, the consumer surplus is $1. For the third unit, it is zero. At the $8 price, this good has a *total consumer surplus* of $3 ($2 + $1). Consumer surplus is the difference between what consumers are willing to pay for a good and what they must pay (as seen in the market price).

Halfway There

Having derived the market demand curve for a good, an economist has one-half of the picture required for a supply-demand analysis—the demand half. The plot of price against quantity demanded is the end product of a series of choices made by consumers, who seek to maximize their utility by

◆ Deciding on what goods to purchase

◆ Deciding on what substitutes are viable alternatives

◆ Deciding on what quantities of goods to purchase, based on income constraints

Driven by these decisions, consumers make purchases to the point where utility (satisfaction) derived per dollar is equalized across all available goods. This behavior results in a downward-sloping demand curve consistent with the laws of demand and of diminishing marginal utility. The overall market demand curve is the sum of the individual demand curves.

In the next chapter, we'll survey what beginning economics students can expect to learn about the other half of the supply-demand analytical picture: the role of the producer.

CHAPTER 9

THE ROLE OF THE PRODUCER

FIRMS ARE PRODUCERS. THEY PRODUCE WHAT THE CONSUMERS IN THE PRECEDING chapter consume. But they are also themselves consumers, who consume (use *inputs*) not to maximize utility, but to achieve the highest level of output, subject to a cost constraint.

From the point of view of the producer, economics seeks first to derive the *production function*, the relationship between inputs used and output produced. At its most basic, the production function is a relationship among

- ◆ Labor input
- ◆ Capital input
- ◆ Product output

Various combinations of labor and capital will produce various amounts of output. That is, more labor may produce more output, but that same quantity of output may also be achieved with relatively less labor and relatively more capital. Analyzing production requires determining what combinations of labor and capital inputs will produce the most output at the lowest cost.

Time Frames

The concept of *short-run* and *long-run* time frames figures importantly in analyzing the production function.

In short-run analysis, the firm has insufficient time to change the level of at least one input. For example, it cannot quickly build a new factory (add a capital input) to increase output.

In the long-run time frame, it is assumed that the firm can change any or all of its inputs. A plant could be built. Labor could be added. And so on.

Measuring Output

For purposes of analysis, the effect that changing input has on production is measured by changing only a single input and holding the others constant. Economists may measure the resulting output in any of three basic ways:

1. **Total physical product** is the total quantity of output produced with a given amount of some input, such as capital or labor.

2. **Average physical product** (also called *average product*) is the *total product* divided by the amount of the variable input used to produce it. If the labor input is varied, then

$$\text{Average product} = Q/L$$

   where Q is the quantity of total product produced and L is the labor input.

3. **Marginal product** is the change in the total product resulting from a change in the variable input. Marginal output is the additional output produced by a 1-unit increase in the amount of the variable input. Add a unit of labor, and you may derive the *marginal product of labor*:

$$\Delta Q/\Delta L$$

   where the delta sign refers to the *change* in the variable it precedes.

Law of Diminishing Returns

Much as marginal utility diminishes for consumers, returns diminish for firms; that is, as the amount of one input used is increased, its effect on productivity will eventually decline. For example, let's say a firm has a production line (a "fixed" input, because it cannot be readily upgraded). To increase output, more labor is put to work on the production line. Output indeed increases, and yet more labor is added. The production line begins to get crowded, workers become less efficient, and production becomes less efficient. The crowded production line still produces more output than it did before additional labor was added, but the addition of the first unit of labor was more productive than the addition of subsequent units of labor.

The implication of the diminishing returns is profound: The amount of variable inputs required to add a given amount to variable output will increase, resulting in greater costs.

Returns to Scale

It is important to note that the law of diminishing returns is a short-run process. It applies when only a single input is varied. In the long run—that is, given a time frame in which all input variables can be changed—*returns to scale* operates. This concept deals with the effect on output of proportional increases or decreases in the use of all inputs simultaneously.

♦ In some cases, scaling up all inputs by the same proportion results in a more than proportional increase in quantity of output. This is called *increasing returns to scale.*

♦ In some cases, this scaling up results in an output increase that is exactly proportional to the increase in input quantities. This is called *constant returns to scale.*

♦ In still other cases, the scaling up of inputs produces output that is less than proportional to the increase in inputs. This is called *decreasing returns to scale.*

Costs

Why are these relationships of input to output so important? As always, the answer is scarcity of resources. All inputs represent cost to the firm. Scarce resources, which are generated by selling goods produced, must be allocated efficiently to cover input costs.

Fixed Costs

A firm's most basic costs are *fixed costs*, which, while essential to production, are independent of production quantity. Increasing or decreasing production will have no effect on these costs. Such costs as rent, some taxes, insurance fees, mortgage payments, and so on are fixed costs.

Variable Costs

Variable costs rise and fall with the level of output. Costs for raw materials, fuel, and labor are prime examples of variable costs. The concepts discussed in relation to diminishing returns and returns to scale mean that variable costs do not behave simply in direct proportion to output, at least not in the short run.

♦ At low levels of production, some resources may not be used efficiently; for example, some workers may be more or less idle.

♦ At high levels of production, diminishing returns creates inefficiencies.

♦ At some level of production between these extremes, variable costs are allocated most efficiently.

More about Fixed vs. Variable Costs

The distinction between fixed and variable costs is not absolute under all circumstances. Viewed in the short-run time frame, costs tend to be fixed. That is, in the short run, relatively few inputs can be changed. But in the long-run time frame, costs tend to be variable, because, given enough time, just about all inputs can be altered.

Total Costs

To make meaningful decisions about production, a firm needs to calculate its *total costs*, the sum of fixed and variable costs. Since total fixed costs do not change, total costs vary with total variable costs. Graphically, fixed costs may be plotted as a straight horizontal line—an unchanging floor from which the curve of variable-costs takes off. Elevated by this floor, the variable-cost curve represents a firm's total costs.

Relationships between fixed, variable, and total costs and output are expressed as

◆ **Average fixed cost** (AFC): Fixed cost divided by output to yield the mean value of fixed cost

◆ **Average variable cost** (AVC): Variable cost divided by output to yield the mean value of variable cost, or variable cost per unit of output

◆ **Average total cost** (ATC): Total cost divided by output to yield the mean value of total cost, or cost per unit of output at each level of output

Marginal Cost

Decisions about allocating inputs may be made by calculating *marginal cost* (MC), the cost a firm incurs to increase output by a single unit. It is calculated in this way:

Assume you want to determine the marginal cost of increasing production from 9 to 10 units. Calculate

$$MC_{10\text{th unit}} = TC_{10 \text{ units}} - TC_{9 \text{ units}}$$

where MC is marginal cost and TC is total cost.

It is very useful to determine marginal cost (MC), because how it relates to average total cost (ATC) and average variable cost (AVC) determines the firm's equilibrium: how much the firm will produce and what price it will get for its product. MC always intersects ATC and AVC at their lowest points:

TIP: Since fixed costs do not change with changes in output, VC (variable cost) could also be substituted for TC to obtain a meaningful figure.

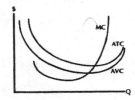

What Happens in the Long Run?

Firms—and economists—must make short-run as well as long-run choices. Remember that in the long run, all costs become variable. The long-run average cost (LRAC) curve is made up of a succession of short-run average cost (SRAC) curves.

At the lowest point of an LRAC curve, optimum plant size occurs. If larger plant and firm sizes increase efficiency, the industry in which that firm operates is said to have *economies of scale*. Economies of scale exist when the LRAC curve declines as production increases. If the curve rises with increased production, the industry has diseconomies of scale.

> **NOTE:** Economies of scale are sometimes called *increasing returns to scale.*

Factors that contribute to economies of scale include

◆ Production processes that operate efficiently only at large scale (mass production, assembly-line industries)

◆ Complex production processes that benefit from specialization of labor and equipment

◆ Industries requiring high capital costs: These costs can be most efficiently spread out over larger outputs, so that long-run average costs decline

It is possible for a firm to become too large and suffer diseconomies of scale. Poor management organization, with excessive bureaucracy, is probably the commonest cause of such a situation.

CHAPTER 10

MODELS OF COMPETITION

ONSUMERS AND PRODUCERS DO NOT EXIST IN A VACUUM. GIVEN SCARCE resources, competition is a fact of economic life. Except in a few societies in which the economy is centrally controlled by government authority, property rights to scarce resources exist and are sanctioned, protected, and enforced by social authority. Without the ability to exchange them, property rights would be essentially meaningless; however, in societies with essentially unregulated economies, property rights are exchanged in competitive markets. The resources are available for those who are willing and able to pay the most for them—presumably in anticipation of realizing greater profit from their use.

Economists recognize four types of market models:

1. **Perfect competition** features many buyers and many small firms making a homogeneous product; entry and exit into this market is free (that is, any firm may enter or exit the market without barriers).

2. **Monopolistic competition** has the same features as perfect competition, except that there is product differentiation.

3. **Oligopoly** is a model of competition in which a few large firms dominate, products are differentiated, and there are barriers to entry and exit.

4. **Monopoly** features a single firm dominant in the marketplace, with formidable barriers to entry.

A word about homogeneous and differentiated products: When firms within an industry produce identical products, it is said that these products are *homogeneous*.

If differences exist or can be perceived among the products of different firms in the same industry, these products are said to be differentiated. With homogeneous products, competition is strictly a matter of price. In the case of differentiated products, competition is based at least in part on the perceived value of differences in the products. Product differentiation can command *customer loyalty*, which, in turn, makes demand for the firm's product less elastic. Product differentiation is enhanced by a firm's ability to establish a valued *brand name*, which may be enhanced through *advertising*. It may also be enhanced, of course, through excellence: creating a product perceived as more useful or desirable than others in the industry.

And a word about ease of entry and exit: Some industries or markets present few or no barriers to firms wishing to enter them. Such industries are usually highly competitive, and ease of entry also generally implies ease of exit as well. Other industries or markets may present various barriers to entry by new firms. These barriers may be economic or noneconomic.

◆ **Economic barriers to entry** include high start-up costs and (related to this) large economies of scale.

◆ **Noneconomic barriers to entry** include government licenses or franchises and private franchises, both of which regulate and reduce competition.

The Model of Perfect Competition

Perfect competition is a model of an ideal case in which competition creates the most beneficial outcome for consumers. Like other economic models, perfect competition is a simplification, but it is an especially important one, as it is a kind of index against which other models as well as real-world competition can be compared and analyzed.

In perfect competition:

◆ Many small firms compete; that is, no single firm is sufficiently large to affect the market as a whole.

◆ All the firms in the industry produce the same (homogeneous) product.

◆ There are no barriers to entry or exit.

◆ It is assumed that firms and consumers have *perfect information* about market prices and product.

◆ In perfect competition, firms are *price takers*; that is, they accept the market price as a given.

◆ In perfect competition, a firm's total revenue (TR) is the total sum for which it can sell the total quantity of its output. Its *marginal revenue* (MR) is the increase in total revenue created by an increase of one unit of output.

◆ In perfect competition, TR rises by the market price P for each additional unit produced. (Therefore, the perfectly competitive firm's TR curve is a straight line rising from left to right.)

◆ In perfect competition, MR = P.

◆ In perfect competition, market demand for the firm's output is perfectly elastic; that is, it can sell all it produces for P, so that demand = MR = P.

Profit Maximization in Perfect Competition

The objective of the perfectly competitive firm is to maximize profits, which means operating such that the difference between total cost and total revenue is as large as possible. This difference may be expressed in an equation:

$$\Pi = TR - TC$$

where Π (pi) is profit, TR is total revenue, and TC is total costs.

Profit maximization (equilibrium) occurs when MR = MC; that is, at the quantity of output where the marginal cost curve intersects the marginal revenue curve. At this intersection, the output of the firm is at its profit maximization point. If the quantity supplied of output exceeds the quantity associated with this point, the cost of these excess units is greater than what the firm will gain in revenue from them (MR). The firm should reduce the quantity supplied. However, if the quantity of output supplied is less than the quantity associated with this maximization point, MC will less than MR for additional units produced *up to* the maximization point. The firm should increase production to this point.

In the model of perfect competition, there is nothing *within* the firm that will disturb equilibrium (move quantity supplied away from the profit maximization point). However, if market demand shifts, then the firm's MR curve will shift, creating a disequilibrium and a need to adjust output. In the real world, where *perfect information* is hard to come by, misreading of market demand and production costs could well lead to disequilibrium. In the long run, market forces will act so that firms produce at the least-cost point, such that MR = MC = ATC.

In the short run, market supply may lag behind market demand, pushing up prices and thereby allowing firms to sell their output for more than their ATC. The result is *excess profit*, profit exceeding normal profit.

Alas for perfectly competitive firms, this situation is not destined to endure. The lure of excess profits will bring more firms into this industry (which offers no barriers to entry), and the market supply curve will shift outward as market supply increases. With increased market supply, prices will fall, and new firms will cease to enter the industry.

We Quit

If the market supply increases sufficiently for market price to fall below a firm's ATC, the firm will sustain losses and may leave the industry to look for profits elsewhere.

A firm sustaining short-term losses does not necessarily have to leave the industry, but may instead *shut down*— temporarily cease production. Management may be tempted to shut down whenever MR falls below ATC; however, if MR still exceeds average variable costs (AVC), the loss sustained is less than fixed costs, so the firm should continue to produce. If, however, MR falls below AVC, the firm cannot cover variable costs and its losses exceed fixed costs. Shutting down in this case will limit the firm's losses to the amount of the fixed costs.

Imperfect Competition

In an industry in which one or more firms are sufficiently large to affect the market or in which product differentiation exists among the firms in the industry, competition is imperfect.

Monopoly

A *monopoly* exists in an industry when a single firm produces the entire quantity supplied in a market. How does a monopoly come into existence?

◆ Very high cost of entry

◆ Great economies of scale

◆ Government protection (franchises, etc.)

◆ No substitutes for a firm's product

◆ Inelastic market demand

Natural monopolies are special cases in which economies of scale are so great that entry into the industry by new firms is very difficult. Railroads and utilities are good examples of natural monopolies.

For the monopolist, the demand curve is the market demand curve. It slopes downward. This presents an interesting situation for the monopolist's marginal revenue curve. Recall that MR is the change in total revenue that results when the firm increases output by one unit. With a downward-sloping demand curve, the monopolist must reduce price on all its output in order to sell each marginal unit; therefore, MR is not the full price of the marginal unit, it is the full price reduced by the amount of revenue lost by reducing the price on the other units sold.

Where MR = MC, profit is maximized; however, in contrast to the situation of perfect competition, where MR = MC = ATC, the downward-sloping demand and MR curves of the monopolist mean that its equilibrium price is not the same as MR or ATC, and, therefore, the MC curve is not the monopolist's supply curve. These downward-sloping demand and MR curves also mean that the output at the profit maximization point will result in excess profits because equilibrium price is higher than ATC. The nature of a monopoly is such that excess profits can be sustained indefinitely.

Therefore, monopolies are not allocatively efficient. They may operate with technical and economic efficiency, but because the monopolist's output is less than the level of lowest ATC, which, furthermore, is higher than the lowest possible ATC, the monopolist is not allocatively efficient.

- ◆ **Technical efficiency** prevails whenever using a lower quantity of any input requires using a higher quantity of at least one other input in order to maintain the same level of output.

- ◆ **Economic efficiency** exists when a firm, at a given level of output, uses the one technically efficient combination of inputs that results in the lowest cost of producing that level of output.

- ◆ **Allocative efficiency** is achieved when the firm produces at the level of output at which its ATC is lowest. At allocative efficiency, output is produced at the lowest possible cost.

Despite the lack of allocative efficiency, a monopoly may realize excess profits. Moreover, the economies of scale possible in some monopolies may not lead to the *lowest possible cost*, but nevertheless yield lower costs than would be possible in a market consisting of many smaller firms.

Monopolistic Competition

Monopolistic competition is differentiated from perfect competition only by the fact that firms do not produce homogeneous output; products are differentiated, but are *close substitutes* for one another. As in perfect competition, there are many firms in the industry, and few barriers to entry and exit exist.

While the competitive market for monopolistic competition resembles that of perfect competition more than it does that of monopoly, the market demand curve for these firms shares an important characteristic with the market demand curve for monopolies: Demand is downward-sloping, as is the marginal revenue curve. This is due to product differentiation.

While products are differentiated, they are also close substitutes, which means that many, though not all, buyers will substitute another product if a firm's output price rises. Moreover, if a firm's output price falls, it will attract buyers from other firms. Demand and MR curves are highly elastic, though not perfectly so.

As in the previous two models of competition, market equilibrium is reached when MR = MC. For the monopolistically competitive firm, however, at this point price and ATC are equal, so that there is no excess profit in the long run. Nor do these firms produce where MR = ATC, which means that they do not achieve allocative efficiency—that is, least-cost production.

In the short run, if excess profits are achieved, new firms will enter the market. The close substitutes that these new firms produce compete sufficiently with the products of the older firms to shift the market demand curve for all firms inward. With this comes an inward shift in the firms' MR curves, reducing and ultimately eliminating excess profit. When excess profit is gone, new firms will stop entering the market. This coincides with price becoming equal to ATC and MR becoming equal to MC.

If too many firms operate in the market, ATC will rise above demand (D) and, therefore, above price as well. Firms will incur losses, and so some will leave the market, thereby shifting the demand curve for the remaining firms outward once again until price again becomes equal to ATC.

Oligopoly

In oligopoly, entry into the industry is difficult (usually because of high start-up costs) and at least some firms are large enough to influence the market. Products may or may not be differentiated. Oligopolists make decisions not just in response to market demand, but also in response to what they perceive other firms will do. This is called *mutual interdependence.*

Flavors of Oligopoly

Oligopolies can be very complex. At the introductory level, three major types are generally presented.

Collusion

In this case, firms in the industry conspire to fix prices, and perhaps even market share. In collusion, firms behave as if they were a single monopolistic firm, enjoying the excess profits of the monopolist.

Price Leadership Model

In this scenario, firms follow the lead of a dominant firm in setting prices. Firms do not adhere to any stated price-fixing agreement, but, once again, the effect may be similar to monopoly.

Kinked-Demand Model

In this case, the industry is dominated by several firms that are sufficiently large to influence the market. While each of these firms makes pricing decisions independently, they each assume that the other firms will match any price reductions, but will not match price increases (making this model significantly different from either collusion or price leadership).

Demand and MR Curves under Oligopoly

As with monopoly, demand and MR curves are downward-sloping, and the firms do not produce at the lowest ATC. Large oligopolies have excess profit and, like monopolies, may be sufficiently large to realize economies of scale that, while failing to produce allocative efficiency, nevertheless lead to lower costs than smaller firms could achieve.

A Special Case: Price Discrimination

One other element is sometimes important in competition. *Price discrimination* occurs when a firm charges different prices to different customers. Examples of price discrimination may be found in industries that offer such things as "senior citizens" prices for goods or services. Airlines may offer lower fares to customers who are willing to book well in advance. Utilities may charge different rates to residential and business customers. Whatever the ostensible rationale for price discrimination, its object is to increase profits by obtaining some consumer surplus—that difference between what a customer is willing to pay and what he or she actually pays.

Price discrimination is not always easy to achieve. After all, the firm is requiring consumers to pay different prices for the same good. Requirements for price discrimination include:

◆ **Absence of a substitute**. A customer facing price discrimination will purchase a cheaper substitute, if one is available.

◆ **Ability to control price.** A monopoly can easily price discriminate, because it controls price. Collusion in an oligopoly can also be used to control prices and allow for price discrimination.

◆ **Customer segregation.** If a firm can identify sets of customers whose demand is inelastic, it may be able to charge them more than it can charge those customers whose demand is more elastic. Customers must also be segregated such that they cannot trade the good among themselves, since this would defeat the attempt at price discrimination.

CHAPTER 11

HOW BUSINESSES ARE BUILT, FINANCED, AND REGULATED

GETTING INTO SYNCH WITH A FIRST-TIME ECONOMICS COURSE REQUIRES A WILL-ingness to work with economic models rather than considering the "real world" directly. Nevertheless, most introductory-level courses do maintain a connection with the real world and, at some point, deal directly with the organization, financing, and regulation of business.

How Businesses Are Organized

Firms have one of three broad forms of organization: individual proprietorship, partnership, and corporation.

Individual Proprietorship

In this, the simplest form of organization, an individual owns (and usually runs) the business. This type of organization appeals to entrepreneurs who are willing and able to take total responsibility for their business decisions. While all profits belong to the owner—and are treated for tax purposes as ordinary income—the owner is also directly responsible for losses. The owner's liability for business debts is unlim-ited, which means that personal assets are necessarily at risk. Another disadvantage of the individual proprietorship is the limitation of financing. To expand an indi-vidual proprietorship requires the owner's use of personal resources or loans, for which the owner remains personally responsible.

Partnership

In this form of organization, more than one individual owns the firm, and the relationship between or among these individuals is usually formalized by legal documentation. Even when the parameters of the partners' individual authority and responsibility are specified by contract, it is all too easy for disputes and disagreements to arise. When partnerships work well, management can be very efficient. When friction develops, inefficiencies can be disastrous. The partnership is also vulnerable to dissolution if a partner dies or decides to withdraw from the enterprise.

In the simplest form of partnership, the partners jointly own the business and share both profits and liabilities. Should one of the partners be unable to cover his or her share of liabilities, the others are legally responsible for them. This situation has led to the creation of various forms of *limited partnership*, in which there is a distinction between a *general partner*—the individual who bears full responsibility for liabilities—and *limited partners*, whose liability extends only to the limits of their actual holdings in the firm.

Partnerships generally provide a firm with access to more funding than is the case with individual proprietorships. Partners pool their resources. The income partners derive from the partnership is taxed as regular income.

Corporation

While individual proprietorships and partnerships abound in free-market economies, most larger (and even many smaller) businesses obtain corporate charters from the state in which they operate. Thus sanctioned by the government, they are corporations and enjoy a number of benefits unavailable to sole proprietorships and partnerships, including these:

- ◆ A corporation can obtain funding through sale of ownership shares (called stocks) to individuals or the public. This allows for greater expansion.
- ◆ Stocks can be freely traded, so ownership transfer does not present a problem, as it often does in the case of partnerships.
- ◆ Legally, the corporation is treated as an individual. The corporation, not the shareholders, borrows funds, for which the corporation bears liability. Shareholders cannot lose more than the value of their stock in the firm. Individual liability is, therefore, significantly limited.

For all its advantages, the corporation has at least one major drawback: Corporate profits are effectively subject to *double taxation*. That is, corporate profits are subject to corporate income tax and, after distribution to shareholders, are taxed as individual income.

Large corporations have many shareholders, so that most or all of the owners of the firm do not directly manage the firm. Managers are hired. Nevertheless, shareholders do participate in control of the corporation by casting votes on various issues affecting the corporation and by casting votes for members of the corporation's board of directors. The number of votes is proportional to the number of shares held. A stockholder with 10 shares has 10 votes; a stockholder with 100 shares has 100 votes. The degree of control shareholders exercise does not necessarily mean that they can always influence management decisions as they might wish; however, a shareholder is always free to sell her stock and exit the corporation.

Stocks are only one way in which corporations are financed. They also use funds produced by product sales, withholding some profits from shareholders as *retained earnings*. Corporations can also borrow money directly from banks and other institutions and can issue bonds.

A bond differs from a stock in that it is *not* a share in the corporation, but rather a loan to the corporation. If the corporation fails, stockholders may lose their investment; bondholders, however, have a prior legal claim on the assets of the corporation. Bonds are, therefore, less risky than stocks. Like stocks, bonds can be bought and sold in a public market.

An Unregulated Economy? Not Really

While capitalism and a free-market economy prevail in the United States, business is nevertheless subject to government regulation. As corporations have grown larger and more powerful, government regulation has also tended to increase. The object of such regulation is to protect the rights of individuals and, most important, to preserve and maintain the benefits of competition by controlling or even barring monopolies and oligopolies.

Safety and the Environment

The government takes an active role in regulating and enforcing worker safety. From an economic point of view, such regulation is justified because

◆ Firms and workers may not understand all the risks involved in a particular occupation.

◆ Because of market conditions, workers may be all too willing to take unreasonable risks.

◆ The cost of occupational injuries is ultimately borne by society, and therefore it is the government's responsibility to minimize such costs for the public good.

Government also takes an active role in regulating and enforcing product safety, again justifying this on the grounds that neither firms nor consumers may fully understand the risks involved with certain products and that because the cost of product-related injuries and health problems is borne to a large extent by society, the government has a responsibility to reduce these costs for the public good. Protecting the public good is also the object of government environmental regulation.

Government regulation has a profound effect on economics, especially in the United States. The subject of pollution controls and management of other so-called *externalities* increasingly figures in introductory economics courses. We will return to this in Chapter 13.

Monopoly Regulation

Perhaps the most important form of government regulation—as far as a direct effect on the economy is concerned—is laws to control monopoly power and promote fair business conduct. While the U.S. economy is not centrally controlled, laws do limit market power with the object of preserving and maintaining competition that is beneficial to the consumer and that gives more businesses an opportunity to operate.

Beginning with the passage of the Sherman Act in 1890, there has been a series of federal laws aimed at regulating monopoly power, in large part by limiting the ability of firms to collude (fix prices) and to merge. Merger is a particularly attractive means by which firms may achieve monopoly or a nearly monopolistic market share. Types of mergers include the following:

◆ **Horizontal mergers** are the union of firms producing the same or very similar products. While it is possible that consumers may benefit from such mergers in some cases (if combined production is more efficient, costs may be lower, and prices may be reduced accordingly) most horizontal mergers between firms with significant market share are prohibited by law.

◆ **Vertical mergers** occur when firms specializing in different stages of a production process join forces. For example, an oil refiner may merge with an oil-drilling firm and with an oil-transport firm. Such mergers are not absolutely prohibited, but are regulated.

◆ **Conglomerate mergers** result when firms producing unrelated products merge. Conglomerate mergers, while regulated, are not prohibited. Conglomerate mergers are often controversial, because it may be argued that inefficiencies develop from the attempt to manage a diverse enterprise.

The role of government regulation in an essentially free-market economy is controversial and is subject to change through legislation, through interpretation of legislation by the courts, and through the way an administration chooses (or fails to choose) to apply the law. It is an area in which the counsel of economists is increasingly sought.

CHAPTER 12

LABOR

MOST OF AN INTRODUCTORY MICROECONOMICS COURSE IS DEVOTED TO QUES-
tions involving *output markets*: the dynamics of selling products to consumers, who obtain from this consumption satisfaction or "utility."
Firms, however, also participate in *input markets*; in these markets, land,
capital, and labor are sold to firms, which use these inputs to produce the
output sold in output markets. While land and capital are discussed in beginning
economics courses, the input market that receives the most attention is labor.

Supply and Demand—Again
In principle, the market for labor functions according to the same mechanisms of
supply and demand that drive any other market.

◆ The *price* of labor is wages.

◆ The *quantity* of labor may be measured in terms of hours worked or number
of workers employed.

◆ The *supply* of labor may be measured by the *labor-force participation rate*, that
fraction of the working- age population that is actually in the labor force

◆ *Demand* for labor is often a complex combination of the amount of output a
firm plans to sell and the technology by which it plans to produce the output.
Of course, these plans are directly influenced by the utility-maximizing behavior of consumers in the output market.

Issues of Demand

The quantity of labor a firm demands is a function of

◆ Productivity of labor

◆ Output price

◆ Prevailing wages

From the perspective of the firm, the optimal quantity of labor input must be determined, such that laborers are hired to the point at which their wage equals the value of their marginal product:

$$W = P \times MP_L$$

where W is the prevailing wage for labor, P is the price per unit of output, and MP_L is the marginal product of labor—that is, the additional output produced by the *last* worker hired.

As with any input, the law of diminishing returns applies, so that the increase that comes with each additional unit of labor decreases. For this reason, the condition used to determine the optimal quantity of labor is sometimes expressed in terms of the *real wage*—the wage rate divided by the price of output:

$$W/P = MP_L$$

Issues of Supply

From the perspective of the household supplying labor, labor is a trade-off between leisure (all nonlabor activities, including such things as child rearing, sleeping, and eating, not just recreational activities) and labor. While time spent supplying labor is time lost to leisure (for the worker, labor has an *opportunity cost*), it is also time that produces income; therefore, at a certain wage level, the household will supply more labor because the opportunity cost of leisure becomes higher.

The situation seems clear: When wages are low, households will supply less labor (because the opportunity cost of labor is high), and when wages are high, they will supply more labor (because the opportunity cost of leisure is high); therefore, the supply curve for labor should be a simple upward-sloping curve. However, the labor-supply curve is more complex. The trade-offs between leisure and labor are *substitution effects*, but where wage rate changes are concerned, an *income effect* is also operative.

When wages rise, workers can consume more without supplying more labor; that is, they can "buy" more leisure by working less time. At some point, increasing wages will actually bend the supply curve for labor backward, so that increasing wages yields a *lower* supply of labor. In this case, the income effect overcomes the substitution effect.

Monopsony

Like most markets, the labor market is subject to competition. Workers may move from employer to employer in search of better work, better working conditions, or higher wages. In the real world, however, it is not unusual to find labor markets in which a single firm provides most of the jobs. This situation, called *monopsony*, provides a convenient model, uncomplicated by issues of competition, for studying optimal input. In the absence of monopsony, the equilibrium wage and quantity of labor occurs at the point at which the labor-demand and labor-supply curves intersect. But the monopsonist faces no competition for labor, so it may fix wages below the level that would be paid under competitive conditions and determine optimal input based solely on the relation of marginal labor cost and the marginal revenue product of labor.

The Role of Labor Unions

Monopsony is both an economic model and, in some labor markets, a real-world fact. Indeed, labor unions came into being in the United States as a means by which workers might avoid exploitation by monopsonistic employers. Unions replace the competitive labor market with *collective bargaining*, a process by which the union negotiates contracts with employers on behalf of all workers.

In economic terms, the objective of the union is to function as a monopolist in the *input* market, so that it can produce monopoly profits for its members. To achieve this objective, unions

◆ Organize available labor in a given market so that the individual workers agree to abide by union negotiations with employers

◆ Negotiate contracts with employers restricting employment to union members

◆ Restrict membership to a level below the labor supply in a competitive market

Why Has Union Membership Declined?

Labor unions assumed an important role in the U.S. labor market at the end of the nineteenth century and reached the height of their power by the mid-twentieth century. Since 1950, however, union membership has generally declined, so that, at century's end, it is about half what it was in the 1950s. Why?

◆ Unions successfully lobbied government for legislation protecting the rights of workers. The very existence of such legislation has reduced the perceived need for union membership.

◆ Union practices perceived as abuses, including stringently restricting membership, forcing employers to hire superfluous workers ("featherbedding"), and corruption, have reduced public acceptance of unions.

◆ Competition from offshore firms producing goods with much lower labor costs has made it increasingly difficult for unions to compel industries to maintain high wages.

◆ Federal regulation formerly protected unions in some industries. The deregulation of many industries during the 1970s and 1980s allowed nonunion firms to begin operating and competing with union firms.

Discrimination and Segregation

Economics, especially as presented at the introductory level, often straddles the realm of modeling and theory, on the one hand, and the "real world," on the other. The economic impact of discrimination and segregation in the labor market figures increasingly not only in economics generally, but in survey-level courses as well.

Two important methods of analyzing the effects of discrimination are the *dual-labor-market model* and the *human-capital model.*

Dual-Labor-Market Model

As conceptualized under this model, the labor market is split into the primary labor market and the secondary labor market. The primary sector consists of the "good jobs"—those offering high wages, career development opportunities, and job security. Workers tend to be promoted from within firms, and their perceived productivity is greatly prized by the employer.

Turned away from this primary sector are those workers who are perceived as being less productive—traditionally blacks, women, and, in some places, members of other minorities (such as new immigrants). These workers are relegated to the secondary labor market, which consists of jobs with minimal skill requirements that offer poor pay, little chance for career development, and little job security. Employees do not work their way up within these firms, because the jobs require little training; that is, the employer's investment in such workers is minimal.

Human-Capital Model

Under this approach, economists assume that individuals make decisions concerning "investments" in themselves, acquiring education and training because they perceive that these will enable them to get more desirable jobs. To assess the role of discrimination in the labor market, an economist might quantify the human-capital characteristics of individuals (such as years of education, special training, on-the-job experience, and so on), then correlate this information with wages earned. Any differences in wages that cannot be accounted for by human-capital factors are the so-called *discriminatory residual,* which represents the effects of discrimination.

More Models of Discrimination

Economists have developed additional models to analyze discriminatory behavior. The purpose of such models is not only to predict the effect of regulation and policies designed to curb discrimination, but also to assess the costs of discrimination. Important models include

◆ **The overcrowding model.** The group discriminated against is crowded into a less desirable sector of the labor market, resulting in an output loss for society. If this group were permitted to enter the more desirable sector, a net gain to society in the value of output would result.

◆ **Employer taste for discrimination model.** In this model, employers are assumed to sacrifice profit maximization for perceived utility gained by discriminating against certain groups.

◆ **Employee discrimination model.** If some workers prefer not to work with members of certain minorities, an employer who hired members of these minorities might have to pay a premium to attract or retain other workers. To avoid this, the employer will discriminate against members of those minorities.

◆ **Customer discrimination model.** In some cases, consumers may be unwilling to purchase goods produced by firms employing certain minorities—unless, perhaps, prices are reduced. To avoid reducing prices, an employer may discriminate.

◆ **Statistical discrimination.** An employer may use some form of average characteristic of a certain sex or race to guide hiring practices. If the employer perceives women to be, on average, less productive than men, he will discriminate against women job applicants—regardless of whether or not the statistical information is relevant to the *individual* applicant.

CHAPTER 13

THE REAL WORLD: PUBLIC GOODS AND EXTERNALITIES

O NE OF THE KEY ASSUMPTIONS OF ECONOMIC THEORY IS THAT GOODS AND SERVICES desired by consumers are always readily supplied by profit-maximizing producers. Yet this is not true in all cases. The fact is that certain classes of goods are not necessarily produced under a free-market system, even though consumers are willing to pay for them. These are called *public goods*. They are distinguished from other classes of goods in that consumption by one person does not diminish consumption by others. Economists call such goods *nonrival* in their consumption. National defense and municipal street lamps are examples of public goods. More specifically, these are examples of *pure public goods*, goods from which it is impossible to exclude anyone from consuming. Not all public goods are pure. For example, a toll road is nonrival (consumption by one does not diminish consumption by others), but the road is unavailable to those who are unwilling or unable to pay the toll.

Special Problems Posed by Public Goods

Because public goods are nonrival, a producer of such goods can sell a unit of output ad infinitum without experiencing an increase in cost. Regardless of the number of consumers, the good is available to be sold again and again. This sounds quite good for the producer, but what about pure public goods, from the consumption of which exclusion is impossible? Who will produce such goods? How will they be paid for? This is known as the *free-rider problem*: Some individuals who enjoy the benefits of a pure public good will pay nothing. This being the case, private markets for pure public goods cannot exist, and the government must devise means for financing such goods.

The pricing of pure public goods is also problematic. Because any number of consumers can benefit from a public good, its marginal cost is zero. That is, it costs no more to provide a corner street lamp for thousands of people who may pass under it than it costs to provide such a lamp for one person who will pass under it. This being the case, efficient pricing of a public good should be zero, since price should equal marginal cost. Of course, this is impossible. No private firm could remain in operation if it charged nothing for its output. For this reason, the private sector cannot provide (finance) pure public goods.

This leaves the government, but it also leaves the government with the problem of creating a demand curve for the public good it proposes to produce. If the government knew the demand for a given public good, it could then determine the quantity of the good to supply and what taxes to assess to pay for the good. The demand curve for a pure public good is the sum of what each citizen-consumer is willing to pay for it.

The optimal provision of a public good is based on the sum of citizen-consumers' valuations of additional units of the good; that is, the demand curve for the good is also society's *marginal benefit schedule* for the public good. It shows the additional benefit society derives from consuming an additional unit of the good. To derive the optimal quantity of a public good, the costs of providing the good must be considered in relation to the benefits derived. Net benefits are positive as long as marginal benefits exceed marginal costs of the good. Where marginal costs intersect the demand curve (which is also the marginal benefit schedule), the optimal provision of the good is found.

In theory, providing the quantity of the good at the intersection of marginal cost and the marginal benefit schedule is optimal. In practice, however, the problem of financing this quantity remains. Remember, the demand curve/marginal benefit schedule is the sum of how citizen-consumers value the good and each additional unit of the good. Because valuations differ across individuals, some will pay too much and others too little for the good if taxes are levied on all citizen-consumers equally. In real-world practice, governments attempt to develop appropriate tax strategies to address this problem.

External Economies and Diseconomies

In terms of costs, there is an equivalent to public goods that economists must take into account. Costs and market prices may not always accurately account for the true costs involved in producing or consuming a good. In these cases, *external economies and diseconomies* (*externalities*) are said to occur. An example of an externality is the pollution of a stream created by an industry that freely uses the waterway to dispose of the waste products of some production process. The firm incurs no cost in dumping its waste, but the people downstream incur the cost of a polluted waterway from which they can no longer drink.

Externalities run counter to what the eighteenth-century economist Adam Smith called the *invisible hand*—the capitalist principle that, driven by their own selfish ends, individuals will collectively create the highest possible state of social welfare. An externality is the result of pursuing a selfish end and causing harm to social welfare in the process.

> **NOTE:** Externalities are not limited to production. Consumption may also create externalities, such as the cigarette smoker's "secondhand smoke" or the rock fan's cacophony. The smoker's externality may damage your health, thereby incurring unwanted costs for you. The rock fan's music may interfere with your sleep or your ability to concentrate productively, thereby incurring costs associated with these problems.

Not all externalities are bad or necessarily adverse. The activity of the Hollywood film industry provides a no-cost benefit to the southern California tourism industry: It attracts tourists. A *pecuniary externality* may benefit some and create diseconomies for others. For example, a new employer may open up a plant in a small town. As a result, wages for all workers in the town rise because of increased competition for the labor supply. The townspeople enjoy the benefits of an externality, but the town's other employers incur diseconomies as a result. They suffer higher input costs.

Insofar as they ignore externalities, private cost curves fail to represent true costs, which means that analyses of optimal output based on private costs alone are inaccurate when externalities are present. Government regulation and/or special taxation may be necessary to ensure that the true costs of production are accounted for.

Pollution Costs—and Benefits!

Pollution is perhaps the most pervasive and vexing of externalities. Common sense would dictate that the optimal level of pollution is zero, but, as is so often the case in economics, common sense can be misleading. When this is analyzed in economic terms, it is quite possible to derive a marginal-pollution-benefit curve, which puts the optimal level of pollution not at zero, but at the point where marginal pollution costs intersect with marginal pollution benefits. Allowing more pollution than this amount will incur excessive costs to society, but the cost of reducing pollution below this amount will deprive society of some of the benefits provided by pollution-producing goods.

The Coase Theorem: An Alternative to Government Regulation

Is government intervention inevitably required in order to control externalities? The *Coase theorem* provides a set of circumstances in which externalities can be managed without government regulation. According to the theorem, if property rights are adequately specified and costless negotiation is allowed, the amount of pollution will be efficient and identical regardless of how property rights are allocated. It is the property rights that provide the basis for negotiating who pays what costs for externalities.

If a town's property rights include the right to clean water, it may declare that the level of acceptable water pollution is zero. Starting from this point, however, the town may choose to *sell* to a firm the right to pollute the town's water to a certain degree. The town would have to determine just where the intersection of marginal pollution costs and marginal pollution benefits occurs and use this as a basis for determining the quantity of pollution rights it will sell.

On the other hand, if a firm's property rights include the right to pollute, the town may pay the firm to reduce its pollution to the point where marginal pollution costs intersect with marginal pollution benefits.

Note that the values negotiated are the same, regardless of whether the town or the firm owns the pollution property rights. If the town has the right to clean water, it sells some portion of that right to the firm in return for income. If the firm has the right to pollute, it sells some portion of that right to the town in return for income. Ideally, in either case, the optimal level of pollution is achieved.

The Coase theorem establishes the conditions necessary for establishing a market for pollution rights. To the degree that these conditions are not satisfied, the government could intervene by creating pollution certificates, giving the holder the right to produce a certain quantity of units of pollution. The certificates would be offered for sale on an auction basis. This would mean that the amount of a firm's bid would be determined by its pollution-abatement costs. It would bid up to but not above the cost of abatement; therefore, firms with the highest abatement costs would make the highest bids. Those firms whose abatement costs are lower would devote funds to abatement rather than to purchasing pollution certificates.

CHAPTER 14

MACROECONOMIC OVERVIEW

W E TURN NOW FROM MICROECONOMICS, THE STUDY OF FACTORS DETERMINING THE relative prices of goods and inputs, to macroeconomics, the study of the economy as a whole. While some introductory economics courses encompass both microeconomics and macroeconomics, the majority of survey-level courses are divided, with a semester spent on microeconomics and a semester on macroeconomics.

Macroeconomics shares many fundamental concepts with microeconomics, including the concept of money—anything that functions as a generally accepted medium of exchange and as a standard unit of account—and the concepts of scarcity, resource allocation, and prices.

- ◆ Whether on a micro or a macro level, resources are always scarce, meaning that wants, needs, and desires always exceed resources.
- ◆ Given the fundamental fact of scarcity, individuals and societies must make decisions about allocating scarce resources to satisfy wants, desires, and needs.
- ◆ Price is the mechanism whereby goods are rationed and resources are allocated.

The Tripartite Economy and the Circular Flow

Economists recognize three major components in our economy.

- ◆ **Households** supply the economy's labor inputs and consume the economy's outputs.

◆ **Firms** are the producers of outputs (goods).

◆ **Government** must be included as an active participant even in an economy like ours, which is not centrally regulated. Government levies and allocates taxes to purchase public goods and to influence the level of employment and business activity. Government provides a central banking authority, which ultimately controls the availability of money and credit. Government also regulates business, exerting controls on the factors of production, including capital and labor. As we have seen, it plays an active role in maintaining competition in the marketplace by discouraging monopolistic behavior among businesses. Government is big and therefore exerts important influences on the redistribution of income through taxation and borrowing.

Among the three major elements of the economy, households, firms, and government, a *circular flow* of income continually circulates. Households purchase goods, thereby furnishing income to firms. In order to produce these goods, firms require inputs from households in the form of labor, land, and capital; the wages, rent, and interest firms must pay for these inputs are the source of the household's income, which is spent on consumption. Government inserts itself into the circular flow as a collector of taxes (on household incomes and firm incomes), a producer of public goods, a regulator of business, and a large employer and consumer.

Viewed from the perspective of microeconomics, the circular flow is a description of output and input markets. Viewed from the perspective of macroeconomics, the circular flow is a model of the national income.

From Flow to Pulse

The circular flow is a highly simplified model of the economy. Certainly in the short run, the economy does not present so static a picture.

One key feature of the economy is the *business cycle*, a pattern of expansion and contraction—or recovery and recession—which affects growth, employment, and inflation. The business cycle goes through a period of expansion, rises to a peak, enters a period of recession, and sinks to a trough, from which it begins to rise again. The working of the cycle is evident in such economic indicators as gross national product (GNP), unemployment rate, prices, and profits. A major focus of macroeconomics is the attempt to forecast business cycles, since they have a profound impact on households, firms, and government.

Unemployment and Full Employment

Inasmuch as full employment is held to be a desired economic goal, macroeconomics is profoundly concerned with studying unemployment as a measure of the economy's health. *Unemployment* is simply the lack of jobs for people willing *and able* to work at the prevailing wage rate. *Full employment* exists when all individuals willing to work at the prevailing wages are employed in tasks appropriate to their skills. Full employment is not synonymous with 100 percent employment, and economists are not in agreement as to what employment figure represents a realistic full employment level. For years, 96 percent employment was considered full employment, but many economists now believe that 93 to 94 percent is a more realistic figure. (Elsewhere in tis book, 96 percent employment is taken to be full employment.)

Reasons why employment never reaches 100 percent include:

- ◆ **Frictional unemployment**—A "normal" level of unemployment due to workers changing jobs, temporary layoffs, and so on. For any individual, frictional unemployment is of short duration.

- ◆ **Structural unemployment**—Unemployment resulting from changes in the economy caused by such things as population shifts, government policies, technological changes, or changes in consumer tastes. In structural unemployment, the economy's aggregate demand is sufficient to provide full employment, but the distribution of that demand is out of synch with the composition of the labor force. For example, a decline in the birth rate may put some teachers out of work, despite the general good health of the economy.

- ◆ **Cyclical unemployment**—Unemployment resulting from a downturn in the business cycle. With the downturn comes a reduced demand for labor, usually beginning with the lowest-paid and least-skilled workers.

- ◆ **Seasonal unemployment**—The unemployment that occurs in certain industries whose production is tied to weather or season. Local construction workers may find themselves out of jobs if their part of the country is subjected to a long siege of inclement weather. Summer resort workers must find alternative employment in the wintertime.

The costs of unemployment may be measured in economic and noneconomic terms.

- ◆ **Economic costs** may be measured in "forgone output": the gap between potential GNP and actual GNP.

- ◆ **Noneconomic costs** are the individual and social impact of loss of income.

Okun's Law

Okun's law states that unemployment declines by 1 percent for every 2.5 percent of growth in real GNP above a trend rate that is sustained for one year. The implication of Okun's law is that the economy must grow substantially indeed to achieve a reduction in unemployment.

Government's Role

Most economists and virtually all politicians deem full employment to be a desirable objective. Accordingly, government may act to maintain aggregate full employment by enacting fiscal and monetary policies that promote business expansion. The trade-off here is the risk of inflation.

Inflation

Yet another focus of the macroeconomist's attention is *inflation*, a general rise in price level, which means that today's dollar buys less than yesterday's.

Demand-pull inflation results from excess demand for goods, which pulls output prices upward. *Cost-push inflation* results from increases in input costs, such as the cost of raw materials and labor, which push the prices of output up. In the case of demand-pull inflation, the government, acting through the Federal Reserve, can intervene by curbing the money supply. The government can also introduce such changes in fiscal policy as increasing taxes and cutting government spending.

Routine government intervention can do less for cost-push inflation, which is most commonly caused by demands for higher wages. (The result of these demands, often called a *price-wage spiral*, is inflation, which tends to cancel out the benefit of increased wages and elicits calls for yet higher wages.) If the price-wage spiral is extreme, the government may take the extraordinary action of introducing wage controls.

Keeping Score

Fundamental to the work of macroeconomics are measures of economic activity. The most common is the gross national product (GNP), which measures the value of all goods and services produced by the economy. GNP data are compiled quarterly, and GNP is considered a prime barometer of economic performance. A decline in GNP over two consecutive quarters is widely interpreted as a recession.

NOTE: Gross domestic product (GDP) includes only the value of goods and services earned by a nation within its boundaries. The U.S. Department of Commerce primarily uses GDP to assess the nation's economic health.

Calculating GNP

There are two major approaches to calculating GNP:

1. **Expenditure approach:** GNP is taken to be the sum of the incomes derived from production of the year's total output.

2. **Income approach:** GNP is taken to be the sum of the wages, interest, rent, and profits earned by the factors of production.

GNP is an economic barometer, but it fails to make any statement about the quality of life or the costs of growth (externalities). Left out of the GNP are all "non-market" activities, such as the work of homemakers.

Other Measures of National Income

The GNP is the source for other major measures that are important in *national income accounting*, the system by which macroeconomists determine the variables by which the state of the economy is calculated. These other measures include the following:

◆ **Net national product (NNP):** The GNP adjusted for capital consumption allowances, which yields a figure for total annual output that the entire economy can consume without affecting the capacity to produce in future years. This corrects a shortcoming of the GNP, which makes no allowance for the portion of current output necessary to replace capital goods used to produce that current output.

◆ **National income (NI):** The income that resource suppliers earn for what they contribute to GNP.

◆ **Personal income (PI):** NI minus social security contributions, corporate income taxes, and retained earnings plus transfer payments.

◆ **Disposable income (DI):** PI less personal taxes.

◆ **Personal savings (S):** DI remaining after personal consumption expenditures.

Price Indexes

National income figures are important, but *price indexes* are required for measuring inflation. The simplest price index is obtained by dividing the price of a good in any chosen year (P_n) by the price of that good in a base year (P_1), then multiplying by 100 to get I, the index number.

While this simple index number is adequate for measuring inflation in terms of a single good, it creates distortions when used to measure several goods, because it fails to take into account the fact that different goods have unequal importance in the total budget. Weighted index numbers are used to address these drawbacks. The Producer Price Index (PPI) and the Consumer Price Index (CPI) compare the costs of a fixed market basket of goods. The GNP deflator is the current GNP in a given year divided by the constant (real) GNP and is another widely used measure of inflation.

Measuring the Money Supply

Another aspect of the economy that macroeconomists track is the *money supply*, the level of funds available at a given time within an economy. The Federal Reserve System publishes four measures of the money supply:

1. *M1* is currency in circulation, checkable deposits, and traveler's checks. This is known as the basic money supply.

2. *M2* is M1 plus "medium-range money," which includes savings deposits, repurchase agreements, money market shares, etc.

3. *M3* is M2 plus "wide-range money" (large-denomination time deposits, term repurchase agreements, etc.).

4. *L* is M3 plus liquid and near-liquid assets (including short-term Treasury securities, commercial paper, etc.).

Unemployment Measures

Finally, unemployment figures are closely monitored. The unemployment rate is the number of unemployed workers divided by the total labor force, multiplied by 100 to yield a percentage.

Plugging Into the Basic Macro Model

The GNP and the numbers derived from it represent the income the nation's firms pay the factors of production, which is equal to the value of output produced. The objective of the basic macroeconomic model, discussed in the next chapter, is to determine the equilibrium level of GNP. This is important because the equilibrium level directly affects the level of unemployment and inflation.

CHAPTER 15

THE BASIC MACRO MODEL

THE BASIC MACRO MODEL BEGINS WITH A FURTHER DEVELOPMENT OF THE CIRCULAR flow of the economy. The major *economic agents* in this flow are consumers, financial intermediaries (such as banks), government, and firms. These agents participate in four major *expenditure categories*: consumption, investment, government spending, and foreign trade. Firms produce output. To do so, they must pay the factors of production an income equal to the value of the output produced. As we saw in the last chapter, this is the GNP. A portion of this income is paid to the government as taxes, and the remainder is *disposable income*, part of which consumers spend on output and part of which is saved. The portion saved is used by financial intermediaries as investment expenditure. A certain portion of consumption, investment, and government expenditure flows out of the system to purchase imports. But foreign trade also involves the sale of exports, which adds to the total expenditure on U.S. goods. When all is in balance, the value of expenditures on U.S. goods equals the value of GNP.

Aggregate Demand

The sum of all expenditure categories is *aggregate demand*. Discounting foreign trade, aggregate demand is expressed as this formula:

$$E = C + I + G$$

where E is aggregate expenditure (i.e., aggregate demand), C is consumption expenditure, I is investment expenditure, and G is government expenditure. If foreign trade is put into the picture, the expression becomes

$$E + C + I + G + (Ex - Im)$$

where Ex is exports from the United States and Im is imports into the United States.

Consumption

The most important element of total expenditure is consumption, which is primarily determined by disposable income. The fraction of a given amount of disposable income spent on consumption is called the *average propensity to consume* (APC). The fraction of any change in income that is subsequently spent on consumption is the *marginal propensity to consume* (MPC). It may be expressed as

$$MPC = \Delta C / \Delta GNP$$

where Δ is the change in the variable it precedes.

Saving

Saving is the difference between income and consumption. The *average propensity to save* (APS) is saving (S) divided by income (Y). The *marginal propensity to save* is the fraction of any change in income that is saved:

$$MPS = \Delta S / \Delta Y$$

The values of MPC and MPS are constant.

Investment

After consumption and saving, the next major component of expenditure is investment—in housing, plant, and equipment. The level of investment is determined by

◆ Revenues produced by investment (directly influenced by the state of the business cycle)

◆ The cost of investment (dependent on interest rate and tax policy)

◆ Expectations for the future

For purposes of forecasting, the investment component is highly interesting and volatile, because the factors that influence investment are themselves difficult to predict.

The *accelerator principle* holds that net investment in capital goods is dependent on changes in GNP: If aggregate demand rises, the economy will have to make additional investments to produce increased GNP. Therefore

$$\text{Net investment} = \text{accelerator} \times \text{change in GNP}$$

and, conversely,

Accelerator = net investment/change in GNP

Government Spending
In today's America, government expenditures account for some 20 percent of GNP, which makes this component of demand very important in macroeconomics. Nevertheless, in the short run, government expenditure is independent of GNP. It does not inevitably change with recessions and booms.

Aggregate Expenditure
Aggregate supply is the goods producers make available for sale. It is equal to the income received by the owners of the factors of production. Aggregate demand—expenditure—is the sum of funds spent on output. In many introductory-level macroeconomics discussions, a *two-sector model* is used, in which aggregate demand is defined as the sum of consumption spending (C) and investment spending (I).

Equilibrium of Output and Income
Equilibrium of output and income is attained when aggregate supply equals aggregate demand. At this point, the economy is operating at maximum efficiency. In a two-sector model, this occurs when consumption and investment combined intersect with the aggregate supply.

The Multiplier Effect: The Role of Investment
Investment is said to have a *multiplier effect* on output in that when the investment level changes, there is an equal primary change in national output; however, as capital-goods producers receive additional investment income, they create additional *secondary* consumption and employment. Hence the multiplier.

A multiplier is the change in GNP that occurs given a change in some component of autonomous expenditure, such as investment.
Other components of expenditure that have multiplier effects include government spending, lump-sum taxes, and autonomous consumption.

In introductory courses, the multiplier is used in two ways:

1. To assess the impact on GNP of a change in any component of autonomous expenditure, such as investment

2. To determine how much a given component must be changed in order to create a desired effect on GNP

If both the change in GNP and the change in autonomous expenditure (such as investment) that brought it about are known, then it is possible to estimate the size of the multiplier and the marginal propensity to consume.

The multiplier is an important concept in the basic macroeconomic model, because it demonstrates how relatively small changes in autonomous consumption, investment, government spending, or taxes can have a major impact on GNP. It takes the model well beyond the basic components of expenditure in the circular flow. Knowledge of the multiplier effect is invaluable in predicting the impact of government policy and making recommendations concerning it.

Foreign Trade

At the introductory level, the foreign trade component plays only a minor role in the presentation of the basic macro model in the form of *net exports*—the difference between exports and imports. While net exports are a component of the economy's aggregate demand, they do not exert a profound influence on overall economic activity, since they represent a small fraction of GNP (usually less than 1 percent).

NOTE: While net exports may not figure prominently in the presentation of the basic macro model at the introductory level, most macro courses do include material on international trade (Chapter 18).

Government policy has a significant impact on net exports, since tariff and quota policies greatly influence the balance between exports and imports. Other factors include foreign exchange rates, currency regulations, and political attitudes toward issues of foreign trade.

CHAPTER 16

FISCAL AND MONETARY POLICY

WHILE ECONOMICS IS DEEPLY INVOLVED IN MODELING AND MANIPULATING MODels, it is, at bottom, an *applied* discipline. The principles of microeconomics can be used by individuals and businesses alike to guide decisions about spending, investment, savings, and production. Likewise, the principles of macroeconomics are employed not merely to study and explain the dynamics of economic behavior, but also to make recommendations as to how government policy makers might alter aspects of policy in order to reduce unemployment, achieve desired growth of GNP, and maintain low rates of inflation.

Fiscal Policy and Monetary Policy

Fiscal policy refers to government spending and taxation policies. *Monetary policy* applies to increasing or decreasing the nation's money supply.

The variables that the government directly controls include, for fiscal policy, spending and taxation and, for monetary policy, the money supply.

Macroeconomics attempts to assess

◆ How effectively specific fiscal and monetary policies achieve desired objectives

◆ The magnitude of an action required to achieve a desired effect

◆ The speed with which policies can be put into place

◆ The speed with which desired changes will occur

◆ The effects of policy on consumption, investment, interest rates, and price levels

◆ Trade-offs between desired objectives, such as unemployment versus inflation

Aspects of Fiscal Policy

The fundamental objective of fiscal policy is to keep actual GNP near the potential full-employment GNP. Since inflation reduces purchasing power and individual wealth, it can create a reduction in output, and so a prime objective of fiscal policy is to control inflation.

Key elements of fiscal policy are taxation and government spending.

A change in personal income taxes affects the size of disposable income, since disposable income is income minus taxes. An increase in tax rates will reduce consumption and savings at each level of income, while a decrease in tax rates will increase these components.

Since government expenditure accounts for some 20 percent of GNP, spending policy has a major impact on the economy. Importantly, government spending is largely autonomous—that is, it is not closely tied to the profit expectations that ultimately drive the spending of firms and households. The government, therefore, bases most of its spending decisions on social and political considerations—and on economic considerations, in so far as it uses spending to effect desired changes in the economy.

Multiplier Effects

Remember that both taxation and government spending have a multiplier effect. That is, changes in taxation or spending bring about magnified changes in real aggregate income. A change in taxation has a smaller multiplier effect on the macroeconomy than an equal change in government spending.

The *balanced budget multiplier* holds that a simultaneous equal increase or decrease in government spending and taxation will create an equal increase or decrease in GNP.

Putting It All Together

Fiscal policy attempts to coordinate and direct government spending and taxation to keep GNP close to potential full-employment GNP, but without reaching that point, which would bring about inflation. To achieve this, excessive unemployment must be avoided and production capability must be maximized such that the economy will grow at a rate that is neither too slow (creating recession) nor too fast (creating inflation).

By purposely creating a budget deficit, through reduced taxation, increased spending, or some combination of the two, the government can inject dollars into the economy and thereby increase spending levels. Increased demand will generate increased output, which will, in turn, create increased income. Because of the multiplier effect, the government does not need to inject into the economy the entire amount of the gap between actual and potential GNP; it need only inject a sufficient amount for the multiplier effect to act on.

Money

At some point before moving from a survey of issues relating fiscal policy to monetary policy, the introductory macroeconomics course will address basic issues of money: what it is, how it functions, and the means and institutions by which it is managed and manipulated.

Money functions in the macroeconomy in four ways:

1. As a medium of exchange
2. As a medium by which value is stored
3. As a unit of account
4. As a standard of deferred payment

Money includes cash, checking accounts, and savings accounts.

Financial Instruments, Institutions, and Markets

It is vital to an economy that money be efficiently managed, manipulated, and transferred.

Financial instruments are documents issued to savers by the government or by firms in exchange for funds and traded on financial markets.

Financial markets include money markets, which deal in short-term debt securities, and capital markets, which deal in long-term securities.

Important financial instruments include:

◆ **Bonds:** Contracts between borrower and lender specifying the repayment amount, the interest amount, and the maturity of the obligation.

◆ **Stocks:** Certificates (shares) of partial ownership of a firm.

◆ **Money market instruments:** Short-term instruments such as U.S. Treasury bills and commercial paper.

◆ **Certificates of deposit:** Savings certificates with a fixed maturity period.

◆ **Commercial paper:** Essentially unsecured, relatively high-yield promissory notes issued by a large corporation and bearing a relatively short-term maturity.

◆ **Treasury bills:** Short-term instruments issued by the government that don't pay interest per se, but are sold at a discount, then redeemed at face value on maturity.

◆ **Repurchase agreements:** Contracts by which a borrower sells securities to a lender, but agrees to repurchase them at a price that produces an agreed-upon yield.

- ◆ **Banker's acceptances:** Drafts drawn by a firm on a bank to purchase merchandise. The draft promises repayment by a specified date. Because the lending bank guarantees payment, however, these instruments may be traded. The BA is especially important in foreign trade.
- ◆ **Capital market instruments:** Long-term securities, which may be issued by the government or by firms.

The Banking System

Most of us are introduced early in life to the concept of banking: the idea that the depositor earns interest on savings deposited with the bank, which, in turn, uses that money to make loans. These loans act to increase demand deposits and the money supply in the economy. Banks, therefore, are essential in creating money.

While the depth of discussion about the banking system varies greatly among introductory macroeconomics courses, you will almost certainly learn something about the turbulent history of banking in the United States, which ultimately motivated the creation of the Federal Reserve System by the 1913 Glass-Owen Bill (Federal Reserve Act).

Before the creation of the Federal Reserve, the U.S. banking system was an unstable collection of government-chartered, state-chartered, and private banks, subject to the vagaries of booms and busts.

The Role of the Federal Reserve

The Federal Reserve was created to bring stability to the U.S. economy by controlling the quantity of money in circulation; therefore, the primary function of the Federal Reserve is to create and conduct the nation's monetary policy. Acting through a seven-member Board of Governors, "the Fed" may

- ◆ Raise or lower reserve requirements
- ◆ Set the discount rate for loans to commercial banks
- ◆ Purchase and sell government securities

The Federal Reserve is also the central bank of the United States, effectively serving banks in much the same way as banks serve their customers.

The Federal Reserve and Monetary Policy

While it is the deposit and loan activity of the commercial banks that creates money, the Federal Reserve System regulates the supply of money in circulation. The Fed's monetary policy bears directly on interest rates (the cost of borrowing), which thereby profoundly influence decisions made by individual consumers and firms. In turn, these decisions affect output, employment, income, and prices.

By increasing commercial bank reserves, the Fed can inject more money into the economy, thereby promoting investment through lowered interest rates and a greater demand for loans. This is an *easy-money policy*.

By lowering reserves, the Fed can reduce the money supply, thereby discouraging investment. This is a *tight money policy*.

In addition, the Fed can ease credit (increase the total money supply) by lowering the discount rate, thereby allowing banks to lower the interest rates they charge their loan customers. This will encourage investment. Or, in inflationary periods, the Fed can raise the discount rate, thereby causing banks to raise their interest rates, which will discourage investment.

Finally, the Fed can buy or sell government securities on the open market; this will raise or lower the reserves of commercial banks and thereby affect their ability to lend money.

Monetary Policy and Inflation

By appropriately managing fiscal policy, the government, through decisions made by the president and Congress, can attempt to address problems of *recession*. By appropriately managing monetary policy, the Federal Reserve can address problems of *inflation*.

Under the *quantity theory of money*, spending and prices are directly proportional to the quantity of money in circulation. It is, therefore, critical to economic stability that the money supply be adequately managed, and that is the role of the Fed. Using the tools at its disposal, as discussed above (changes in the reserve ratio, changes in the discount rate, and trading government securities on the open market), the Fed can

- ◆ Act to curb inflation
- ◆ Act to achieve price stability
- ◆ Act to smooth out business cycles
- ◆ Act to bring employment and output to desired levels

According to the macroeconomic model, "desired levels" are those that create *equilibrium income*, where planned saving and planned investment are equal.

CHAPTER 17

THE FULL MACRO MODEL

THE BASIC MACROECONOMIC MODEL THAT IS PRESENTED EARLY IN AN INTRODUC-
tory course is relatively straightforward because it represents a very high
degree of simplification. The full macro model, which takes into account
more real-world parameters, is more complex. The most significant dimensions added to the full macro model are differences in the short-run and
long-run time frames, the use of the Phillips curve to study the relation between
unemployment and inflation, the subject of stagflation, and the hotly debated issue
of federal deficits versus a balanced budget.

Equilibrium

Where the aggregate supply and aggregate demand curves intersect, overall macroeconomic equilibrium is reached. These AS and AD curves look like the supply and
demand curves fundamental to microeconomics, although the macro curves result
from different causes. In the short run, the AD curve slopes downward, reflecting
the fact that consumers spend more on real output at a lower average price level
than they do at a higher average price level. Conversely, the AS curve slopes upward
because rising prices create higher levels of real GNP and employment.

Before we look a little more closely at the short-run AD and AS curves, we might
contrast the long-run AS curve. Instead of being gently upward-sloping, AS in the
long run is vertical. Remember, in the long run, all costs are variable; therefore, cost
structure will simply follow output prices. Price levels are plotted on the vertical
axis; therefore, the long-run AS will be a vertical line. The significance of the rela-

tionship of short-run AS and AD to long-run AS can be readily plotted:

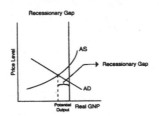

Potential GNP is the GNP level attainable under full employment (that is, if unemployment is at 4 percent). If the equilibrium level of real GNP falls below potential GNP, a *recessionary gap* results between the equilibrium level (the intersection of short-run AS and AD) and the long-run AS (the vertical curve).

Conversely, should the equilibrium level of real GNP exceed potential GNP, an *inflationary gap* between the long-run AS and the intersection of short-run AS and AD will exist.

Recessionary gaps result in high unemployment and/or underemployment of resources. Economic growth is slower than would be the case at potential GNP. Keynsian theory holds that in a recessionary gap, upward pressure on prices is minimal because of competition between underemployed plants and unemployed workers.

Inflationary gaps produce lower unemployment rates and higher use of resources. In this situation, Keynesian economists predict upward pressure on prices due to demand-pull inflation.

Role of Labor

The labor supply and wages are an important component of the full macro model. The macroeconomist is more interested in *real wages* than in the *money-wage rate*. Real wages is the money-wage rate divided by the price index, which effectively yields the purchasing power of money wages. The level of real wages are related to the productivity of labor. The more capital available per worker, the higher the real wages. The more advanced the technology of production, the higher the real wages. The more readily available natural resources are, the higher real wages. All of these inputs tend to make labor more productive.

Where the market demand for labor and the market supply of labor intersect, the *competitive equilibrium real-wage rate* is determined. As established by microeconomic theory, a firm hires labor to the point where its *marginal revenue product of labor* (MRP_L) equals its marginal resource cost of labor (MRC_L).

NOTE: The student in a survey-level macro course will encounter the work of British economist John Maynard Keynes extensively. Keynes (1883–1946) took exception to the long-held contention of the eighteenth-century economist Adam Smith (1723–1790) that business cycles ultimately corrected themselves. Smith believed that, in sum, the selfish actions of individuals and firms ultimately move the economy—as by an "invisible hand"—toward the best possible state; therefore, the free market should be left precisely that way: free. Keynes, working in the midst of the Great Depression of the 1930s, suggested that economic depression was not necessarily temporary and self-correcting. His advocacy of government intervention drove the New Deal programs of Franklin Delano Roosevelt and has been highly influential (often controversially so) in U.S. fiscal and monetary policy ever since.

The full macro model also takes into account, as necessary, the role of labor unions in the labor market and the role of *imperfect markets*, in which firms and workers are influenced by such factors as lack of information, minimum-wage laws, an unwillingness to move out of a "company town," and so on.

The Phillips Curve

The Phillips curve plots the statistical relationship between unemployment and inflation, the two major extremes between which macroeconomic theory attempts to navigate. Regarded from a historical perspective, the objective generally set for national fiscal and monetary policy—providing price stability (avoiding inflation) while maintaining full employment (that is, a 4 percent unemployment rate)—is extremely difficult to achieve. The Phillips curve suggests that these objectives inevitably conflict. A movement toward full employment creates a higher level of inflation. A movement toward lower inflation results in reduced employment.

Stagflation

Recent experience has suggested that the situation described by the Phillips curve may not be inevitable. The mid to late 1990s saw a prolonged period of low unemployment *and* low inflation. Even more dramatically, part of the 1970s and 1980s was plagued by *stagflation*, an economic condition combining some of the features of both inflation and recession.

Stagflation is not only a theoretically vexing situation but a socioeconomically frustrating and urgent one. While demand-pull inflation responds to monetary and fiscal policies intended to counteract inflation, such measures aggravate stagflation, slowing an already sluggish economy and increasing unemployment without sufficiently reining in inflation. Stagflation does respond to such measures as

◆ Public-service employment programs

◆ Programs to stimulate investment in physical and human capital

◆ Welfare reform (to reduce the welfare rolls by encouraging welfare recipients to seek employment)

◆ Wage-price controls (to curb inflation by imposing price ceilings)

Deficit Spending or Balanced Budget?

Economic policy founded on the ideas of John Maynard Keynes has favored sacrificing a balanced federal budget in order to maintain economic stability. Yet the notion of perpetual debt is repellent to many, even as the prospect of a balanced budget is a powerful lure.

The Keynesians' arguments for deficit spending were especially compelling in the depths of a profound economic depression; however, many more recent policy makers and legislators have attempted to act on their beliefs that debt is inherently a bad thing, that it is a burden to the present as well as to future generations, that debt represents government competition for resources that could be better used by the private sector, and that financing government debt unduly disrupts private capital markets and investment.

While the Gramm-Rudman-Hollings Act, signed into law in 1985, mandated a balanced budget by 1991, and while the 1997 federal budget actually saw a surplus, the debate between deficit spending to stabilize the economy and maintaining a balanced budget regardless of social costs is likely to continue as a centerpiece of national economic policy.

CHAPTER 18

INTERNATIONAL TRADE AND OTHER ISSUES IN MACROECONOMICS

W HILE INTERNATIONAL TRADE ACCOUNTS FOR A RELATIVELY SMALL PERCENTAGE OF the U.S. GNP, the subject is an important one in most macroeconomics courses, especially insofar as it brings into discussion the issue of free trade versus restricted trade.

Why Trade?

International trade is driven by *interdependency*, which, indeed, is the concept that drives all trade. If two nations—or two other entities or individuals—were *independent*, so that each was capable of producing efficiently on the basis of its own needs, there would be no need for trade. The *law of comparative advantage* applies when two countries (or individuals) each produces the same two types of goods, but one country specializes in one type of good over the other. This being the case, both countries derive benefit from trade. The country that specializes in producing one of the goods and so produces it at a lower opportunity cost, benefits from selling some of the good to a trading partner. For the trading partner, it is less costly to buy this good than to produce it domestically, so it, too, reaps the benefit of reduced opportunity cost.

Should Trade Be Free?

The case for free trade is simply stated: Through specialization, in a free-trade situation, nations can achieve the most efficient possible allocation of scarce world resources. This is true (advocates of free trade argue) whether an *absolute advantage* or a *comparative advantage* is operative.

In the case of an absolute advantage, one nation can produce a good more efficiently than another nation can. The basis for trade is thereby created, because, when each nation specializes in the good it can produce more efficiently, both trading partners can obtain the two goods at lower opportunity costs. If country A has an absolute advantage in producing product X and country B has an absolute advantage in producing product Y, both countries can obtain X and Y at lower opportunity costs if they trade.

In the case of comparative advantage, a nation may be able to produce two goods more efficiently than another nation, yet still be able to establish a basis for trade. If country A can produce both good X and good Y efficiently, but finds that producing X is more profitable than producing Y, it may wish to concentrate on X and trade with country B for Y.

Restricting free trade forces the PPF of each potential trading partner to the left, thereby preventing the economies of both nations from achieving maximum efficiency.

Should Trade Be Restricted?

The chief arguments against free trade include the following:

◆ **Protection of "infant industries"**. A nation may want to aid its domestic industries in their development by protecting them from competition from well-developed foreign industries supplying the same products.

◆ **National security.** A nation may benefit from protecting industries that are vital to the national defense. Nations do not want to be dependent on foreign imports where defense goods are concerned.

◆ **Wage protection.** U.S. workers are generally more highly paid than workers in most other countries. Without trade restrictions, competition from foreign goods produced by low-cost labor would threaten the wages and standard of living of American workers.

◆ **Employment protection.** Related to wage protection, this argument holds that import restrictions will promote increased domestic production and, therefore, increased domestic employment.

Accounting for International Trade

International trade is accounted for by calculating the *balance of payments*, a statistical tabulation of a nation's transactions with all other nations during a specified (usually annual) period. The balance of payments takes into account not only exports and imports, but the movement of investments, currency, and gold. Two major categories of transactions are recognized:

1. **Current account** transactions include commodity exports and imports of goods and services. "Unilateral transfers", such as grants of foreign aid, are also included. The difference between goods exported and goods imported is called the *balance of trade*.

2. **Capital account** transactions are the flows of investment capital into and out of a country.

Payments must balance over a given period, so that debits equal credits. If the combined current and capital accounts show a deficit (that is, if more goods, capital investment, etc., are flowing into a nation than are going out), it must meet its obligations by exporting some of its gold reserves or spending some of its foreign-currency reserves. If a nation shows a surplus, its payments are brought into balance by an inflow of gold and foreign currency.

Balance of payments must not be confused with balance of trade, which, as mentioned, is the difference between a nation's merchandise imports and exports over a given period. When exports exceed imports, the nation's balance of trade is "favorable"; when imports exceed exports, the balance of trade is "unfavorable." If a *trade deficit* is significantly large, the nation may experience higher interest rates and correspondingly depressed stock prices and lower currency prices as the nation resorts to foreign capital to finance its deficit.

Policies to Correct Payment Imbalances

A persistent payments deficit can be corrected through any of three occurrences:

1. An increase in the (home country's) price of imports
2. A fall in the (foreign country's) price of exports
3. A rise in interest rates

One way to make imports more expensive is to *depreciate* the home country's currency, so that it will purchase fewer units of the exporting country's currency, thus making imports more costly. The danger in this strategy is inflation, of course, since it will take more units of currency to buy goods, whether imported or domestic. Therefore, contractionary monetary and fiscal policies may be introduced instead, although this brings the risk of recession. As usual, correcting an adverse economic condition requires trade-offs.

Other Macroeconomic Issues

Free trade versus restricted trade and the benefits and disadvantages of each is an important and controversial issue generally raised in introductory macro courses. There are numerous other areas of debate and controversy as well. Chief among these are the relative merits of the major macroeconomic models:

◆ **The classical model.** Assuming operation of a free- enterprise and highly competitive economic system, the classical model holds that prices will, of themselves, adjust to changes in supply and demand.

◆ **Keynesianism.** Introduced by John Maynard Keynes in the 1930s, this presents a grave challenge to classical economics by claiming that an economy may achieve equilibrium at *any* employment level, not necessarily at (or even near) full employment. Thus, without government intervention, free enterprise may result in permanent depression. Because Keynesian economics stresses the necessity of stimulating aggregate demand, it is often called *demand-side economics*.

◆ **Monetarism.** Monetarism holds that the rate of growth of the quantity of money is consistently related to the rate of growth of income. If the quantity of money grows rapidly, so will income. If the rate of monetary growth is reduced, the rate of growth of income and physical output will decline, but the rate of price rise will be affected very little. Monetarists conclude that inflation is a monetary phenomenon. A change in monetary growth affects interest rates in one direction at first, then in the opposite direction later. In the monetarist view, monetary policy is important because of its effect on the quantity of money, not on bank credit or total credit or interest rates.

◆ **Supply-side economics.** In contrast to Keynesian "demand-side economics," supply-side theory focuses on incentives to stimulate production. The theory holds that reductions in marginal tax rates (taxes paid on the last dollar of taxable income) provide incentives to work, save, and invest. Supply-side economics rose to public prominence during the administration of President Ronald Reagan, whose economic advisers proposed a program of tax incentives to "jump-start" the economy.

PART THREE

MIDTERMS AND FINALS

CHAPTER 19

ECONOMICS 19.200: MICROECONOMICS

Robert M. Feinberg, Professor

T HE PRIMARY OBJECTIVES OF THIS COURSE INCLUDE GETTING STUDENTS TO UNDER-
stand some key concepts of microeconomics at the intuitive level, to appreci-
ate the application of microeconomics to real problems, and to gain an
understanding of the way in which economists think about the world. I want
my students to understand concepts such as opportunity cost, elasticity, supply and demand, and market structure, as well as the powerful force of incentives.

In the two to three course exams, problems tend to focus on elasticity and supply
and demand, with some consideration of the effects of different market structures
on market pricing. Multiple-choice and definition questions are more useful in
exploring the understanding of opportunity cost, scarcity, and how incentives can
influence behavior.

MIDTERM EXAM

While course credit is sometimes given for a short paper and problem sets, the exams are of greatest importance in determining the final grade. The midterm accounts for 30 to 40 percent of the
grade, and the final for another 30 to 40 percent.

Part A. Multiple Choice *(4 points each)*

1. If some prices increase and income remains unchanged, the budget line will
    A. not change
    B. show a parallel shift away from the origin

    C. move in toward the origin

    D. move out away from the origin

Answer: C

2. **The price elasticity of demand for Wheaties (breakfast cereal)—in absolute value terms—is likely to be**

    A. smaller than the price elasticity of demand for all breakfast cereals.

    B. greater than the price elasticity of demand for prescription drugs.

    C. zero because of strong brand loyalty.

    D. smaller in the long run than in the short run.

Answer: B

3. **A drought affecting wheat farmers in the Midwest is likely to lead to the following:**

    A. Lower wheat prices.

    B. Reduced wheat consumption.

    C. Lower wheat-farmer incomes.

    D. All of the above.

Answer: B

4. **The quantity of McDonald's cheeseburgers that households are willing to purchase is predicted to rise if there is**

    A. an increase in the price of McDonald's fish filet sandwiches.

    B. a decrease in the price of Burger King cheeseburgers.

    C. a fall in the price of umbrellas.

    D. a reduction in incomes (especially of low- to moderate-income households).

Answer: A

5. **The production-possibilities curve (or frontier)**

    A. shows the bundles of goods that use up a household's income.

    B. shows the trade-offs society faces because of scarcity.

    C. shows all combinations of goods that yield the same satisfaction.

    D. changes its slope when the price of a product changes.

Answer: B

6. **Which of the following is a normative statement?**

    A. Expenditures on crime prevention are effective in limiting the loss of jobs in the inner cities.

    B. The North American Free Trade Agreement (NAFTA) has led to increased unemployment in Texas.

C. A $1 increase in the minimum wage will increase unemployment nationally by 1 percentage point.

D. Inflation is a more important national problem than unemployment.

Answer: D

7. An increase in taxi fares will result in increased revenues for taxi drivers if the price elasticity of demand for taxi rides (in absolute value) is

A. unity (one).

B. less than one.

C. greater than one.

D. infinity.

Answer: B

8. The marginal revenue obtained by a farmer from producing an additional bushel of wheat is equal to a constant market price. Which of the following best explains why this is true?

A. She supplies a negligible fraction of the total supply of wheat.

B. There are no good substitutes for this particular farmer's wheat.

C. Other farmers are free to change from the production of other crops to the production of wheat.

D The market demand curve for wheat is infinitely elastic.

Answer: A

9. The opportunity cost of producing an additional unit of good A can be defined as

A. the profit to be made from producing good A.

B. the retail price of good A.

C. the cheapest method of producing A.

D. what must be sacrificed of other goods to get an additional unit of good A.

Answer: D

10. As a general rule, it will always pay a firm to expand output whenever

A. average revenue exceeds average cost.

B. marginal revenue exceeds marginal cost.

C. average product is rising.

D. total product is rising.

Answer: B

Part B. Define and Explain *(6 points each)* ANSWER 5 OF 6

1. Consumer surplus

Answer: The difference between the total value that consumers place on all units consumed of a particular good and the payment they must make to purchase that amount.

The existence of consumers surplus reflects the fact that, given downward-sloping demand curves, consumers would be willing to pay more for earlier units of consumption than is required when a fixed market price is charged.

> Look for *key words* in the question. Here those key words are obvious: *define* and *explain*. Having identified the key words, make certain that your answer supplies what the key words ask for. Note that these short answers fill the bill precisely, supplying one sentence (or sentence fragment) of concise definition followed by a sentence or two of explanation. Not only are the two halves of the response kept distinct from each other, they are delivered in the order that the question asks for: first definition, then explanation.

2. Revealed preference analysis of demand choices

Answer: The practice of observing consumer decisions in evaluating the likely responses to price changes. For example, by using revealed preference, we can determine that the demand curve for normal goods must always slope downward.

3. Indifference curve

Answer: The locus of all combinations of consumption of two goods which leave the individual with the same level of utility (and so equally well off). By combining indifference curves and budget lines, we can formally derive demand curves.

4. Black market

Answer: Any market in which goods are sold illegally or at prices which violate a legal price control (either a maximum or a minimum price). Examples would be smuggling cigarettes across state lines to evade taxes, or subletting rent-controlled apartments at market rates.

5. Economies of scale

Answer: Technologies which exhibit falling long-run average costs with the expansion of output. This is associated with increasing returns to scale, in which the proportionate increase in output is greater than the increase in all inputs in the production process.

6. Assumptions of perfect competition

Answer: There are a number of these—the most important are that all firms sell the same homogeneous product, all parties have perfect information, there are a large number of firms in the market, each firm's output is small relative to total industry output, and in the long run, entry and exit are possible. Under these assumption we know that, in the short run, firms will equate price to marginal cost and, in the long run, profits will be driven to zero.

> Some short-answer questions seem to require more than a *short* answer. Don't let yourself get over-whelmed. Take control of the question, as this student does, by noting that there are "a number of" assumptions of perfect competition, then going on to identify only the "most important" of them.

Part C. Problems *(15 points each) ANSWER BOTH PROBLEMS*

1. Suppose a consumer has an income of $250 and faces market prices of $10 per unit of good X and $25 per unit of good Y.

   a. Draw the budget line she faces.

Answer:

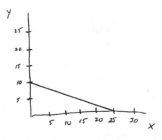

> On a graph with *Y* on the vertical axis and *X* on the horizontal axis, the budget line will be a straight line connecting the points 10 on the vertical axis and 25 on the horizontal axis. The best way to see this is to say, if I spend all my money on Y what is the most I can buy? (So it is my income of $250 divided by its price of $25 per unit.) Alternatively, if I were to spend all my money on X, what is the most I can buy? Another strategy is to see the equation of the budget line as $I = p_x x + p_y y$, or $250 = 10x + 25y$ and then solve for $y = 10 - 0.4x$.

   b. Is the combination 20 of X and 5 of Y attainable?
   Answer: No

> You can see this in two ways. If you plot that point, you see that it is outside the budget line. Also, if you multiply those amounts by the prices and add them up, you see that that combination would cost $325, which exceeds the consumer's income.

c. The price of good X now falls to $5 per unit; draw the new budget line.
Answer:

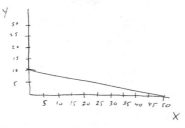

> Now the budget line is a straight line connecting the points 10 on the vertical axis and 50 on the horizontal axis (or the plotting of the equation $250 = 5x + 25y$, or $y = 10 - 0.2x$)."

d. Is the combination of 20 X and 5 Y now attainable?
Answer: Yes

> It's inside the new budget line, and you can also see that at the new prices, it can be purchased for a total of $225, which is within the income of $250.

2. Given the demand schedule for donuts consumed per week given below, calculate the price elasticity of demand when the price is between 45 cents and 55 cents per donut. In this range, is demand price-elastic or price-inelastic?

Price of Donuts	Donuts Demanded per Week
75 cents	8
65	9
55	11
45	15
35	25

Answer: The price elasticity of demand is -30.8/20 = -1.53.
Demand is price-elastic.

> The price elasticity of demand is the percentage change in donuts divided by the percentage change in the price. We usually use the average of the starting and ending values as the base for calculating percentages when we compute elasticities. Since when price increases from 45 to 55, quantity demanded falls from 15 to 11, the percentage change in quantity is 100(-4/13), or -30.8 percent. The percentage change in price is 100(10/50), or 20 percent. The demand is price-elastic because the elasticity is greater than 1 in absolute value.

The best approach to preparing for the exams is to read and review the book (it's amazing how often students don't spend much time doing this) and to work out problems either from the text or from old exams (I make mine available). I also stress that class lecture notes are the best indication of the material the professor thinks is most important and should be studied carefully.

Part A. Multiple Choice *(4 points each)*

1. The allocative inefficiency of monopoly arises because
   - A. the price exceeds the opportunity cost of the last unit produced.
   - B. the average cost is not at a minimum for the quantity produced.
   - C. the opportunity cost exceeds the marginal cost for the last unit produced.
   - D. the marginal cost exceeds the average cost for the last unit produced.

Answer: A

2. The widget industry is composed of a large number of small firms. In recent years, firms in the industry have suffered economic losses, and many sellers have left the industry. Economic theory suggests that these conditions will
   - A. cause the demand curve to shift outward, so that price will rise to the level of production cost.
   - B. cause the remaining firms to collude so that they can produce more efficiently.
   - C. cause the market supply to decline and the price to rise.
   - D. cause firms in the industry to suffer long-run economic losses.

Answer: C

3. Aggregate taxes from all levels of government amount to approximately _____ percent of GDP in the United States.
   - A. 10
   - B. 18
   - C. 33
   - D. 50

Answer: C

4. When an externality is internalized,
   - A. the firm produces at less than the optimal level of output.
   - B. marginal social costs are zero.
   - C. allocative efficiency is not achieved.
   - D. the firm bears the entire social cost of production.

Answer: D

5. The federal personal income tax deduction for charitable contributions
    A. is equally valuable regardless of the level of taxable income.
    B. amounts to a federal subsidy of personal charitable giving.
    C. is worth less to an individual in the 31% tax bracket than to one in the 15% tax bracket.
    D. is none of the above.

Answer: B

6. The advantage of emissions taxes as a means of pollution control is that they
    A. centralize decision making in the hands of government bureaucrats.
    B. internalize the externality in the most efficient way.
    C. require all firms to adopt the most up-to-date abatement techniques.
    D. eliminate all pollution in an industry.

Answer: B

7. The *per se* rule in antitrust law means that
    A. all monopolies other than regulated public utilities are automatically illegal.
    B. all price fixing is automatically illegal.
    C. one firm cannot buy up a competitor if the new firm created by the merger would have more than a 35 percent market share.
    D. large size by itself is illegal.

Answer: B

8. Health and safety regulation is *not* generally motivated by
    A. economies of scale in production.
    B. paternalism.
    C. information asymmetries between firms and consumers, or between firms and workers.
    D. externalities from private consumption decisions.

Answer: A

9. The prediction of the model of perfect competition that firms will earn zero profits in the long run means that
    A. perfectly competitive firms are always on the verge of bankruptcy.
    B. firms have no incentive to minimize costs.
    C. firms will earn a normal return on investment in the long run.
    D. short-run profits will also be zero.

Answer: C

10. In the short run, firms will exit an industry if
    A. the price they charge is less than average variable cost.
    B. they have negative economic profits.
    C. their price is less than average total cost.
    D. a competitor enters the industry.

Answer: A

> Students often seem not to carefully read and think about a question before starting to answer it. This is probably why students who finish an exam early (and think it is easy) sometimes get the lowest scores.

Part B. Define and Explain *(6 points each). ANSWER 5 OF 6*

1. Externality

Answer: Effects on parties that are not directly involved in the production or use of a commodity. Also known as "third party effects." Examples of externalities are pollution problems, solutions to which involve methods of imposing the full social costs of actions on those causing the externality.

> Note here that the student provides something extra by mentioning the synonym "third party effects." In this case, the explanation part of the answer is an example rather than a straight explanation; however, note that the example is explained. Without the second part of the second sentence of the answer, this response would have received half credit. An example is not an explanation—although it can be an effective *part* of an explanation.

2. Progressive tax

Answer: A type of tax in which the ratio of total tax paid to income (the average tax rate) increases with increases in income. The federal personal income tax in the U.S. is a progressive tax, due to increasing marginal tax rates, but so is a "flat tax" with an initial exemption amount. Taxes that tend to be regressive (with the ratio of total tax paid to income falling with increased income) include the social security payroll tax and sales taxes.

> After supplying the definition, the student explains progressive tax with a well-explained example, and also refines the concept of a progressive tax by showing how a so-called flat tax may be progressive and by *contrasting* progressive tax with regressive tax. Many concepts are best explained by contrasting them with their opposite.

3. Price discrimination

Answer: The charging of different prices to different consumers of a good (or to the same consumer for different amounts purchased), when these different prices are not accounted for by differences in the costs of providing those units of the good. Examples would be senior citizen discounts and student discounts at movie theaters, and electricity rates that decline with increases in monthly consumption.

Again, providing explained examples is the only practical way to explain this definition.

4. Prisoner's dilemma

Answer: A "game" in which each firm, acting independently in its own interest, is led to a second-best result. This is the dilemma. It is based on a story in which two prisoners both confess to a crime, even though it would have been to their advantage to both stick to the same story and deny everything. Similarly, this game can be used to explain oligopoly behavior in which firms choose to compete when collusion would be to their mutual advantage.

The first three sentences are essential to the answer. The last sentence is not essential, but it will certainly impress the grader with the student's depth of understanding of the concept. In short answers, it is often to your advantage to go the extra mile, to extend the answer a little further, *provided that* you have fully answered the question first.

5. Scarcity

Answer: Existing resources are inadequate to satisfy all desires. The implication is that choices must be made between competing uses for these resources. These choices reflect the fact that the opportunity cost of obtaining more of one thing is the other item(s) which must be given up. The production possibilities frontier illustrates this. Without scarcity, economics ceases to be an interesting subject for study.

The last two sentences are extra and interestingly extend the question, showing a firm grasp of more profound concepts in economics. You don't have to think of short-answer questions as calling exclusively for cut-and-dried responses.

6. Deadweight loss from monopoly

Answer: A measure of the inefficiency (allocative inefficiency) of monopoly, this is the area under the demand curve and above marginal cost between the output chosen by the monopolist and the output society would like to see the firm produce (which is where the demand curve and marginal cost intersect). One can think of the deadweight loss as the potential gains from exchange that the economy is losing out on as a result of the output restriction of monopoly.

Part C. Problems *(15 points each). ANSWER BOTH PROBLEMS.*

1a. Fill in the missing items below.

P	Q	TR	MR	TC	MC
$15	7		—	$ 8	—
14	8			10	
13	9			20	
12	10			38	

Answer:

P	Q	TR	MR	TC	MC
$15	7	*105*	—	$8	—
14	8	*112*	*7*	10	*2*
13	9	*117*	*5*	20	*10*
12	10	*120*	*3*	38	*18*

Here you just need to know that total revenue is P times Q, that marginal revenue is the additional revenue from the last unit sold, and that marginal cost is the additional cost of the last item sold.

1b. What is this monopolist's profit-maximizing quantity of output?
   Answer: 8

This is the level of output for which the marginal revenue of the last unit exceeds the marginal cost, and for which the next unit's production would involve a marginal revenue below marginal cost. In a table like that above, the answer can also be gotten simply by realizing that profit is TR - TC, and seeing where this is greatest. (Here profit is $102 at Q=8, which is the highest it gets.)"

1c. What level of output would society like to see produced? (Or: What is the allocatively efficient level of output?)
   Answer: 9

This is the highest level of output for which price exceeds marginal cost.

2. The government is considering placing a $1 per unit tax on one of the two following products: (a) prescription drugs; and (b) oatmeal. Using supply and demand curves, determine which will be most effective at raising revenues, and which will

likely have the most impact in reducing consumption. For each tax, estimate roughly how much of the $1 tax will eventually be paid by consumers in the form of higher prices.

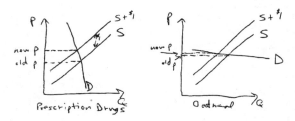

Answer: A $1 tax will shift the supply curves up in a parallel fashion by a constant $1 amount for both. The new equilibrium price for prescription drugs will go up by almost the full $1 tax (intuitively, since consumers have little choice but to pay the higher price), while the new equilibrium price for oatmeal will go up by a smaller amount (since consumers would switch to other products if the seller tried to pass the tax on fully).

We expect that, having few substitutes, prescription drugs will have very inelastic demand curves, whereas oatmeal (with many substitute breakfast foods) will have relatively elastic demand. This means that the demand curve for prescription drugs will be relatively steep (with price on the vertical axis) and that for oatmeal relatively flat. Assume that the supply curves look the same for both."

CHAPTER 20

ECO 2306: PRINCIPLES OF MICROECONOMICS

Beck Taylor, Assistant Professor

THREE EXAMS ARE GIVEN IN THE COURSE, TWO "MIDTERMS" AND A FINAL. THE TWO midterms each account for 25 percent of the course grade, as does the final. Quizzes account for the remaining 25 percent.

My primary aim in this course is to help students attain a basic understanding of the 'economic way of thinking,' improve their ability to reason and think critically, and critically disseminate economic information presented in the popular media. The course requires students to develop high-level synthesis skills, which enable them to take concepts and definitions and apply them to solve unfamiliar problems. They must also learn the language of economics and be able to use theoretical models to explain real-world observations.

I advise students to attend class regularly, read the text before the lecture, complete homework in a timely and conscientious way, and spend approximately 10 hours per week studying economics, including class time.

MIDTERM EXAM 1

The exams are generally broken into three different types of questions: The first type tests basic understanding and definitional material; the second type requires students to think conceptually about a problem, possibly utilizing specific models to answer the question; and the third type of question presents a scenario with which the student is probably unfamiliar, requiring the student to apply his or her knowledge and reasoning ability to work out a solution.

I. Multiple Choice

Instructions: Answer each of the following questions by choosing the best response. Mark your answers clearly on the scantron form provided. Only answers recorded on the scantron will be counted.

1. Which of the following is a normative economic statement?

   (a) "Given an elastic demand curve, an increase in price will decrease total revenue."

   (b) "Trade policies which have opened American markets to foreign competition have caused too much unemployment."

   (c) "When consumers are less responsive to a price change than suppliers, an excise tax will be passed along to consumers."

   (d) "The demand for a normal good will increase when income increases."

   (e) All of the above are normative economic statements.

Answer: b

> A positive economic statement is one that can be refuted. Any statement that cannot be refuted because it is grounded in opinion is a normative statement.

2. Suppose that in one hour the U.S. can produce 50,000 pounds of steel or 30,000 barrels of beer. Great Britain, on the other hand, can produce 15,000 pounds of steel or 20,000 barrels of beer in one hour. Which of the following is true?

   (a) Great Britain has an absolute advantage in the production of both goods.

   (b) The U.S. has a comparative advantage in the production of beer.

   (c) Great Britain has a comparative advantage in the production of steel.

   (d) Great Britain has a comparative advantage in the production of beer.

   (e) None of the above is true.

Answer: d

> It costs Great Britain 0.75 unit of steel to produce one more unit of beer. On the other hand, it costs the U.S. 1.67 units of steel to produce one more unit of beer. Therefore, Great Britain has the comparative advantage in the production of beer."

3. Suppose that the demand for good X is $q^D(p) = 30 - p$ and the supply of good X is $q^S(p) = p$. What is the equilibrium quantity traded in this market?

   (a) 15

   (b) 12

   (c) 30

(d) 20

(e) none of the above

Answer: a

Equating supply and demand and solving for price yields an equilibrium price of $15. Substituting this value into either supply or demand yields an equilibrium quantity traded of 15 units.

4. Suppose that the government places a price floor of $5 in the market described in the previous question. What is the effect of this policy?

(a) The market price will fall to $5.

(b) Quantity supplied will increase.

(c) Quantity demanded will decrease.

(d) The market price will remain unchanged.

(e) None of the above.

Answer: d

To be effective, a price floor must be set above the equilibrium price. Therefore, this market will remain unaffected.

5. Suppose Julie's marginal values for her consumption of gasoline are given below. If the market price is $1.20 per gallon, what is Julie's total consumer surplus on all units consumed?

Gallons Consumed/Week	Marginal Value
1	$5
2	$4
3	$3
4	$2
5	$1

(a) $3.80

(b) $0.80

(c) $9.20

(d) $9.00

(e) None of the above

Answer: c

Consumer surplus is defined as the difference between the consumer's marginal value and the market price. At an equilibrium price of $ 1.20, Julie will purchase 4 units. Taking the difference between marginal value and market price for each of the 4 units and adding them together yields a surplus of $9.20.

6. Suppose that the supply of apartments is fixed at 100. In other words, regardless of the price, 100 apartments will be supplied. Demand for apartments adheres to the Law of Demand. Suppose that the price of town houses (a substitute) decreases. What will happen in the market for apartments?

 (a) Quantity supplied will decrease.
 (b) Equilibrium price will decrease.
 (c) Equilibrium quantity traded will decrease.
 (d) Quantity demanded will increase.
 (e) Both (b) and (c) are correct.

Answer: b

Supply of apartments is perfectly inelastic (vertical) at 100 units. The decrease in the price of town houses (a substitute) will reduce the demand for apartments, thus decreasing the equilibrium price of apartments. Note that quantity traded is unaffected.

7. Suppose the demand for Internet access increases. What will be the effect in the market for Internet service?

 (a) Equilibrium price will fall.
 (b) Quantity supplied will increase.
 (c) Supply will increase.
 (d) Equilibrium quantity traded will decrease.
 (e) None of the above.

Answer: b

An increase in demand will cause the equilibrium price to rise. This, in turn, will cause quantity supplied to increase (a movement along the supply curve).

8. Suppose that UPS experiences higher marginal costs because of a new labor agreement. At the same time, Federal Express (a substitute) lowers its price. What will be the effect in the market for UPS service?

 (a) Equilibrium quantity traded will decrease and price is indeterminate.
 (b) Equilibrium price will increase and quantity traded is indeterminate.
 (c) Equilibrium quantity traded will increase and price will increase.
 (d) Equilibrium price will decrease and quantity traded is indeterminate.
 (e) None of the above.

Answer: a

The higher marginal cost will decrease UPS supply. The lower price for FedEx will lower demand for UPS. Thus, quantity traded will definitely decrease, but the effect on price depends on the magnitudes of the shifts, which are not given in the problem.

9. A local cinema increases the price of a movie ticket from $5 to $6.50. At the same time, it lowers the price of popcorn from $3 to $1.50. Total revenues for both goods decrease, so we can conclude that the demand for movies is _____ and the demand for popcorn is _____ .

   (a) elastic; elastic
   (b) inelastic; elastic
   (c) elastic; inelastic
   (d) inelastic; inelastic
   (e) none of the above

Answer: c

> A price change and total revenue are inversely related on the elastic portion of the demand curve. Price changes and total revenue are positively related on the inelastic portion of the demand curve. Thus the demand for movie tickets is elastic and that for popcorn is inelastic.

10. If quantity demanded decreases from 100 units to 95 units when price increases from $3 to $3.50, then we can conclude that demand is

   (a) elastic.
   (b) unit elastic.
   (c) inelastic.
   (d) Cannot answer with the information given.
   (e) none of the above.

Answer: c

> Price elasticity of demand is calculated as -0.33, which indicates that demand is price inelastic.

11. Suppose that the income elasticity of demand for good X is 1.56. We can conclude that good X is

   (a) a normal good.
   (b) a necessity good.
   (c) a luxury good.
   (d) both (a) and (b).
   (e) both (a) and (c).

Answer: e

> Income elasticities greater than zero indicate normal goods. Income elasticities greater than unity indicate luxuries.

12. Suppose Jack consumes two goods: A and B. You are told that Jack is spending his entire income on these two goods. If the marginal utility per dollar spent on good A is less than the marginal utility per dollar spent on good B, then Jack should

(a) increase consumption of both A and B.
(b) increase consumption of A and decrease consumption of B.
(c) increase consumption of B and decrease consumption of A.
(d) decrease consumption of both A and B.
(e) do none of the above.

Answer: c

Consumer equilibrium requires that marginal utilities per dollar spent be equal across all goods consumed. If the 'bang for the buck' for product B is greater than that for product A, then the consumer should consume more of B and less of A until their marginal utilities per dollar spent are equal.

13. Suppose the Acme Widget Company is earning just enough revenue to cover only its explicit costs. We can conclude that:

(a) Acme is earning zero economic profits.
(b) Acme is earning normal profits.
(c) Acme is earning positive economic profits.
(d) Acme is earning negative economic profits.
(e) both (a) and (b) are correct.

Answer: d

Economic profit is defined as revenues minus both explicit and implicit costs. If the firm is covering only its explicit costs, then economic profit must be negative.

14. Total product is maximized when

(a) marginal product is maximized.
(b) diminishing marginal returns set in.
(c) marginal product is zero.
(d) marginal product is minimized.
(e) none of the above.

Answer: c

Marginal product is the slope of the total product curve (first derivative). At its maximum, total product should not be changing. Marginal product, therefore, must be zero.

15. Study the following table. Marginal costs begin to increase with the hiring of the _____ worker. (Assume each worker is paid $15 per hour.)

Units of Labor	Total Product
0	0
1	5
2	15
3	35
4	60

(a) 1st
(b) 2nd
(c) 3rd
(d) 4th
(e) 5th

Answer: d

Marginal cost decreases as marginal product increases, and increases as marginal product decreases. The hiring of the 4th worker yields diminishing marginal product.

II. Problems

Instructions: Answer each of the following problems in the blue book provided. Only answers recorded in the blue book will be counted.

1. Suppose supply and demand for product X are shown in the following graph:

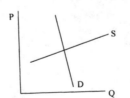

(a) Demonstrate on the graph the effects of an excise tax of $t per unit.
(b) What is the tax incidence of this particular tax? In other words, who pays this tax?
(c) Graphically show the tax revenue generated by this tax. Would tax revenue be higher or lower if the price elasticity of demand were higher?

Answers:

(a)

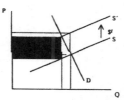

(b) Consumers will pay the majority of the tax, but not all of it.

(c) See diagram below. If the elasticity of demand had been higher, tax revenue would have fallen.

2. Suppose the demand for good X is $q^D(p) = 50 - 2p$ and the supply for good X is $q^s(p) = 5 + p$. If the government imposes a price ceiling of $10 in the market for good X, what is the "black market price" that can be charged in this market?

Answer:

$q^S(10) = 5 + 10 = 15$

$15 = 50 - 2p => p - \$17.50$

3. Suppose that a production possibilities curve includes the following data points:

Wheat	Cotton
0	50
40	25
45	0

(a) Graph the production possibilities curve, assuming that it has no curved segments.

(b) What is the cost of one additional unit of cotton when 5 units of cotton are already being produced? When 45 units are already being produced?

(c) What is the cost of one more unit of wheat when 30 units of wheat are already being produced? When 42 units are already being produced?

Answers:

(a)

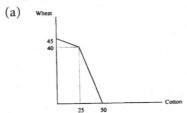

(b) When 5 units of cotton are being produced, the 6th unit of cotton will cost 0.20 unit of wheat. When 45 units of cotton are being produced, the 46th unit of cotton will cost 1.6 units of wheat.

(c) When 30 units of wheat are being produced, the 31st unit of wheat will cost 0.625 unit of cotton. When 42 units of wheat are being produced, the 43rd unit of wheat will cost 5 units of cotton.

4. **Fill in the following table with the correct values for (a) to (e).**

Labor	TP	MP	TFC	TVC	TC	AFC	AVC	ATC	MC
0	0	--	--	--	--	--	--	--	--
1	10	10	100	10	110	10	1	11	1
2	25	15	100	20	120	(c)	0.80	4.80	0.67
3	(a)	5	100	30	(b)	3.33	1	4.33	2
4	31	1	100	40	140	3.23	1.29	(d)	(e)

Answer:

Labor	TP	MP	TFC	TVC	TC	AFC	AVC	ATC	MC
0	0	--	--	--	--	--	--	--	--
1	10	10	100	10	110	10	1	11	1
2	25	15	100	20	120	**4**	0.80	4.80	0.67
3	**30**	5	100	30	**130**	3.33	1	4.33	2
4	31	1	100	40	140	3.23	1.29	**4.52**	**10**

III. Short Answer

Instructions: Answer each of the following questions in the blue book provided. Answers will be evaluated based on accuracy, completeness, and clarity. You may include graphs or examples to support your answers. Only answers recorded in the blue book will be counted.

1. Explain the "minimum wage paradox."

Answer: The minimum wage paradox is the result of an effective price floor being placed in the market for low-wage workers. At the elevated wage rate, suppliers of labor increase their quantity supplied of labor. At the same time, consumers of such labor (firms) reduce their quantity demanded, creating a surplus in the market. This surplus of labor translates into unemployment. Thus the paradox is that the price support was intended to benefit laborers, yet many laborers will forfeit their jobs as a result.

> A good short answer consists of a definition, an explanation, and a description of consequences or effects.

2. What is a sunk cost? What do economists have to say about sunk costs?

> Read the question carefully. Note that there are two parts to this question. Be sure to answer both.

Answer: A sunk cost is an unrecoverable cost. No matter what decision is made, the sunk cost cannot be retrieved. Economists insist that rational economic agents should not consider these costs in economic decision making, but rather should rely on marginal analysis.

MIDTERM EXAM 2

> I give very detailed class notes. After they read the text initially, I recommend that students use it as a reference. To study, I recommend that students review old quizzes, class notes, old exams, and lecture notes. I warn students not to expect 'easy,' low-level, regurgitation-type questions.

I. Multiple Choice

Instructions: Answer each of the following questions by choosing the best *response. Mark your answers clearly on the scantron form provided. Only answers recorded on the scantron will be counted.*

1. Suppose that a firm in a perfectly competitive industry is currently earning positive economic profits in the short run. Suddenly, market demand for the product decreases. Which of the following is *always* true, given that the firm has upward-sloping marginal cost?

   (a) The firm's profits will increase.
   (b) The firm's profits will become losses.
   (c) The firm's profits will decrease.
   (d) The firm's marginal costs will increase.
   (e) None of the above.

Answer: c

A decrease in market demand will decrease the price that the firm charges for its product. Thus, economic profits must decrease.

2. The perfectly competitive firm charges a price equal to _____ in the long run.
   (a) the market price
   (b) marginal cost
   (c) the minimum of average total cost
   (d) the minimum of long-run average cost
   (e) all of the above

Answer: e

In the long run, the perfectly competitive firm is a price taker, prices at marginal cost, and earns normal profits.

3. Suppose that the market price in a perfectly competitive industry is equal to $5. At that price, XYZ Company produces 500 units per period. Suppose that the marginal cost of producing the 500th unit is $4.50. To maximize profits, XYZ should
   (a) maintain the current production rate.
   (b) decrease production.
   (c) increase production.
   (d) Cannot answer with the given information.
   (e) do none of the above.

Answer: c

Since the marginal revenue of $5 is greater than the marginal cost of $4.50, the firm should increase production to maximize profits.

4. Because the perfectly competitive firm has zero market power,
   (a) price equals marginal cost.
   (b) price is greater than marginal cost.
   (c) price is equal to the minimum of average total cost.
   (d) price is less than marginal cost.
   (e) none of the above is correct.

Answer: a

Zero market power leads to no markup by the firm. Free entry and exit yields zero profits. Compare perfect competition with monopolistic competition.

5. Which of the following is the *primary* reason for the existence of natural monopolies?
   (a) patents
   (b) antitrust exemptions
   (c) economies of scale over the entire range of market demand
   (d) illegal anticompetitive behavior
   (e) none of the above

Answer: c

> Natural monopolies are characterized by economies of scale over the entire range of market demand.

6. For the monopolist, total revenue is maximized when
   (a) marginal revenue equals 1.
   (b) marginal revenue equals -1.
   (c) price elasticity of demand equals -1.
   (d) price elasticity of demand equals 0.
   (e) none of the above is true.

Answer: c

> Total revenue (not profits!) is maximized when the firm prices at the unit-elastic point on the demand curve.

7. Suppose a monopolist can sell 8 units at $12 per unit and 7 units at $14 per unit. The marginal revenue for the 8th unit is
   (a) $2.
   (b) $96.
   (c) $98.
   (d) -$2.
   (e) none of the above.

Answer: d

> At 8 units, revenue is $8 \times 12 = 96$. At 7 units, revenue is $7 \times 14 = 98$. Thus, marginal revenue for the 8th unit is -2.

8. In the long run, monopolistically competitive firms will
   (a) earn normal profits.
   (b) exit the industry.

(c) shut down.

(d) earn positive profits equal to each firm's implicit costs.

(e) do none of the above.

Answer: a

Monopolistic competition is characterized by zero entry barriers. Thus firms earn normal profits in the long run, just as in perfect competition.

9. Oligopolists are somewhat different from firms in other market structures, as evidenced by

(a) their ability to earn short-run profits.

(b) the strategic nature of competition between firms.

(c) the large degree of independence in decision making.

(d) the ease of entry into and exit from markets.

(e) all of the above.

Answer: b

Strategic behavior is what differentiates oligopolists from firms in other market structures.

10. The recent rash of mergers in the accountancy/consulting industry between firms like Ernst & Young and KPMG Peat Marwick is an example of

(a) vertical mergers.

(b) S&P 500 mergers.

(c) horizontal mergers.

(d) corporate raids.

(e) none of the above.

Answer: c

Horizontal mergers are mergers between firms producing the same product line.

11. A firm's demand for any particular resource is that firm's marginal value curve for the resource. This curve is also known as

(a) the marginal resource cost curve.

(b) the marginal revenue curve.

(c) the marginal cost curve.

(d) the marginal revenue product curve.

(e) none of the above.

Answer: d

Marginal revenue product is the most a firm would be willing and able to pay for a resource. It is therefore the firm's demand for the resource.

12. Suppose that the supply and demand for a particular resource are represented in the following graph. Which of the following statements is true?

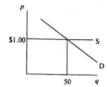

(a) The resource will earn a rent equal to $50.
(b) The resource will earn a profit equal to $50.
(c) The resource will earn revenue equal to $50.
(d) The resource's opportunity cost is $50.
(e) Both (c) and (d).

Answer: e

Since the supply for the resource is perfectly elastic, the resource can be considered very generic and not specialized. Therefore, the revenue the resource earns is all opportunity cost and no economic rent.

13. Which of the following is true if a firm is a price taker in a resource market?

(a) The firm has zero market power in the output market.
(b) The firm will hire the resource until marginal revenue product equals marginal resource cost.
(c) The firm has zero market power in the resource market.
(d) The resource's equilibrium wage will equal the firm's marginal revenue product.
(e) All are true except (a).

Answer: e

The level of market power in either the output or the resource market generally has no bearing on the market power enjoyed in the other market.

14. A firm that is the sole buyer of a particular resource is called

(a) a monopolist.
(b) an oligopolist buyer.

(c) a monopsonist.

(d) a price-taker in the resource market.

(e) none of the above.

Answer: c

15. **Which of the following is true for a monopsonist?**

(a) The firm has market power in the resource market.

(b) The firm will earn a profit.

(c) The firm will pay the resource less than its marginal revenue product.

(d) Both (a) and (b).

(e) Both (a) and (c).

Answer: e

> A monopsonist has market power in the resource market, and this market power is shown by the firm's ability to pay a resource less than its marginal revenue product.

II. Problem

Instructions: Answer the following problem in the blue book provided. Only answers recorded in the blue book will be counted.

1.

(a) Define Nash equilibrium.

(b) Solve the following game for its Nash equilibrium. Write the corresponding strategies in your blue book. Be careful, there may be more than one. All pay-offs are positive; i.e., each player will choose the highest number, positives are always chosen over negatives, etc.

		PLAYER 2			
		I	II	III	IV
PLAYER 1	I	5 / 2	7 / 7	3 / -3	0 / 1
	II	6 / 3	12 / 5	9 / 2	-8 / -5
	III	10 / 12	1 / 1	0 / 0	1 / 13
	IV	-1 / -1	-3 / -5	0 / 1	-5 / -5

Answers:

(a) In a 2-player game, a Nash equilibrium is a pair of strategies such that each player chooses his or her optimal choice given the other player's optimal choice. Nash equilibria can usually be determined through the elimination of strictly dominated strategies.

(b) There are two Nash equilibria in this game: (II, II) and (III, IV).

III. Short Answer

Instructions: Answer each of the following questions in the blue book provided. Answers will be evaluated based on accuracy, completeness, and clarity. You may include graphs or examples to support your answers. Only answers recorded in the blue book will be counted.

1. Describe the shutdown condition for any firm.

Answer: If a firm is operating with a loss in the short run, it must consider the relationship between its average revenue per unit (price) and its average variable cost per unit. If average revenue is greater than average variable cost, the firm should continue operating in the short run. However, if average revenue is less than average variable cost, the firm should shut down and pay only fixed costs.

2. Why is marginal revenue less than price for a monopolist?

Answer: Marginal revenue for the monopolist consists of two factors. First, the firm gains revenue by selling one more unit of the product. But the firm must also decrease the price on all units. This effect offsets the first, causing marginal revenue to be less than price.

> Whenever possible, quantify your response. The student mentions *two* factors, not something vague such as "certain factors" or "several factors."

3. Describe kinked-demand theory.

Answer: Kinked-demand theory is a theory which seems to explain price rigidity in oligopolistic markets very well. Two assumptions are made concerning the behavior of firms. First, rival firms are assumed to react to and follow price decreases, leaving the firm with relatively inelastic demand at lower prices. Second, rival firms are assumed not to react to price increases, causing the firm's demand to be relatively elastic at higher prices. This generates the "kinked" demand. After the construction of demand, marginal revenue can be constructed and will appear discontinuous. If marginal costs equal marginal revenue in the "vertical" section of marginal revenue, the profit-maximizing price will remain constant.

4. Explain the difference between the "short run" and the "long run."

Answer: In the "short run," at least one of the firm's inputs is fixed. In the "long run," all the firm's inputs are variable.

Instructions: Answer each of the following questions by choosing the best *response. Mark your answers clearly on the scantron form provided. Only answers recorded on the scantron will be counted.*

1. Because people's wants are unlimited but resources are scarce,

    (a) only the rich get everything they want.
    (b) choices must be made.
    (c) there will be more services produced than goods.
    (d) poor people never get anything they want.
    (e) none of the above is true.

Answer: b

Scarcity implies that humans must make choices. This is why economics is a behavioral science.

2. Which of the following is *not* a resource?

    (a) land
    (b) labor
    (c) entrepreneurial ability
    (d) patents
    (e) All of the above are resources.

Answer: d

Resources are defined as land, labor, capital, and entrepreneurial ability. Read questions carefully! Don't trip over that "*not.*"

3. When economists say that people act rationally, they mean

    (a) that people gather all relevant information before making their decisions.
    (b) that once a pattern of behavior has been established, people tend to become set in their ways.
    (c) that people respond in predictable ways to changes in costs and benefits.
    (d) that people rarely make errors when they are permitted to exchange or trade for themselves.
    (e) none of the above

Answer: c

Rationality assumes that people gather as much information as possible and make the best decision possible, weighing costs and benefits at the margin.

4. In economics, the term *marginal* means

(a) incremental or decremental, extra.
(b) unimportant.
(c) level or size.
(d) a bad alternative.
(e) none of the above.

Answer: a

5. The basic purpose of economic models is to

(a) construct simplifying assumptions about the real world.
(b) explain reality in all its complexity.
(c) collect empirical data to support the observed facts.
(d) provide explanations for, and predictions of, economic events.
(e) do none of the above.

Answer: d

Economic models are powerful tools for explaining and predicting human behavior.

6. Which of the following is a positive economic statement?

(a) An unemployment rate of 7 percent is a national disgrace.
(b) Unemployment is less important than inflation.
(c) When the national unemployment rate is 7 percent, the unemployment rate for inner-city youth is often close to 40 percent.
(d) Unemployment and inflation are equally important problems.
(e) None of the above.

Answer: c

Positive economic statements are those that can be refuted. Any statement that cannot be refuted because it is grounded in opinion is a normative statement.

7. Opportunity cost is defined

(a) only in terms of money spent.
(b) as the value of alternatives not chosen.
(c) as the value of the best alternative not chosen.
(d) as the difference between the benefits from your choice and the costs of that choice.
(e) as none of the above.

Answer: c

8. Sunk costs

(a) can be measured only in monetary terms.

(b) are not opportunity costs.

(c) lower the efficiency of production.

(d) should be considered in economic decisions.

(e) are none of the above.

Answer: e

Sunk costs, like all costs, are opportunity costs.

9. According to the law of comparative advantage, a person should produce a good if he or she

(a) can produce it with the fewest resources.

(b) has the lowest opportunity cost of producing the good and can produce it with the fewest resources.

(c) has the greatest opportunity cost of producing the good regardless of whether it is produced with the fewest resources.

(d) has the lowest opportunity cost of producing the good regardless of whether it is produced with the fewest resources.

(e) has none of the above.

Answer: d

The law of comparative advantage states that only relative cost advantages should determine the allocation of production. Absolute advantages are unimportant.

Consider the following production possibilities table for Questions 10 and 11.

	United States	JAPAN
Wheat	200	150
Rice	400	100

10. If the numbers in the table represent outputs per worker, what is the opportunity cost for Japan of producing one more unit of rice?

(a) 1.5 units of wheat

(b) 0.67 unit of wheat

(c) 4 units of wheat

(d) 0.25 unit of wheat

(e) None of the above

Answer: a

150/100 = 1.5

11. Which of the following statements is *true* if the numbers in the table represent the number of workers required per unit of output?

(a) The U.S. has an absolute advantage in the production of both goods.
(b) The U.S. should produce rice.
(c) Japan should produce both goods.
(d) Japan has a comparative advantage in the production of wheat.
(e) None of the above is a true statement.

Answer: e

Japan has an absolute advantage in the production of both goods. The U.S. has a comparative advantage in the production of wheat, and Japan has a comparative advantage in the production of rice.

12. If the production possibilities frontier is a straight line,

(a) its slope will equal -1.
(b) resources must not be used efficiently.
(c) resources must be unemployed.
(d) opportunity costs are not constant.
(e) none of the above is true.

Answer: e

A linear production possibility curve implies that resources are equally adept at producing both goods. Opportunity costs are constant.

13. Suppose that you drink more tea because the price of coffee has increased. Which of the following best explains your behavior?

(a) The law of demand
(b) The fact that tea and coffee are complements
(c) The substitution effect of a price change
(d) The income effect of a price change
(e) None of the above

Answer: c

The substitution effect of a price change explains changes in consumption due to changes in relative prices.

14. Suppose there are only two goods, apples and oranges. What happens if the price of each good increases by 15 percent?

   (a) The consumer will substitute apples for oranges.
   (b) The consumer will substitute oranges for apples.
   (c) There is no substitution effect because the relative prices have remained constant.
   (d) Demand for both goods decreases.
   (e) Both (c) and (d).

Answer: c

No relative price change implies that the substitution effect is zero. A change in price does not cause a change in demand!

15. Which of the following will not cause a change in demand for peanuts?

   (a) A change in the price of cashews
   (b) A change in consumer income
   (c) A change in the price of peanuts
   (d) A change in consumer expectations about the future price of peanuts
   (e) None of the above

Answer: c

A change in the price causes a change in quantity demanded, not in demand.

16. Suppose that there are 3 consumers in the market for yo-yos: Don, John, and Ron. At a price of $5 per yo-yo, the quantities demanded by each are 3, 2, and 1, respectively. At a price of $3 per yo-yo, the quantities demanded are 4, 5, and 3, respectively. Which of the following is *true*?

   (a) The market demand for yo-yos does not obey the law of demand.
   (b) The price decrease causes the quantity demanded in this market to increase by 6.
   (c) The price decrease causes John's demand curve to shift the most.
   (d) At a price of $1, the quantity demanded in this market must be 20.
   (e) None of the above.

Answer: b

Market demand is the sum of individual demands.

17. Which of the following is the best example of complementary goods?

   (a) milk and cheese
   (b) coffee and tea
   (c) CDs and tapes
   (d) film and film processing
   (e) none of the above

Answer: d

Film and film processing are goods that are typically consumed together.

18. Suppose Julie's marginal values for her consumption of gasoline are given below. If the market price is $1.20 per gallon, what is Julie's total consumer surplus on all units consumed?

Gallons/Week	Marginal Value
1	$5
2	$4
3	$3
4	$2
5	$1

   (a) $3.80
   (b) $0.80
   (c) $9.20
   (d) $9.00
   (e) None of the above

Answer: c

Consumer surplus is defined as the difference between marginal value and market price. At a market price of $1.20, Julie will consume 4 gallons. Adding the difference between marginal value and price for each unit consumed yields a consumer surplus of $9.20.

19. Suppose that demand is given by the function $q^D(p) = 96 - 4p$ and supply is given by $q^S(p) = 2p$. What are the equilibrium price and quantity traded in this market?

   (a) Price is $10, and quantity traded is 56 units.
   (b) Price is $16, and quantity traded is 30 units.
   (c) Price is $10, and quantity traded is 30 units.
   (d) Price is $16, and quantity traded is 33 units.
   (e) None of the above.

Answer: e

Setting supply equal to demand and solving for price yields an equilibrium price of $16. Substituting this back into either supply or demand yields an equilibrium quantity traded of 32.

20. In the previous problem, if the government forced firms to charge a price of $10, this would be an example of

    (a) a price ceiling.

    (b) an ineffective price ceiling.

    (c) an ineffective price floor.

    (d) a price floor.

    (e) both (a) and (c).

Answer: e

A price set below equilibrium is both an effective price ceiling and an ineffective price floor.

21. Assume that the market for bubble gum is competitive and that current conditions yield an equilibrium at a price of 25 cents and a quantity of 100,000 units. Which of the following events would imply a new equilibrium price of 30 cents and a quantity of 90,000 units?

    (a) An increase in the price of other kinds of gum and candy

    (b) An increase in the price of ingredients used to make bubble gum

    (c) A decrease in the number of young people in the population

    (d) An increase in consumer income

    (e) None of the above

Answer: b

An increase in production costs will decrease supply, increasing price and decreasing quantity

22. If both supply and demand increase, price will

    (a) always increase.

    (b) always decrease.

    (c) increase only if supply increases more than demand.

    (d) increase only if supply increases less than demand.

    (e) do none of the above.

Answer: d

A bigger increase in demand will increase price.

23. The law of demand implies that the price elasticity of demand (without taking absolute values) should always be

   (a) less than zero.
   (b) less than -1.
   (c) greater than zero.
   (d) greater than 1.
   (e) none of the above

Answer: a

> Price elasticity of demand is the percentage change in quantity demanded divided by the percentage change in price. The law of demand says that price and quantity demanded are inversely related.

24. Another word for elasticity is

   (a) happiness.
   (b) responsiveness.
   (c) bonus.
   (d) surplus.
   (e) none of the above.

Answer: b

25. If an increase in the price of a product from $1 to $2 per unit leads to a decrease in quantity demanded from 100 to 80 units, then the value of price elasticity of demand is

   (a) elastic.
   (b) inelastic.
   (c) unit elastic.
   (d) suggestive of an inferior good.
   (e) none of the above.

Answer: b

> The price elasticity of demand is -0.33, implying that demand is price-inelastic.

26. If demand for good X is inelastic, then

   (a) total revenue increases as quantity demanded increases.
   (b) total revenue increases as price decreases.
   (c) total revenue remains constant as quantity demanded increases.
   (d) total revenue decreases as price increases.

(e) none of the above is true.

Answer: e

Price and quantity demanded are inversely related. Price and total revenue are positively related for inelastic demand.

27. Along a linear demand curve, total revenues are maximized when demand is

(a) elastic.
(b) inelastic.
(c) unit elastic.
(d) perfectly elastic.
(e) none of the above.

Answer: c

The relationship between total revenue and elasticity dictates that revenue is highest when demand is unit elastic.

28. For which of the following is demand most likely to be perfectly inelastic?

(a) BMW autos
(b) Dr. Pepper
(c) Hot dogs
(d) Insulin
(e) Tylenol

Answer: d

A necessity like insulin is likely to have inelastic demand, indicating that consumers are not very price responsive.

29. Suppose that at equilibrium, $P = \$8$ and $Q = 30$. If demand is perfectly inelastic and supply is upward sloping, a \$2 excise tax will yield which of the following?

(a) $P = \$8$, $Q = 32$
(b) $P = \$9$, $Q = 31$
(c) $P = \$10$, $Q = 30$
(d) $P = \$10$, $Q = 31$
(e) None of the above

Answer: c

With perfectly inelastic demand, the entire tax will be passed along to consumers.

30. "The second glass of Pepsi was good. May I have another?" Which of the following
    is *necessarily* true regarding this statement?

    (a) The marginal utility of the second glass is negative.
    (b) The marginal utility of the second glass is less than the marginal utility of
        the first.
    (c) The marginal utility of the second glass is positive.
    (d) The glass of Pepsi is "free."
    (e) none of the above.

Answer: b

The law of diminishing marginal utility.

31. Which of the following can be considered implicit costs for a firm?

    (a) Insurance costs
    (b) Electricity costs
    (c) Opportunity costs of capital owned and used by the firm
    (d) The cost of raw materials
    (e) None of the above

Answer: c

32. Economic profit is defined as

    (a) total revenue minus total costs.
    (b) total revenue minus marginal costs.
    (c) total revenue minus variable costs.
    (d) total revenue minus fixed costs.
    (e) none of the above.

Answer: a

33. If General Motors earns normal profits this year,

    (a) its economic profit is equal to its accounting profit.
    (b) its economic profit is zero.
    (c) its economic profit is equal to the average accounting profit in other industries.
    (d) its accounting profit is less than its economic profit.
    (e) none of the above is true.

Answer: b

34. Which of the following probably has the shortest short run?

    (a) A law firm

(b) A steel mill

(c) An automobile plant

(d) A tire factory

(e) An aircraft manufacturer

Answer: a

The short run is defined as the period of time in the future for which at least one factor of production is fixed. A law firm is very labor-oriented, and therefore is likely to be able to change the scale of operation very quickly.

35. With increasing marginal returns, total product is

(a) increasing at a constant rate.

(b) increasing at an increasing rate.

(c) increasing at a decreasing rate.

(d) decreasing at a decreasing rate.

(e) doing none of the above.

Answer: b

If each additional input yields more output, then total output must be increasing at an increasing rate.

36. What is true of marginal cost if marginal product is decreasing?

(a) It is negative and increasing.

(b) It is negative and decreasing.

(c) It is positive and increasing.

(d) It is positive and decreasing.

(e) None of the above.

Answer: c

When marginal product eventually declines, marginal cost increases.

37. If labor is a firm's only variable input, its marginal cost ultimately depends on

(a) fixed cost.

(b) how much profit is made.

(c) the price of the good produced.

(d) how much output each worker produces.

(e) none of the above.

Answer: d

The marginal cost will be the wage rate over the marginal product.

38. If marginal cost exceeds average variable cost,

(a) average variable cost is negative.
(b) average variable cost is increasing.
(c) marginal cost is greater than average total cost.
(d) average variable cost is decreasing.
(e) none of the above is true

Answer: b

The marginal-average rule states that if marginal is greater than average, then average must be increasing.

39. Generally, as a cinema adds more movie screens, it experiences

(a) economies of scale.
(b) higher prices.
(c) diseconomies of scale.
(d) declining profit.
(e) none of the above.

Answer: a

Adding screens will increase output, but is not likely to increase the number of other factors needed. Average costs are likely to decline.

40. The price charged by a perfectly competitive firm is determined by

(a) each individual firm.
(b) a group of firms acting together.
(c) market demand and market supply.
(d) the firm's average variable cost.
(e) none of the above.

Answer: c

Perfectly competitive firms are price takers.

41. What is always true at the quantity where average total cost equals average revenue?

(a) Profit is zero.
(b) Marginal cost equals marginal revenue.
(c) Profit is maximized.

(d) Cost is minimized.

(e) None of the above.

Answer: a

Profit is always zero when average cost equals average revenue (price).

42. Which of the following occurs at each level of output for the perfectly competitive firm?

(a) MC = AVC = ATC

(b) MR = MC

(c) P > AVC

(d) AR = MR = P

(e) None of the above

Answer: d

Average revenue always equals price, which, for the perfectly competitive firm, is also equal to marginal revenue.

43. If a monopolist must lower the price on all units in order to sell an additional unit,

(a) it is impossible for the monopolist to maximize profit.

(b) the monopolist will always lose profit when it increases quantity.

(c) the monopolist will always lose revenue when it increases quantity.

(d) price will always be greater than marginal revenue.

(e) none of the above is true.

Answer: d

A nondiscriminating monopolist must lower price when it increases output, causing marginal revenue to be less than price (for every unit after the first).

44. If marginal revenue is negative,

(a) total revenue must be zero.

(b) total revenue must be decreasing.

(c) total revenue must be increasing.

(d) total revenue must be negative.

(e) none of the above is true.

Answer: b

Marginal revenue is the slope of the total revenue curve. If the slope is negative, then total revenue must be decreasing.

45. Which of the following market structures is both allocatively and productively efficient?

(a) Perfect competition
(b) Monopoly
(c) Monopolistic competition
(d) Oligopoly
(e) None of the above

Answer: a

Perfect competition is the only market structure that is both allocatively (price = marginal cost) and productively (price = minimum average cost) efficient.

46. The distinguishing characteristic of monopolistic competition is

(a) ease of exit and entry.
(b) no entry barriers.
(c) product differentiation.
(d) standardized products.
(e) none of the above.

Answer: c

47. The chances of successful collusion are greatest when

(a) firms are producing a differentiated product.
(b) there are many firms in the industry.
(c) there are huge firms together with very small firms.
(d) costs are similar across firms.
(e) all of the above are true.

Answer: d

Success of collusion diminishes as more firms are involved and the product is highly differentiated.

48. If Michael Jordan earns millions of dollars playing professional basketball but would earn only $100,000 playing professional baseball instead,

(a) all of his present salary is economic rent.
(b) none of his present salary is economic rent because he has an alternative.
(c) $100,000 of his salary is rent.
(d) all but $100,000 of his salary is rent.
(e) none of the above is true

Answer: d

The $100,000 is opportunity cost. Therefore, the rest is economic rent.

49. What is the annual installment on a 7 percent 4-year simple-interest loan of $4000? (Round to the nearest cent.)

   (a) $1180.91
   (b) $1089.40
   (c) $1345.99
   (d) $999.00
   (e) None of the above

Answer: a

The loan amount represents the present value of 4 equal installments of $1180.91 at 7 percent interest.

50. If a negative externality exists,

   (a) too much is consumed and produced, and the price is too high.
   (b) not enough is consumed and produced, and the price is too high.
   (c) too much is consumed and produced, and the price is too low.
   (d) not enough is consumed and produced, and the price is too low.
   (e) none of the above is true.

Answer: c

A negative externality exists when social costs are higher than private costs. Prices should be raised and output decreased to internalize the external costs imposed on society.

CHAPTER 21

CLEMSON UNIVERSITY

50322 ECON 211: PRINCIPLES OF MICROECONOMICS

Yesim Subasim, Graduate Teaching Assistant

I STATE THE OBJECTIVE OF THE COURSE IN MY SYLLABUS: 'ECONOMICS IS THE SCIENCE OF allocation of scarce resources among unlimited wants. Our objective in this course is to learn to think in a manner consistent with the existence of scarcity.' Further, my own objective is to teach the students an understanding of the decision-making process of the economic agents in the economy: the individual buyer, the individual seller, and the government.

A student who has taken this course will have an idea about the economic environment around him or her. He or she will be able to apply the material of this course to the real world. I believe that economics is a way of looking at and thinking about life—and that it is an efficient way of doing so; therefore, by taking this course, students will acquire a way of thinking that will be useful in their business and personal lives.

I have observed that economics is a hard subject for most students. Generally, interpreting the graphs—of which there are many in this course—is a big problem. I advise students to attend lectures and participate in class discussions. The best time to learn is *in the classroom*. It is unlikely that a student who has not understood in class will go home, read the book or go over notes, and then clearly understand the subject. It is in the student's best interest to read the assigned chapters from the book before coming to the lecture. Never be ashamed to ask questions in the classroom."

This is the first midterm exam given in the course. It covers scarcity, sunk cost, the production possibilities frontier, opportunity cost and comparative and absolute advantage, demand and supply curves, market equilibrium, excess supply and demand, and distortions in the market such as taxes and price ceilings.

1. The reason that opportunity costs arise is that
   a. there are no alternative decisions that could be made.
   b. people have limited wants.
   c. an economy relies on money to facilitate exchange of goods and services.
   d. resources are scarce.

Answer: d

This is a question about scarcity. It emphasizes the fact that because resources are scarce, people have to make choices and incur costs. These costs are called opportunity costs. When a choice is made, something is forgone, sacrificed. The value of the sacrifice is the opportunity cost. This does not mean that there are no alternative choices. There is always an alternative choice. Obviously, people do not have limited wants. We all want to have more and more goods. Opportunity cost applies to any economy, both one with money as a medium of exchange and one without money, which we call barter. If there is no money, we would express the opportunity cost in terms of goods."

2. Suppose that Mr. Smith decides to open a bookstore in downtown Clemson. He spends $15,000 to buy all the necessary equipment and books. But after a few months, the store doesn't have any business at all. So he thinks that he has made a bad decision, and he makes all the necessary moves to open a nightclub, which costs him $25,000. What is the actual cost of the nightclub to Mr. Smith?
   a. $10,000
   b. $15,000
   c. $25,000
   d. $40,000

Answer: c

This is a question about sunk cost. The student is expected to know that a sunk cost is a cost that is already lost and does not have any relevance to decision making. In the example above, Mr. Smith spends $15,000 on the bookstore, but then he decides to open a nightclub, which costs him $25,000. It would seem that the cost of the nightclub is $25,000 + $15,000 = $40,000. But does the initial cost of the bookstore have any effect on the decision to open a nightclub? No. The actual cost of the nightclub is only $25,000, because the $15,000 is already lost. Whether or not he spent that money does not affect Mr. Smith's decision.

Answer Questions 3 to 6 by using the following production possibilities frontier (PPF) for a country in autarchy producing goods X and Y.

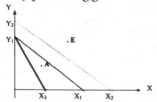

3. Which of the following is a reason for a shift of the PPF above from Y_1X_1 to Y_2X_2?
   a. natural disaster (e.g., earthquake)
   b. an improvement in the production technology
   c. a decrease in the labor force
   d. both a and c

Answer: b

> For this question, first of all, the student has to know what *autarchy* means. It means that the country is self-sufficient and doesn't trade with other countries. Second, the student must know what a *production possibilities frontier* is: the graph that shows all the goods and services that can be produced if all the country's resources are used efficiently. Third, the student must know what causes a production possibilities frontier to shift outward and inward. If it shifts outward (as in the question), this means that the country can produce more than it could before. Obviously, $Y_2 > Y_1$ and $X_2 > X_1$. There are basically two things that shift the PPF outward in parallel, as in this question: (1) technology improvement in the production of both goods and (2) economic growth, such that more of both goods can be produced than before. Answer b gives one of these. Answers a and c would lead to a downward shift in the production possibilities frontier.

4. Suppose that, currently, this country is producing according to PPF shown by Y_1X_1. Which one of the following is true for point *A*?
   a. It indicates that some resources are used inefficiently (wasted).
   b. It is impossible to attain.
   c. It is always better than a point outside the production possibilities frontier.
   d. It implies that the country is self-sufficient.

Answer: a

> The student is expected to interpret the graph. Point *A* is inside the production possibilities frontier given by Y_1X_1. Points on the production possibilities frontier mean that all the resources are used efficiently. They also mean that the country is self-sufficient, that it doesn't trade with other countries. If not all the resources are used efficiently, then fewer goods will be produced, which will result in a point inside the production possibilities frontier. So it is possible to attain point *A*, and it is always worse than a point outside the production possibilities frontier, because it means that fewer of both goods are produced.

5. Which one of the following is a reason for the shift of the PPF from Y_1X_1 to Y_1X_3?

    a. There must have been a productivity increase in the production of good X.

    b. There must have been a productivity increase in the production of good Y.

    c. There must have been a productivity decrease in the production of good X.

    d. There must have been a productivity decrease in the production of good Y.

Answer: c

This question is about the rotation of the production possibilities frontier. First of all, the student has to see that the point on the Y axis hasn't changed, but the point on the X axis has shifted inward and the production of X has decreased from X_1 to X_3. When the PPF rotates inward from the X axis like this, it means that there has been a productivity decrease in the production of X. The country continues to produce the same amount of Y, so there is no change in productivity in the production of Y.

6. Assuming that the current PPF is shown by Y_2X_2 in autarchy, point E might become attainable for this country if it were to

    a. become more inefficient.

    b. trade with other countries.

    c. increase input costs.

    d. discourage fertility increase.

Answer: b

With the resources available, the country can attain only points on the production possibilities frontier. They are the maximum amounts with all resources being used efficiently. The only way to attain a point outside the PPF like E is to trade with other countries. Trading leads to specialization and allows the country to obtain more of the goods than in autarchy. Point E doesn't have anything to do with increasing costs or decreasing the labor cost or becoming inefficient. Actually, any of these would lead to a point inside the PPF.

Questions 7 through 10 are based on the following information:

There are two people, David and Alison, who have to take care of a very fun job. They have to copy and staple the tests for all the courses in the Economics Department.

If David spends all his time copying, he can produce a maximum of 50 tests in a day, leaving him no time for stapling. Alternatively, if he spends all his time stapling, he can do 100 tests in a day, leaving no time for copying. David is also capable of producing any linear combination of these.

Being more experienced and faster, Alison is capable of daily production of at most 100 copies and no stapling, if she specializes completely in copying, or a maximum of 300 stapling operations and no copying, if she only staples. Like David, she is able to produce any linear combination of these extremes. For simplicity, assume that both can use their time only for copying and stapling.

7. Who is the low-cost producer of stapling?

    a. David, because he can produce the least of them

    b. Alison, because she can produce the most of them

    c. Alison, because she must sacrifice only one-third of a copy to perform a staple

    d. David, because he must sacrifice only two staples to make a copy

Answer: c

First of all, the student must read the information carefully and know how to interpret it. The question asks for the *low-cost producer* of stapling. Low-cost producer means that the producer has the least cost for producing that good, or he or she has a comparative advantage in producing that good. A person or a country has a comparative advantage in producing a good over another if it can produce the good at lower cost, in terms of the other good, than the other person or country; that is, less of the other good is sacrificed (or the opportunity cost is lower) when production of this good is chosen. The student needs to know all these definitions, then figure out what the opportunity costs of producing one unit of stapling for both David and Alison are. The one who has to sacrifice the fewest copy jobs will be the low-cost producer. The easiest way to figure this out is to create a chart like this:

David		Alison	
Staple	**Copy**	**Staple**	**Copy**
0	50	0	100
100	0	300	0

    The student should be able to draw up the chart using the given information. It shows that David has to sacrifice 50 copy jobs to produce 100 staple jobs, so 100 staples cost him 50 copies, and 1 staple will cost him 1/2 copy. The opportunity cost of a staple for David is 1/2 copy. Alison, on the other hand, has to sacrifice 100 copy jobs for 300 staple jobs. So 300 staples cost her 100 copies, and 1 staple will cost her 1/3 copy. The opportunity cost of a staple is 1/3 copy for Alison. As 1/3 < 1/2, Alison has a lower opportunity cost of stapling, and so she is the low-cost producer.

    Notice that the answer is not b, which relates to the *absolute advantage principle*. That principle says that a person has an absolute advantage in the production of one good if he or she can produce the most of it. But this does not mean that he or she is the low-cost producer, so b is not the answer."

8. Who has a comparative advantage in copying?

    a. David, because he can produce the least of them

    b. Alison, because she can produce the most of them

    c. David, because he is the low-cost producer of copies

    d. Alison, because she is the low-cost producer of copies

Answer: c

By making use of the definitions and the chart created to answer Question 7, it can be concluded that David has a lower opportunity cost for copying. David has to sacrifice 100 staples for 50 copies, so 50 copies cost him 100 staples and 1 copy will cost him 2 staples. Alison has to sacrifice 300 staples for 100 copies, so 100 copies cost her 300 staples, and 1 copy costs her 3 staples. As 2 < 3, David has the comparative advantage in copying. Notice that a is not the answer. (The reason is the same as the reason for why b is not the answer in 7.)"

9. Suppose that there is an urgent need for 100 copies and 150 staples. How should the job be organized?

   a. Have David staple only and have Alison make copies only.
   b. Have David and Alison each make 50 copies, with Alison spending the rest of her time stapling.
   c. Have David only make copies and Alison only staple.
   d. Have Alison make the 100 copies and spend the rest of her time on stapling, allowing David to do nothing but staple.

Answer: b

To answer this question, the student has to proceed alternative by alternative. In a, David can produce 100 staples if he doesn't do anything else, and Alison can produce 100 copies if she doesn't do anything else. This results in 100 staples and 100 copies. It's not the answer.

In b, they each makes 50 copies, resulting in 100 copies. Alison spends the rest of her time stapling. Now, let's remember that 1 copy costs Alison 3 staples, and so 50 copies will cost her 150 staples. Thus, if she produces 50 copies, with the rest of the time she has she can produce 150 fewer staples than she could have produced if she had devoted all of her time to stapling. That would have produced 300 staples; therefore, in the rest of her time, she will produce 300 - 150 = 150 staples. This leads to 100 copies and 150 staples. This is the answer: b.

But it is always safest to check the other options. In c, David makes only copies; this means 50 copies. Alison makes only staples; this means 300 staples. This is not the answer. In d, David staples only, which means 100 staples. Alison makes 100 copies and spends the rest of her time stapling. Again remember that 1 copy costs her 3 staples, so 100 copies cost her 300 staples, and she does not have any time to staple. This can be seen from the chart for Question 7: If Alison makes 100 copies in a day, she cannot do anything else. This results in 100 copies and 100 staples, which is not the answer.

10. Who has an absolute advantage in stapling?

    a. Alison, because she has a comparative advantage in stapling
    b. David, because he has a comparative advantage in copying
    c. Alison, because she can produce the most of them
    d. Neither of them

Answer: c

Absolute advantage means that one person or country can produce more of a good with the given resources than the other person or country. It is completely different from *comparative advantage*. There are no costs involved here. The only thing to look for is who produces the most staples. As is obvious from the chart created for Question 7, Alison can produce 300, whereas David can produce only 100; therefore, Alison has an absolute advantage in stapling.

11. The height of an individual's demand curve (measured at some quantity Q) shows

  a. the marginal value of consuming the Qth unit.

  b. the equilibrium price of the good.

  c. the total value of consuming Q units.

  d. none of the above.

Answer: a

The student has to know what an individual's demand curve for a good looks like:

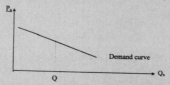

The above shows an individual's demand curve for good X. The height of the demand curve measured at Q is the marginal value of that Qth unit. *Marginal* means incremental, additional. *Marginal value* means what an additional amount of good X is worth to the individual, what the additional value of that Qth unit is. So the height of the demand curve at any point like Q shows how much money this individual is ready to give up to receive the Qth unit. That height is the marginal value of the Qth unit. The total value of the Qth unit would be the area under the demand curve, from the origin to the Qth unit. (To find the *equilibrium price*, we need the supply curve.)

12. The First Law of Demand implies that when the price of good X increases, the result will be

  a. an increase in the demand for good X.

  b. a decrease in the quantity of good X demanded.

  c. a decrease in the supply of good X.

  d. an increase in the quantity of good X demanded.

Answer: b

First, of course, the student needs to know the First Law of Demand, which is, "With everything else held constant, when the price of a good decreases (increases), the quantity demanded of that good increases (decreases)." Notice that it is the *quantity demanded*, not the *demand*. As can be seen from the graph below, the demand curve shows a relationship between the price of the good and the quantity demanded of that good. When the price increases from P_1 to P_2, the quantity demanded decreases from Q_1 to Q_2. Nothing happens to the demand curve, so there is no change in the demand, but the quantity demanded changes. When the *own price* of the good changes, the result is a change in the quantity demanded, not the demand.

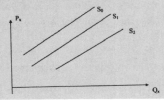

13. Socks and shoes are complements. The demand for shoes will increase if
    a. the price of shoes falls.
    b. the quantity of shoes demanded falls.
    c. the price of socks decreases.
    d. the supply of socks increases.

Answer: c

Price of other goods is one of the things that affect the demand curve. If goods X and Y are complements, it means that they are used together, like cars and gasoline or tapes and tape recorders. So if the price of X increases, then the demand for Y goes down. Or if the price of Y decreases, then the demand for X goes up. In this question, the demand for shoes goes up. Notice that the word is *demand*, not *quantity demanded*.

One option is to proceed alternative by alternative. Answer a cannot be true, because if the price of shoes falls, the *quantity demanded* of shoes will increase, not the *demand*. Answer b cannot be true, because it does not make any sense. C is right because when the price of socks decreases, it becomes cheaper to buy socks, and the fact that socks and shoes are used together leads to an increase in the demand for shoes. This is the same as the idea that when gasoline becomes cheaper, car sales go up. Answer d cannot be true because demand and supply cannot be explained by each other.

14. Lacrosse sticks are a superior good. A decrease in the demand for lacrosse sticks could be caused by
    a. an increase in the price of lacrosse sticks.
    b. a decrease in the price of a complement.
    c. a decrease in the price of a substitute.
    d. a decrease in income of consumers.

Answer: d

Income is one of the things that affect demand. If the good is a superior good, then when the consumers' income increases, the demand for that good also increases, and when the consumers' income decreases, the demand for that good decreases. Lacrosse sticks are given as a superior good, and demand for them has fallen. The only answer that corresponds to this situation is a decrease in the income of consumers. In a, the price of lacrosse sticks increases. This leads to a decrease in the quantity demanded, not the demand. In b, there is a decrease in the price of a complement to lacrosse sticks. This leads to an increase in the demand curve. In c, the price of a substitute decreases, which also leads to a decrease in the demand for lacrosse sticks because substitutes are things used instead of the good in question. If the price of a good that can be used instead of lacrosse sticks decreases, then consumers will buy fewer lacrosse sticks, and, therefore, demand for it will fall.

15. The market demand curve for a good shows us

    a. that as the price of that good falls, people will spend more on that good.
    b. the price of the good that will be observed as the incomes of consumers rise.
    c. that purchases of that good will decrease as the incomes of consumers rise.
    d. how many of that good will be bought at any given price during a specified time period.

Answer: d

The market demand curve for a good is the horizontal summation of the demand curves of all consumers of that good; that is, the quantities demanded at each price are added together. The market demand is also downward sloping, expressing the First Law of Demand. It shows the total amount of the good that will be bought by consumers at any given price. This corresponds to answer d.

In a, the price of the good falls, but we cannot know if the total amount of money spent on the good will increase or decrease. We know only that quantity demanded will increase. Answer b does not make any sense, and c also makes no sense because, along a market demand curve, incomes of the consumers are assumed to be constant. If incomes rise, demand will rise or fall, depending on whether the good is superior or inferior."

16. If unusually good weather results in a large kumquat crop, the result will be

    a. an increase in the demand for kumquats.
    b. an increase in the supply of kumquats.
    c. a decrease in the demand for kumquats.
    d. no change in the demand and supply of kumquats.

Answer: b

The question states that good weather results in a large crop of kumquats. This is clearly a question about supply. Good weather enables the farmers to produce more kumquats than they did before. This has nothing to do with demand.

17. A decrease in the supply of K-juice (made from kumquats) could be caused by

a. a rise in the price of K-juice.

b. a decline in the price of kumquats.

c. an increase in the price of kumquats.

d. a decline in the price of K-juice.

Answer: c

"The question states that K-juice is made from kumquats, which means that kumquats are *inputs* to K-juice; that is, kumquats are used in the production of K-juice. A change in the price of kumquats will affect the supply of K-juice, because suppliers of K-juice have to pay for the kumquats. If the supply of K-juice falls, less K-juice is supplied at all prices. A decrease in the supply of K-juice in this case results from an increase in the price of kumquats, because this increases the cost of K-juice suppliers, who consequently supply less at all prices. Answers a and d cannot be true because they result in a change in the *quantity supplied*, not the *supply*."

18. A decrease in the supply of a good means that

a. there is a movement along the supply curve.

b. the supply curve shifts to the right.

c. the demand curve shifts to the right.

d. the supply curve shifts to the left.

Answer: d

A decrease or an increase in the supply indicates a change in the whole supply curve:

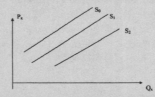

A decrease in the supply of good X is shown as the shift from S_1 to S_0 or from S_2 to S_1 or from S_2 to S_0. This is because, at all prices, less of good X is supplied in S_0 than in S_1. An increase in the supply is shown as the shift from S_0 to S_1 or from S_1 to S_2 or from S_0 to S_2. Therefore, a decrease in the supply means a shift of the supply curve to the left. It has nothing to do with the demand curve.

19. Kumquats and chewing gum are substitutes. If a technological innovation results in a larger than average crop of kumquats, what will be the impact on the price and quantity of chewing gum?

a. Higher price and lower quantity

b. Lower price and lower quantity

c. Uncertain price and higher quantity

d. Higher price and uncertain quantity

Answer: b

This question requires that demand and supply be brought together. First of all, there are two markets here: the kumquat and chewing gum markets. There is an increase in the crop of kumquats. The student should immediately understand that this means an increase in the supply of kumquats. Having figured that out, you have to think about how that affects the price and quantity of chewing gum.

"Let's draw the market for kumquats first:

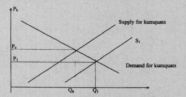

When supply and demand curves intersect, the intersection point is called the *equilibrium*. P_e is the equilibrium price for the kumquats, and Q_e is the equilibrium quantity of kumquats in the market. When the supply of kumquats increases, it means a shift of the supply curve to the right to S_1. Then the intersection point of demand and supply changes, leading to a change in the equilibrium price and quantity of kumquats. The equilibrium price falls to P_1 and quantity falls to Q_1. This is all the information the student has to get from the technological innovation resulting in a large kumquat crop.

How does this affect the chewing gum industry? These two goods are assumed to be substitutes, so if the price of kumquats falls, people will buy more kumquats and less chewing gum. Buying more kumquats is already seen from the increase in the quantity from Q_e to Q_1 in the above graph. Now we have to look at the chewing gum market:

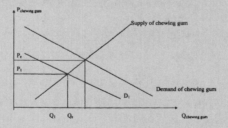

As the price of kumquats falls, people will buy less chewing gum. You may conclude that this means that the demand for chewing gum will decrease to D_1. This results in a new intersection of the supply and demand curves for chewing gum. With the new demand curve, the new equilibrium price P_1 is less than P_e, and the new equilibrium quantity Q_1 is less than Q_e. As a result, the technological innovation in kumquat production leads to lower price and lower quantity of chewing gum.

20. If demand and supply of a good both increase, the result will be

  a. higher price and lower quantity.
  b. higher price and higher quantity.
  c. uncertain price and higher quantity.
  d. higher price and uncertain quantity.

Answer: c

"First of all, the student has to know what increases in demand and supply mean. An increase in demand means that the demand curve shifts upward to the right, and an increase in supply means a shift downward. It is impossible to answer this question without drawing a graph that shows both changes:

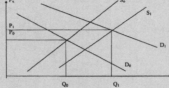

"The above graph shows an increase in demand from D_0 to D_1 and an increase in supply from S_0 to S_1. The initial equilibrium price and quantity are P_0 and Q_0. After the changes, it seems from the graph that the equilibrium price rises to P_1, and the equilibrium quantity increases to Q_1. Notice, however, that the answer is not b (higher price, higher quantity). To see why it is not, you can draw another graph showing the same changes but resulting in a different conclusion:

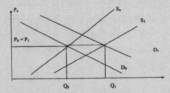

As this graph shows, the equilibrium price does not change. So what is the correct answer? The quantity is going to increase, that is for sure, because consumers demand more and sellers offer more of the good, but the effect on the price depends on the magnitude of the changes in demand and supply. In the second graph, the increase in the demand is less than that in the first graph. So the price is uncertain, unless we know how much demand and supply shift.

21. A decrease in the consumption of a good results from

    a. an increase in supply combined with an increase in demand.

    b. an increase in demand combined with no change in supply.

    c. an increase in supply combined with no change in demand.

    d. none of the above.

Answer: d

First, interpret the question. A decrease in the consumption of a good means that the equilibrium quantity of that good has fallen. People are buying less of that good. Then, the best way to proceed is alternative answer by alternative answer. This requires drawing a graph for each alternative. Without graphs, the question is very hard to answer.

(a)

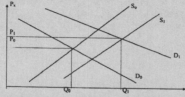

When both demand and supply increase, quantity always increases. There is no possibility for quantity to decrease (see previous question).

(b)

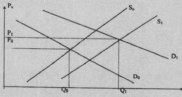

When only demand increases, obviously quantity also increases.

(c)

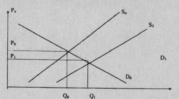

Again, when only supply increases, quantity increases. Therefore, the answer is d, none of the above.

22. If government authorities set a price ceiling for in-line skates that is substantially above the equilibrium price (maximum price),

a. there will be excess demand for in-line skates.

b. there will be excess supply of in-line skates.

c. it will not have any effect on the in-line skates market.

d. both a and c are correct.

Answer: c

It is important to understand the question very well. It says that the government imposes a maximum price, which is above the equilibrium price of the good. *Maximum price* means that the producers aren't allowed to sell at a higher price than the price set by the government. However, this is effective (binding) only when this price is less than the equilibrium price, because at the equilibrium price, the producers and consumers are already in agreement. Maximum price is a tool government uses to protect individuals who cannot afford such necessities as milk. It forces the milk producers to charge no more than a given price ceiling, which should be below the equilibrium price.

Sometimes the government wants to stop unfair acts by landlords who charge very high rental rates. It forces them to reduce the rental rates to a given value. In sum, a price ceiling, by definition, should be lower than the equilibrium price; otherwise it has no effect.

23. Which one of the following statements is true?

a. When a tax is levied on suppliers, demanders are not affected at all.

b. The full price paid by consumers is the same whether the tax is on suppliers or demanders.

c. The quantity traded increases when a tax is levied on demanders.

d. None of the above.

Answer: b

This is a question about distortions to the market, one of which is the imposition of taxes by government. The student is expected to know how to show graphically the effect of a tax on demand and supply. Once again, drawing a graph is crucial to answering this question. Draw a graph and check the options:

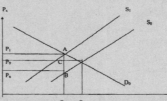

When a government levies a tax on suppliers, the supply curve shifts to the left because the tax increases the suppliers' cost. When the government levies a tax on demanders, the demand curve shifts to the left because they have to pay more to buy the good. Although it seems that the effects of these two cases would be completely different, this is not so. The above graph shows a tax levied on suppliers. The amount of the tax is given by the distance *AB*. Notice that the increase in the price is only *AC*. Because demand and supply curves are assumed to be well behaved (downward sloping and upward sloping), the price does not increase by the full amount of the tax, and so demanders pay P_1 now. This is called the full price paid by the demanders. The suppliers, on the other hand, receive only P_n because they have to pay tax to the government. So suppliers receive P_1 from demanders and give the amount shown by *AB* to the government as tax. This leaves them with only P_n, which is called the net price received by the suppliers. Thus, when a tax is levied on the suppliers, the latter receive a lower net price and the demanders pay a higher full price.

Now let's examine the case when a tax is levied on demanders:

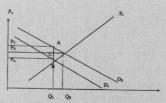

When the government levies a tax on demanders, the demand curve shifts to the left from D_0 to D_1. The amount of the tax is given by the distance AB. Notice that the increase in the price is only AC. Because demand and supply curves are assumed to be well behaved (downward sloping and upward sloping), the price does not increase by the full amount of the tax, so demanders now pay P_f, the full price paid by the demanders. However, some portion of this full price has to go to the government as tax, which is the difference between P_f and P_n. Then the suppliers, as in the previous case, receive only P_n. Thus, when a tax is levied on the demanders, the latter pay a higher full price, and the suppliers receive a lower net price.

Notice that the two cases are identical, except for the party that pays the government. Let's examine the answers:

Answer a is not correct because we have shown that demanders pay a higher price even when the suppliers are taxed.

Answer b is correct because we have proved it above.

Answer c is not correct because, when a tax is levied on demanders, they have to pay a higher price, and therefore the demand curve shifts to the left, indicating that demanders will buy less of the good at any price than they were buying before.

The process of answering this question seems rather long, but students are expected to know all this information from the lectures rather than having to derive them on their own. A careful understanding of underlying principles is much more important than memorizing detailed definitions. Rote memorization is never encouraged."

FINAL EXAM

Success on the exams requires knowledge of the contents of the subject material sufficiently thorough that it can be applied in a practical manner to the exam questions. To practice such application, you might try to answer the questions in the course study guide and those at the end of each textbook chapter. The course homework is also a perfect study guide. Also: learn from the exams themselves. After you have taken the first one, think about how you might better prepare for the next. Look at the structure and content of the questions.

1. When a person makes a choice, that person
    a. discriminates.
    b. incurs a cost.
    c. must give up money.
    d. Only a and b are correct.

e. All of the above are correct.

Answer: d

> This is the starting point for the lecture. The student has to know that resources are scarce in this world and that people have to make choices between their wants. Making a choice always incurs a cost; that is, the individual faces certain trade-offs. When the individual makes a choice between two of the things he or she wants to have, he or she sacrifices one for the other. This means that he or she discriminates, so a choice leads to discrimination and sacrificing, which incurs a cost.

2. If a country's production possibilities frontier shifts to the left (a parallel shift), this means

    a. that the opportunity cost of producing one good has decreased.

    b. that the opportunity cost of producing one good has increased.

    c. that the country has begun trading goods with other countries.

    d. that there has been a reduction in the resources of the country.

    e. that there has been economic growth.

Answer: d

> For this question, the student must first know what a *production possibilities frontier* is. It is the graph showing all the goods and services that can be produced if all of the country's resources are used efficiently. Second, the student needs to know what causes a production possibilities frontier to shift to the left or right. A shift to the left (as in the question) means that the country cannot produce as many goods as it did before. There are basically two things that shift the production possibilities frontier to the left: (1) reduction in resources (e.g., due to a natural disaster) and (2) a productivity decrease such that less of both goods can be produced than before. Answer d gives one of these factors.
>
> *Opportunity cost* is the slope of the production possibilities frontier. It doesn't change because of the parallel shift. Trading with other countries enables the country to move to a point outside its production possibilities frontier, but it does not shift it. Economic growth shifts the production possibilities frontier to the right."

3. If country A has an absolute advantage in the production of everything,

    a. trade probably takes place and all countries gain.

    b. no trade takes place because country B has a comparative advantage in everything.

    c. no trade takes place because country A has a comparative advantage in everything.

    d. no trade takes place because no country has comparative advantage in anything.

    e. trade probably takes place, but country A does not gain.

Answer: a

For this question, the student needs to know what *absolute* and *comparative advantage* mean. A country has a comparative advantage in producing a good over another if it can produce the good at lower cost in terms of the other good than the other country. That is: less of the other good is sacrificed or the opportunity cost is lower when production of this good is chosen. Absolute advantage means that a country can produce more of the good with the given resources than the other country. It is completely different from comparative advantage. That a country has an absolute advantage in producing a good tells us nothing about its comparative advantage. The only information it gives is that the country can produce the most of the good with the given resources. However, having an absolute advantage in the production of everything does not rule out trade taking place. We have to look at the opportunity cost of producing a good (that is, comparative advantage). It is probably true that country A will have a comparative advantage in the production of some goods and country B will have a comparative advantage in the production of other goods, and that they will trade these goods and gain from trade.

4. If the price of bicycles decreases, there will be

    a. an increase in the demand for bicycles.

    b. an increase in the demand for motorcycles, if bicycles and motorcycles are substitutes.

    c. an increase in the demand for kumquats, if bicycles and kumquats are complements.

    d. an increase in income, if bicycles are superior goods.

    e. an increase in the quantity of kumquats demanded, if bicycles and kumquats are complements.

Answer: c

"It is best to proceed alternative by alternative. Answer a is not correct because when the price of bicycles increases, the *quantity demanded* of bicycles decreases, but nothing happens to *demand*. This is the First Law of Demand. Answer b is not correct because if motorcycles and bicycles are substitutes, and if bicycles become cheaper, the demand for motorcycles should decrease, not increase. Answer c is correct because if bicycles and kumquats are complements, things that are used together, and bicycles become cheaper, people will buy more kumquats; therefore, the demand for kumquats increases. Answer d does not make sense because income and prices are not related. Income and demand are related to each other. Answer e is not correct because it says that the *quantity demanded* of kumquats increases, whereas the correct answer is the *demand* for kumquats. The quantity demanded of a good changes only when its *own* price changes."

5. If the price of apples increases, there will be

    a. a movement along the supply curve for apple juice.

    b. a movement along the supply curve for apples.

    c. a leftward shift in the supply curve for apple juice.

    d. a leftward shift in the supply curve for apples.

e. both b and c.

Answer: e

The best way to answer this question is to look at each option. Answer a is not true because apples are obviously used in the production of apple juice, and a change in the price of apples causes a shift in the supply of apple juice, not a movement along the supply curve. Answer b is correct because when the price of apples increases, the supply of apples doesn't change, but the *quantity supplied* changes. A change in the quantity supplied means a movement along the supply curve. Answer c is also correct because, since apples are inputs for apple juice, an increase in the price of apples means an increase in the cost of apple juice. So the supply of apple juice decreases, which means a leftward shift in the supply curve. Answer d is not correct because a change in the *own* price of a good does not change the supply, but changes the quantity supplied. Answer e encompasses both b and c, and is the correct response."

6. Cheeseburgers are an inferior good, and cheese is a factor of production for pizza. The price of pizza will *increase* and the quantity of pizza will be *uncertain* if

    a. incomes of pizza consumers and the price of cheese increase at the same time.

    b. incomes of pizza consumers and the price of cheese fall at the same time.

    c. incomes of pizza consumers increase and the price of cheese decreases at the same time.

    d. incomes of pizza consumers decrease and the price of cheese increases at the same time.

    e. only the price of cheese increases.

Answer: d

The student is expected to know the concepts of *inferior good* and *factor of production*. A good is inferior if demand for it falls when consumer income increases, and demand for it increases when consumer income falls. A factor of production is a good that is used in the production of other goods. Again, the best way to find the right answer is to proceed alternative by alternative, drawing graphs for each.

    Answer a: If incomes of pizza consumers increase, people will buy more pizzas and fewer cheeseburgers because the latter are an inferior good, and so the demand for cheeseburgers will decrease. If the price of cheese increases, the cost of making a cheeseburger increases, and so the supply of cheeseburgers will decrease:

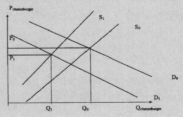

"Before demand and supply change, the equilibrium price in the cheeseburger market is P_0 and the quantity of cheeseburgers is Q_0. When demand and supply decrease at the same time, price decreases to P_1 and quantity decreases to Q_1. However, you should be able to figure out that the outcome of this situation is *not* lower price and lower quantity, but *uncertain* price and lower quantity, because the intersection of the new supply and demand can lead to a price that is less than, equal to, or greater than P_0, but the quantity will *always* be lower.

Another way to see this is to take each change individually. When demand decreases, price goes down and quantity goes down. When supply decreases, price goes up and quantity goes down. Bringing these two together, we get price uncertain and quantity lower. So this is not the right answer.

Answer b: When income falls, demand for cheeseburgers increases, and when the price of cheese falls, the supply of cheeseburgers increases. Therefore, a demand increase means price increases and quantity increases; a supply increase means prices going down and quantity decreasing. As a result, we have uncertain price and higher quantity:

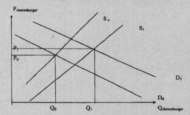

Answer c: If income increases, demand for cheeseburgers decreases, and if the price of cheese falls, the supply of cheeseburgers increases. A decrease in the demand means a decrease in the price and a decrease in the quantity. An increase in the supply means a decrease in the price and an increase in the quantity. As a result, we have lower price and uncertain quantity:

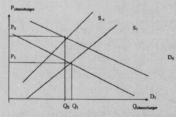

Answer d: When income decreases, the demand for cheeseburgers increases, and when the price of cheese increases, the supply of cheeseburgers decreases. An increase in the demand means an increase in the price, and an increase in the quantity and a decrease in the supply means an increase in the price and a decrease in the quantity. As a result, we have higher price and uncertain quantity—the correct answer:

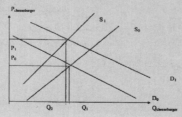

7. The market supply curve

    a. is derived from individual demand curves.

    b. is the horizontal sum of the quantities demanded by each consumer in the market.

    c. is the horizontal sum of individual supply curves.

    d. shows the maximum amount that is demanded at each price level.

    e. is none of the above.

Answer: c

The market supply curve is derived by adding individual supply curves horizontally. This means that the quantities of the good that each producer supplies at each price are added together. The answer that corresponds to this is c. All the other options have demand in the statements; *demand* has no relevance for the market supply curve .

8.) If the elasticity of demand for jeans is -0.5, a 10 percent increase in the quantity of jeans demanded will be a result of

    a. a 50 percent increase in the price of jeans.

    b. a 50 percent decrease in the price of jeans.

    c. a 20 percent increase in the price of jeans.

    d. a 20 percent decrease in the price of jeans.

    e. a 10 percent decrease in the price of jeans.

Answer: d

For this question, the student is expected to know the elasticity of demand formula. Elasticity of demand measures the responsiveness of demand to a change in the own price of the good. The formula is

    E = percent change in the quantity demanded of X/percent change in the price of X

    The answer is always negative because demand is downward-sloping. When price increases, quantity demanded falls, and vice versa. The student must be able to put the right numbers in the right places as below:

    E = -0.5 = +10 percent/percent change in the price of jeans

The - and + signs are crucial because they tell increases and decreases: +10 percent means a 10 percent increase. The answer must be negative because of the negative relation between the price and quantity for demand. Solving the above elasticity formula, we get

    -0.5 (percent change in the price of jeans) = +10 percent
    percent change in the price of jeans = +10 percent/-0.5 = -20 percent

which means a 20 percent decrease in the price of jeans.

9. If the prices of perfumes increase and the expenditures on perfumes decrease, what must be the elasticity of demand for perfumes (in absolute value)?

    a. Greater than 1

    b. Less than 1

    c. Equal to 1

    d. Equal to zero

    e. Equal to infinity

Answer: a

The student is expected to know the relationship between the price of a good and the expenditures on it. By expenditures, we mean the money spent on the good, which is the quantity of the good bought times the price of the good. The question says that the price of perfumes increases and expenditures on perfumes decrease. It must be true that demanders of perfumes are responsive to the price changes. When price increases, they must decrease their quantities bought sufficiently that the expenditures on them fall. Let's look at the expenditures as Expenditures = $P_{perfumes} \times Q_{perfumes}$ bought. The price of perfumes increases, so for the expenditures to fall, $Q_{perfumes}$ bought must have fallen by a value that is greater than the increase in the price. But this means that the demand is elastic. That is, when the price of a good increases by Y percent, the quantity of that good demanded falls more than Y percent, which means that the elasticity is greater than 1 in absolute value. Absolute value makes a negative number positive. It is used to make comparisons easier.

10. If the cross-price elasticity between goods A and B is +2.0, and the price of A increases by 10 percent, then

    a. A and B are substitutes, and the demand for B decreases by 20 percent.

    b. A and B are substitutes, and the demand for B increases by 20 percent.

    c. A and B are substitutes, and the demand for A increases by 20 percent.

    d. A and B are complements, and the demand for B decreases by 20 percent.

    e. A and B are complements, and the demand for B increases by 20 percent.

Answer: b

The student needs to know the definition of the *cross-price elasticity of demand*, which shows not only whether two goods are substitutes or complements but also how a change in the price of one affects the demand for the other. The formula is

    percent change in the demand for good B/percent change in the price of good A

The answer can be positive or negative. If it is positive, goods A and B are substitutes, and if it is negative, they are complements. The question gives the value as +2.0, so they are substitutes. Then, putting the numbers in the formula, we get

    +2.0 = percent change in the demand for good B/+10 percent

so,

    percent change in the demand for good B = +2.0 × 10 percent = 20 percent.

Because the number is positive, it means that the demand for good B increases by 20 percent.

11. Suppose that Fred has $50 to spend on books (leisure books, not school books) and magazines. If the price of a book on average is $5 and the price of a magazine on average is $2, which one of the following will not be correct?

    a. The maximum amount of books that Fred can buy is 10.
    b. The maximum amount of magazines that Fred can buy is 25.
    c. A combination of 6 books and 10 magazines is a point on his budget line.
    d. A combination of 4 books and 15 magazines is a point inside his budget line.
    e. A combination of 8 books and 6 magazines is a point outside his budget line.

Answer: d

To begin with, the student needs to know the definition of a *budget line*. A budget line shows all the combinations of two goods that an individual can buy with a given income if the individual spends all his or her income on those two goods. Therefore, points on the budget line exhaust the income, and they are attainable. Points inside the budget line leave some amount of income unspent, and points outside the budget line are not attainable, because they require more money than the available income. With this information, we can draw the budget line for Fred as follows:

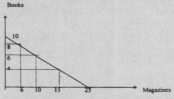

Statement a is correct because $10 \cdot 5 = \$50$, and that is the left corner of his budget line.
Statement b is correct because $25 \cdot 2 = \$50$, and that is the right corner of his budget line.
Statement c is correct because $6 \cdot 5 + 10 \cdot 2 = \$50$, which is on the budget line.
Only d is incorrect, because $4 \cdot 5 + 15 \cdot 2 = \$50$, which is *on* the budget line.
And e is correct because $8 \cdot 5 + 6 \cdot 2 = \$52$, which is outside the budget constraint.

12. If marginal product is increasing and is greater than the average product, then

    a. the average product curve reaches a maximum.
    b. average product increases.
    c. average product decreases.
    d. average product intersects the marginal product curve at the minimum of the marginal cost curve.
    e. average product intersects the marginal product curve at the minimum of the average cost curve.

Answer: b

The student is expected to know the definitions of *average* and *marginal product* and the relation between them. Marginal product shows the additional output produced by an additional input. For example, suppose there are 10 workers in a restaurant who produce 100 meals in a day. If 1 more worker is hired, and, the total output increases to 115 meals, then the marginal product of the 11th worker is 15 meals. Average product shows how much output is produced on average. In the previous example, 10 workers produce 100 meals, so the average product of 10 workers is 10 meals. The average product of 11 workers is 115/11 = 10.45 meals. The relationship between marginal product and average product can be summarized as follows:

as MP (marginal product) increases and MP > AP, AP (average product) increases, and as MP decreases and MP < AP, AP decreases.

Suppose that a student gets 80 on the first exam. This is the marginal product of the first exam. He or she gets 70 on the second exam. His or her average in the first exam was 80, but after the second exam, the average falls to 75. The second marginal product was 70, and it is less than 80, so marginal product falls and, therefore, average product falls. However, if the student gets 90 on the second exam, the average increases to 85, and so marginal product increases from 80 to 90, and the average also increases from 80 to 85. Graphically, the relation can be shown as:"

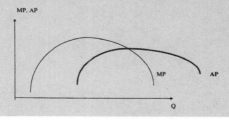

13. Marginal cost is U-shaped because

    a. average cost is also U-shaped.

    b. there are diminishing returns to the variable inputs.

    c. marginal cost is always less than average cost.

    d. average cost is always less than marginal cost.

    e. marginal cost is always greater than average cost.

Answer: b

The student is expected to know the definition of *marginal cost*: the additional cost of producing one more unit of a good. Marginal cost is U-shaped because it decreases until a certain point and then begins to increase. The reason for this is that there are diminishing returns to the variable input. In the short run, some inputs, such as land, buildings, etc., are not variable, while some goods, such as workers, are variable. If more and more of the variable input is added to the fixed inputs, it will become very costly to have those additional workers. The situation will become too "crowded" because even if those additional workers are unable to produce anything, they still have to be paid. Thus they add to the cost without adding to the output and therefore increase the marginal cost. The shape of the marginal cost is not related to its relation with the average cost.

14. Increasing returns to scale indicate that

    a. a decrease in the scale of production will cause average cost to increase.

    b. a decrease in the scale of production will cause average cost to decrease.

    c. an increase in the scale of production will cause average cost to increase.

    d. an increase in the scale of production will cause average cost to decrease.

    e. both a and d are correct.

Answer: e

The student is expected to know the definition of *increasing returns to scale*. Returns to scale show the effect on average cost of an increase in the scale (size) of the firm. Increasing returns to scale means that when the scale of the firm is increased, the average cost falls. The returns from increasing the scale are positive. Showing this on a graph is useful:

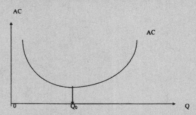

From 0 to Q_0, there are increasing returns to scale because, as the quantity increases, the cost falls. Therefore, decreasing the scale in that range would cause the average cost to increase, and increasing the scale would cause the average cost to fall.

15. Each of the following is a decision that must be made by a perfectly competitive firm *except*

    a. which price level to set for its output.

    b. how much labor to employ.

    c. how much capital to rent.

    d. how to produce the output.

    e. how much output to supply.

Answer: a

The answer is a. A perfectly competitive firm is by definition a price taker. It decides on the quantities of labor, capital, and output, but it has no power to set the price because there are a lot of firms like it in a perfectly competitive market that produce the same product. The price of the product is determined in the market, and all the perfectly competitive firms take it as given.

16. If a perfectly competitive firm is producing 7 units of output where the market price of the good it sells is $25, its average total cost for 7 units is $10, and its average variable cost for 7 units is $5, the profit of this firm is

a. $175.
b. $70.
c. $105.
d. $140.
e. $35.

Answer: c

The student is expected to know the definition of *profit*, which is total revenue of the firm minus total cost. Total revenue is equal to price times the quantity sold, which is $25 \times 7 = 175$. Total cost is average total cost times quantity, which is $10 \times 7 = 70$. Subtracting gives us $175 - 70 = 105$.

17. If the price of the good that a *perfectly competitive firm* is selling is greater than its average variable cost but less than its average total cost,

   a. the firm is making operating profits.
   b. the firm is making operating losses.
   c. the firm increases the price.
   d. the firm decreases the fixed cost in the short run.
   e. all of the above are true.

Answer: a

The student needs to know that when the price of the good that the perfectly competitive firm is selling is less than its average total cost, the firm suffers losses. However, if the price is still higher than its average variable cost, the firm makes operating profits in the short run and is expected to exit the industry in the long run. The perfectly competitive firm has no power over the price and cannot change the fixed cost in the short run.

18. Which one of the following is true?

   a. Market power can occur only when the demand curve facing the firm is downward sloping; therefore, a monopoly has market power.
   b. No profit-maximizing monopolist will produce along the inelastic portion of its demand curve.
   c. A monopolist's profit-maximizing decision leads to efficiency gain.
   d. If a monopolist earns short-run economic profits, market forces will operate to reduce profits to normal levels in the long run.
   e. Both c and d are true.

Answer: b

The best way to find the right answer is to proceed alternative by alternative. Answer a is not correct because perfectly competitive firms also have downward-sloping demand curves, but they don't have any market power. A monopoly has market power because it is the only firm in the market.

Answer b is correct because, in the inelastic portion of the demand curve, people are not responsive to the price changes, and when the monopolist decreases its price at that range, the quantity will not increase as much, and the monopolist's revenue will fall. It is best to show this on a graph:

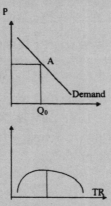

At the midpoint of any demand curve (like point A), the elasticity of demand is -1. To the left of that point, the elasticity falls, and to the right of that point, elasticity increases. So beyond point A, when the monopolist decreases price, total revenue (as shown in the graph) will fall. Therefore, a monopolist never produces in the range beyond point A.

Answer c is not correct because the monopolist's decision results in an efficiency loss, since the monopolist always charges a price higher than the marginal cost.

Answer d is wrong because if a monopolist earns profits in the short run, it will continue to do so in the long run, as it does not face any competition from any other firm.

19. Which one of the following is true for monopolistic competition and oligopoly?

   a. A monopolistically competitive firm faces a downward-sloping demand curve, but an oligopolist doesn't.

   b. A natural monopoly acts exactly like an oligopolist and a monopolistically competitive firm.

   c. A monopolistically competitive firm tries to differentiate its products from those of rivals, but an oligopolist doesn't.

   d. A monopolistically competitive firm may compete with others on price, but an oligopolist never does.

   e. A monopolistically competitive firm is small relative to the size of its industry, whereas an oligopolist frequently is large relative to the size of its industry.

Answer: e

The student must be able to distinguish among monopoly, monopolistic competition, and oligopoly. Monopoly is the case where there is only one firm in the market. In a natural monopoly, large economies of scale (decreasing average cost for large quantities) make production by a single firm the most efficient. Monopolistic competition describes an industry with a few firms that produce differentiated forms of the same product, such as cars. Oligopoly describes an industry with a few firms that may differentiate the product and act strategically.

Answer a is not correct because both face a downward-sloping demand curve.

Answer b is not correct because a natural monopoly acts like a monopoly.

Answer c is not correct because in some forms of oligopoly, differentiated products are sold.

Answer d is not correct because in oligopoly, there are a few firms that compete with one another.

Answer e is correct.

20. If firms in a monopolistically competitive industry are making profits, then

    a. the demand curve faced by an individual firm shifts up.

    b. the marginal revenue curve for an individual firm shifts up.

    c. each individual firm's share of the market demand goes down.

    d. each individual firm's share of the market demand goes up.

    e. answers a, b, and c are correct.

Answer: c

If a monopolistically competitive firm is making profits in the short run (because it cannot make any profits in the long run), it will attract firms outside the industry, which will enter the industry because there is free entry and exit in a monopolistically competitive industry. This will lead to a decrease in the share of each existing firm in the industry. Each of them will have a smaller share of the market, because the number of the firms in the industry will increase. This means a downward shift of each firm's demand curve."

21. Which one of the following is not a source of market failure?

    a. Existence of a public good

    b. Lack of market power by individual firms

    c. Existence of a negative or positive externality

    d. Lack of perfect information

    e. Existence of imperfect competition among producers

Answer: b

The student is expected to know what *market failure* means and what the reasons for it are. Market failure means that resources are misallocated or allocated inefficiently. There are four causes of market failure:

    1. The existence of public goods, which are goods that bestow collective benefits on the members

of the society, which are consumed collectively, and that no one can be excluded from enjoying (such as national defense, parks, highways, etc.).

2. Imperfect markets where there is not perfect competition; any kind of industry structure other than perfect competition leads to resource misallocations.

3. Externalities that result from a cost or benefit from an activity or transaction that is imposed or bestowed upon parties outside the activity. Examples of negative externalities are pollution and toxic waste dumping; an example of a positive externality is education.

4. Imperfect information that leads to resource misallocations. If parties don't have enough information about product quality and prices, they can make the wrong decisions.

Answer b is the only circumstance that doesn't fit one of these causes. Market power actually leads to market failure (e.g., monopoly).

Questions 22 to 24 are based on the following information: Silver is an important ingredient in making photographic film. A major deposit of silver has been discovered in Colorado. You don't know whether the discovery was made by Homesteak, a mining company, or by Cojak, a film manufacturer. (Hints: In answering the three questions that follow, (i) assume that the conditions of the Coase theorem are satisfied, (ii) assume that Homesteak and Cojak act as though they are price takers.)

22. Which of the following statements is correct?

a. The impact of the discovery on the price of silver will be the same, whichever firm made the discovery.

b. The cost of silver to Cojak will be the same, whichever firm made the discovery.

c. The impact of the discovery on the price of *film* will be the same, whichever firm made the discovery.

d. All of the above are correct.

e. Only a and b are correct.

Answer: d

The student needs to understand the information in terms of the Coase theorem. The Coase theorem says that if property rights are fully defined, cheaply enforceable, and transferable, then the ultimate utilization of resources will be independent of the initial allocation of these resources. So regardless of who has made the discovery, the price of the silver, the cost to any of the firms, and the price of the film will be the same; therefore, the answer is d."

23. Which of the following statements is correct?

a. Silver production will rise more if it is Homesteak that made the discovery.

b. Silver production will rise by the same amount regardless of who made the discovery.

c. Film production will rise by the same amount regardless of who made the discovery.

d. The price of film will rise if it is Homesteak that made the discovery.

e. Both b and c are correct.

Answer: e

Again, as the Coase theorem says, the ultimate utilization of resources is independent of the initial allocation of resources. Regardless of which firm makes the discovery, silver production, film production, and the price of the film will be the same. So b and c are correct.

24. **Which of the following statements is correct?**

a. Film users don't care which firm made the discovery.

b. The owners of the two companies don't care which firm made the discovery.

c. Although the owners of *other* silver mines might be unhappy that the discovery took place, they don't care whether it was Cojak or Homesteak that made the discovery.

d. All of the above are correct.

e. Only a and c are correct.

Answer: d

The answer is obvious and follows from the two previous questions.

25. **To attain efficiency in the production of a good,**

a. all costs of production must be borne by producers.

b. all benefits of consumption must be received by consumers.

c. marginal benefits must equal marginal costs.

d. all of the above are required.

e. only a and b are required.

Answer: d

Efficiency is a condition in which the economy produces what people want at the least possible cost. It requires (1) that the supply curve show all costs, (2) that the demand curve show all benefits, and (3) that demand and supply intersect at one point. These are given in answers a through c."

Questions 26 to 30 are based on the following graph. The line labeled D *shows the marginal benefits from consuming kumquats, and the line labeled* S *shows the marginal private costs of producing kumquats. The act of producing kumquats generates external costs that are borne by persons other than the producers of the kumquats. When these external costs are added to the private costs, the result is line* S', *which shows the marginal social costs of kumquat production.*

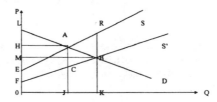

26. What is the *marginal* benefit of producing *OJ* units of kumquats?

   a. *AJ*

   b. *OH*

   c. *OL*

   d. *OM*

   e. both a and b

Answer: e

> The first requirement is to interpret the graph and know the *external cost.* The existence of external cost means that the production of this good leads the supply curve to shift to the left because real costs (social costs) are greater than the private costs. The marginal benefit is measured by the distance under the demand curve at that quantity. For *OJ* units, the height of the demand curve is given by *AJ* or *HO*, both of which give the marginal benefit of that quantity.

27. What is the *marginal* social cost of producing *OK* units of kumquats?

   a. *BK*

   b. *ERKO*

   c. *RB*

   d. *RK*

   e. *EABKO*

Answer: d

> The marginal social cost is the height of the supply curve at the given quantity. Because the supply *S'* shows the marginal social costs of kumquat production, the student should look at the height of *S'* at *OK* units, which is given by *RK*. Notice that *BK* gives only marginal private costs and *BR* gives the external costs. The sum of these two is the marginal social cost.

28. What are the *net benefits* of producing *OJ* units of kumquats?

    a. *LAJO*

    b. *LBKO*

    c. *LBF*

    d. *LAE*

    e. *HAJO*

Answer: d

Net benefits are equal to total benefits minus total social costs. Total benefits are the area under the demand curve at the given quantity, so, for *OJ* units, the total benefits are *LAJO*. Total social costs are given by the area under the marginal social cost curve, which is *S'*, so, for *OJ* units, total social costs are equal to *EAJO*. Subtracting this from benefits we get *LAE*.

29. What are the additional social costs of producing *OK* units? (*Hint:* Compare the total social costs of *OJ* and *OK*.)

    a. *EAJO*

    b. *ERKO*

    c. *ARCB*

    d. *CBKJ*

    e. *ARKJ*

Answer: e

The total social costs of producing *OJ* units are given by *EAJO*, and the total social costs of producing *OK* units are given by *ERKO*; therefore, the additional costs of producing *OK* units are *ERKO - EAJO*, which is *ARKJ*."

30. What is the efficiency loss from producing the inefficient level of kumquats?

    a. *ABC*

    b. *ARB*

    c. *LAE*

    d. *LBF*

    e. *ARBC*

Answer: b

First figure out the efficient level of kumquat production, which is found where the marginal social cost and marginal benefit intersect; that results in *OJ* units for this question. Producing *OK* units is inefficient because this is greater than the efficient level; *OK* is found at the intersection of marginal private cost and marginal benefits—that is, at *OK* units, external costs are ignored, which is why producing *OK* units is inefficient. The efficiency loss from producing *OK* units is found by subtracting the total social costs of *OK* units from the total benefits of *OK* units. Total benefits of *OK* units are *LBKO*, the area under the demand curve at *OK* units. The total social costs of *OK* units are *ERKO*, the area under the marginal social cost curve at *OK* units. Subtracting gives *ARB*, which is a part of the total social cost called the efficiency loss.

The following six questions are on interest rates and present value. Here, briefly, is what the student needs to know about these in order to answer the questions:
   Real interest rate is defined as

   1. Premium on earlier availability
   2. Discount on later availability

(That is, if you want to get the money now, you have to pay a premium, but if you are willing to wait, you can get it for a discount.)
   Differently dated goods and money are different economic identities. They cannot be compared unless the real interest rate is known. Then these differently dated goods and money have to be converted to the same date in order to compare them. The conclusion will be the same whichever date is used. Differently dated goods and money can be converted into their present or future values. For decisions on goods and money that have future value after *one* period (usually a year), the following formulas are used:

$A/P = (1 + r)$

where A = future amount, P = present amount, and r = real interest rate.

$A = (1 + r)P$
$P = A / (1 + r)$

   If the future amount A is n years from now, then the present value becomes

$P = A_n /(1+r)^n$

where A_n = future amount to be received n years later.
   If there are multiple future amounts A_s, the formula for present value is

$P = A_n /(1 + r)^n + A_m/(1 + r)^m$

where A_n = future amount to be received n years later and A_m = future amount to be received m years later.
   An annuity is a series of annual payments, a, for n years, which has the following present-value formula:

$$P = a/(1+r) + a/(1+r)^2 + a/(1+r)^3 + \ldots + a/(1+r)^n = a\sum_{i=1}^{n}\left(\frac{1}{1+r}\right)$$

   If an annuity lasts forever, it is called a perpetuity, and its present value is

$$P = a\sum_{i=1}^{\infty}\left(\frac{1}{1+r}\right)^i = a/r$$

Suppose you have a nice uncle, Uncle DeeBee, who wants to give you a present. This is the good news. The bad news is that Questions 31 to 35 are based on this fact and on the following information. You can collect the money in any one of three ways:

A. $750 on June 19, 1999, and every June 19 thereafter forever

or

B. $1000 on June 19, 1999

or

C. $1500 today

31. If the interest rate is 50 percent, you will

    a. choose A.

    b. choose B.

    c. choose C.

    d. be indifferent between A and C.

    e. be indifferent between A and B.

Answer: d

> The easiest way to answer this question is to compare the present value of each option. Notice that A is a perpetuity and its present value is equal to $P_A = \$750/0.50 = \$1500$. The present value of B is $P_B = \$1000/(1 + 0.50) = \$666.67$, and the present value of C is $1500 because it will be given today. You should choose the option with the highest present value. It turns out that A and C have the same present value, so you should be indifferent between those two.

32. If the interest rate is 100 percent, you will

    a. choose A.

    b. choose B.

    c. choose C.

    d. be indifferent between A and C.

    e. be indifferent between A and B.

Answer: c

> The procedure is the same as that used in the previous question, only the interest rate is different. $P_A = \$750/1 = \$750$, $P_B = \$1000/(1 + 1) = \$500$ and $P_C = \$1500$. So, obviously, C dominates the other two at the interest rate 100 percent.

33. If the interest rate is 200 percent, you will

    a. choose A.

    b. choose B.

    c. choose C.

    d. be indifferent between A and C.

e. be indifferent between A and B.

Answer: c

The procedure is the same as for the previous question; only the interest rate is different. $P_A = \$750/2 = \$375$, $P_B = \$1000 (1 + 2) = \$333$, and $P_C = \$1500$. C dominates the other two at the interest rate 200 percent.

34. Suppose that, just before you make your decisions, Uncle DeeBee decides to "sweeten the pot" by adding $500 to option A only. How many of the correct answers to the previous three questions will change?

a. None

b. One

c. Two

d. Three

e. There is not enough information.

Answer: b

Now option A becomes $1,250 forever. The student has to find the option with the highest present value for each of the above three questions.

For Question 31: $P_A = \$1250/0.5 = \$2500$, $P_B = \$1000/ (1 + 0.5) = \$666.67$, and $P_C = \$1500$, so now A has the highest present value, and so the answer to 31 becomes a.

For Question 32: $P_A = \$1250/1 = \$1250$, $P_B = \$1000/ (1 + 1) = \$500$, and $P_C = \$1500$, so C still has the highest present value. The answer to 32 doesn't change. It remains c.

For Question 33: $P_A = \$1250/2 = \$625$, $P_B = \$1000/ (1 + 2) = \$333$, and $P_C = \$1500$, so C still has the highest present value. The answer to 32, therefore, doesn't change. It remains c.

Only the answer to Question 31 changes.

35. What is the interest rate that makes you indifferent between offers B and C?

a. 33 percent

b. -33 percent

c. 66 percent

d. -66 percent

e. None of the above

Answer: b

For the previous questions, the interest rate was given, but now the student is expected to find the interest rate that makes B and C the same. This means that their present or future values have to be the same, so that someone would be indifferent between them. Answer the question with both present and future amounts.

The present value of B is $P_B = \$1000/(1 + r)$, and the present value of C is $P_C = \$1500$. Thus:

$P_B = P_C$ gives $\$1500 = \$1000/(1 + r)$
and solving this equation for r gives

$r = -500/1500 = -0.33$ or -33 percent

So, at this interest rate, the present values of both offers are equal to $1500.
    We can find the same answer by calculating the future amount. The future amount of B after one year is $A_B = \$1000$. The future amount of C after one year is $A_C = \$1500 (1 + r)$. Thus

$A_B = A_C$ gives $\$1000 = \$1500 (1 + r)$

and solving this equation for r gives

$r = -500/1500 = -0.33$ or -33 percent.

So at this interest rate, the future values of both offers are equal to $1000. This is the exact same answer we got by using the present value formulas. If the answers are different, then one of them must be wrong.

36. Suppose that you bought a certificate of deposit from your bank five years ago at 10 percent, and you have $805.255 in the bank today. What is the amount of money you deposited in the bank five years ago?

   a. $310
   b. $500
   c. $1296
   d. $146
   e. None of the above

Answer: b

The student must interpret the numbers in the question; $805.255 is the money that is received five years later, and that is the future amount that you have today. The amount of the certificate five years ago is asked for. So, the student should treat $805.255 as a future amount and use the following formula:

$P = A_n/(1 + r)n$

where $n = 5$ and $A_n = \$805.255$. Then

$P = \$805.255/(1.1)^5 = \$500$

A $500 certificate bought five years ago yields $805.255 today, with a 10 percent interest rate.

The graph below shows the market for nuts in Pistachio, a small country in terms of trade in nuts. You are the Chief Trade Adviser of Pistachio, and your job is to decide whether Pistachio should trade with the rest of the world or not. P_p shows the price of nuts in Pistachio. P_w shows the price of nuts in the rest of the world. Q_0 shows the quantity of nuts traded in Pistachio without any trade with the rest of the world. If Pistachio decides to trade with the rest of the world, it can buy the nuts at P_w while producing Q_s units at home and consuming Q_d units, the difference being the imports.

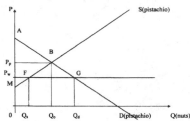

37. What is the consumer surplus if Pistachio *doesn't trade* with the rest of the world?

    a. AGP_w

    b. BFG

    c. P_pBA

    d. P_pBM

    e. ABQ_0O

Answer: c

It must be understood that if the country doesn't trade with the rest of the world, the price of nuts will be P_p. The student also has to understand the concept of *consumer surplus*—the difference between what people are willing to pay at the maximum for a quantity and the market price of that good. Therefore, it is the area under the demand curve and above the market price up to the equilibrium quantity. So, at P_p, the consumer surplus is P_pBA."

38. What is the consumer surplus if Pistachio *trades* with the rest of the world?

    a. AGP_w

    b. BFG

    c. P_pBA

    d. P_pBM

    e. AGQ_dO

Answer: a

If the country trades with the rest of the world, the price of nuts will be P_w. Then the consumer surplus is the area under the demand curve above the market price, which is P_w. So, at P_w, the consumer surplus is P_wGA. Notice that, since the price is now lower, the consumer can consume more—as much as Q_d. Of that amount Q_d, Q_s is produced at home and the rest is imported from the rest of the world.

39. What is the total loss of producer surplus if Pistachio *decides to trade* with the rest of the world?

    a. BFG
    b. P_pBFP_w
    c. GFQ_sQ_d
    d. P_wFM
    e. MBQ_0O

Answer: b

In this case, it is necessary to understand the concept of *producer surplus*—the difference between what it costs the producers to produce the good and the market price of that good. This is the area under the market price and above the supply curve up to the equilibrium quantity. To find the total loss of producer surplus, we have to find the producer surplus with and without trade and compare them. Without trade, the price is P_p, so the producer surplus is P_pBM. With trade, the price falls to P_w, so the producer surplus falls to P_wFM. Notice that at P_w, the producer produces only Q_s units. The difference between P_pBM and P_wFM is the area P_pBFP_w.

40. What is the loss in gains from trade if Pistachio *doesn't trade* with the rest of the world?

    a. $ABFP_w$
    b. ABM
    c. BFG
    d. P_pBFP_w
    e. P_wFM

Answer: c

The student is expected to know what *gains from trade* means: the sum of consumer surplus and producer surplus—that is, the total gain when two parties trade, and both parties are happy about it. Producers are happy to sell, and so they get the producer surplus, and consumers are happy to buy, and so they get the consumer surplus. The addition of these two gives the gains from trade. To find the loss in gains from trade, again we have to compare gains from trade with and without trade. The gains from trade without trade is ABM, which is the addition of ABP_p (consumer surplus without trade) and P_pBM (producer surplus without trade). The gains from trade with trade is $AGFM$, which is the addition of AGP_w (consumer surplus with trade) and $PWFM$ (producer surplus with trade). The difference between ABM and $AGFM$ is BFG. (Notice that $AGFM$ is greater than ABM.)

CHAPTER 22

COLORADO STATE UNIVERSITY

EC 100H: PRINCIPLES OF MACROECONOMICS (HONORS)

Charles F. Revier, Associate Professor

FOUR EXAMS ARE GIVEN IN THIS COURSE: THREE 'MIDTERMS' AND A FINAL. (ONE midterm and the final are presented here.) All the exams require short essay responses.

For a class of twenty-five honors students, the course objectives are that, by the end of the term, students will be able to

1. Explain the causes of the key macroeconomic concerns—unemployment, inflation, economic growth, and exchange rate fluctuations—and assess their consequences for society

2. Understand both the prospects for and the limitations of government macro-economic policy

3. Conduct their own analyses of the likely effects of specific macroeconomic disturbances or policy actions

4. Watch the macroeconomic news items in the media with both greater interest and greater understanding

5. Follow both current and future political debates over economic policy with an ability to separate the sense from the nonsense, and to vote accordingly

Examination questions are intended specifically to test the ability to apply macroeconomic models for the purposes described above. Success in the course requires reading the textbook carefully *before* lectures, with pencil in hand to sketch the key relationships discussed. The student should use all homework assignments and Study Guide problems as opportunities to practice *using* and *applying* the analytical apparatus to understand real-world phenomena. It is also important to attend class and participate actively in all lectures and class discussions.

Students should develop an ability to apply the mainstream macroeconomic models to understand the causes, consequences, and cures for unemployment, inflation, slow growth, and exchange rate fluctuations; to assess the likely impact of government policy actions on macroeconomic performance; and to predict the consequences of various disturbances. In general, they should work toward an appreciation of and a facility with the economic way of thinking.

MIDTERM EXAM

1a. (10 points) Under what circumstances would consumption and saving both change in the same direction (both increase or both decrease)? Under what circumstances would they change in opposite directions? Explain.

ANSWER

Consumption and saving would both increase if there were an increase in disposable income. Similarly, consumption and saving would both decrease if there were a decrease in disposable income. A change in disposable income will bring a movement along the consumption function, which will cause changes in consumption and saving in the same direction. The marginal propensity to consume indicates what fraction of an increase in disposable income will be spent on additional consumption. The reason this increase in consumption is only a fraction and not the full amount of the increase in income is because the rest of the increase will be added to saving.

On the other hand, a change in any determinant of consumption other than disposable income, such as a change in households' tastes or attitude toward saving, will shift the consumption function. At any given level of disposable income, consumption and saving will then change in opposite directions. Since, by definition, saving is the part of disposable income not spent on consumption, an increase in consumption must bring a decrease in saving, and vice versa, if income remains constant.

This answer indicates what it would take for consumption and saving to change in the same direction or in opposite directions, and it also does a good job of providing the explanation for each of these phenomena. It makes use of the analytical apparatus of the consumption function and the concept of the marginal propensity to consume to distinguish the two situations. It therefore provides a complete answer to the question asked without adding superfluous material that was not solicited.

A successful response must make the distinction that an income change would bring consumption and saving changes in the same direction, whereas a change in anything else with income fixed would require inverse movements, since saving is just the part of income not consumed.

> Since the question is asking about the relation between consumption and saving, the appropriate strategy is to begin with that relation, as contained in the definition of saving. It then becomes clear that both saving and consumption will increase if and only if there is an increase in disposable income.

1b. (15 points) Suppose a financial guru publishes a new book that convinces large numbers of households to increase their saving. Discuss what the consequences would be, using our income-determination model.

ANSWER

An increase in the desire to save at any income level will correspond to a downward shift of the consumption function, since at any given income, greater saving must mean less consumption. This decrease in consumption brings a downward shift in the total expenditure schedule, C + I + G + NX. The autonomous drop in consumption spending sets off a multiplier process in which consumption continues to fall as the drop in spending leads producers to cut their output, and this in turn leaves households with less disposable income. As a result, the total drop in real GDP demanded is equal to the initial drop in consumption (increase in saving) times the multiplier. This drop represents the horizontal shift in the aggregate demand schedule, the drop in GDP demanded at a given price level. With an upward-sloping aggregate supply curve, the drop in aggregate demand will bring both a drop in equilibrium output and a drop in the price level.

> This answer is successful because it demonstrates an ability to utilize the income-determination model to predict the consequences of this particular event. It shows mastery of the ability to *apply* that model in a particular circumstance. The important ingredient in the successful answer is to explain what will happen to equilibrium in the income-determination model. The student could go on to describe how a paradox of thrift could arise here: Because saving falls with income, it is possible that the end result of an increased desire to save is a decrease in the level of saving. But the essential ingredient of a correct answer is to describe how the event affects real GDP and the price level.

2. (20 points) Why does desired spending on goods and services fall as the general price level rises?

ANSWER

One reason why desired spending varies inversely with the price level is that an increase in the price level lowers the purchasing power of household assets whose values are fixed in money terms, such as money and government bonds. With this reduction in the purchasing power of wealth, households will reduce their consumption spending.

A second reason is that if the domestic price level rises while foreign price levels remain constant, the demand for imports from abroad will increase, and the demand for our exports will decrease. The net exports component of desired spending will drop, both because of the increase in imports and because of the decrease in exports.

> The successful answer describes the two explanations for the downward-sloping aggregate demand curve that have been addressed in the course up to this point: the real wealth effect and the net exports effect. Later in the course, the effect of the price level on the demand for money balances and, therefore, on interest rates will be added to the list. But given what has been studied up to the time of this exam, the important thing is to describe the two effects and to explain *why* they would imply an inverse association between desired spending and price level.

3a. (15 points) Suppose the economy has a recessionary gap, and government policy-makers have decided to try to close the gap by means of an increase in government purchases of goods and services. Explain as clearly as you can why the increase in government purchases should be (less than, the same as, more than) the magnitude of the recessionary gap.

ANSWER

The increase in government purchases should be less than the magnitude of the recessionary gap. This is because the increase in government purchases will generate a multiplier effect, as producers step up their production to meet the increased demand and avoid undesired decreases in their inventories. This increase in production raises national income as well, which induces households to increase their consumption. Producers will then expand production once again, and the various rounds of the multiplier process will continue until the economy reaches a new equilibrium GDP, with a total increase in real GDP, which is a multiple of the initial increase in government purchases. The initial increase in government purchases should be equal to the magnitude of the recessionary gap divided by the value of the multiplier.

> This answer provides a clear explanation of why an increase in government purchases will lead to a total increase in equilibrium GDP, which is a multiple of the purchases increase. It describes all the steps in the process that lead to the multiplier phenomenon. It also illustrates an understanding that the recessionary gap is the amount by which the economy's equilibrium GDP falls short of the full-employment level. Thus the two concepts essential for a successful answer are this definition of recessionary gap and the concept of the multiplier process. A one-sentence answer that merely asserts that the increase in G should be less than the recessionary gap because of the multiplier would be a start, but it would not provide the details of the clear explanation that the question is asking for."

3b. (15 points) If the government decided instead to close the recessionary gap by means of a permanent tax cut rather than an increase in government purchases, would the required tax cut be smaller than, the same as, or greater than the government purchases increase needed to close the gap? Explain your reasoning.

ANSWER

The required tax cut would be greater than the government purchases increase needed to close the gap. There is a bigger bang for the buck for an increase in G than for a decrease in T. This is because part of the tax cut will be saved, and only a fraction given by the marginal propensity to consume will go into increased spending. So, in the first round of the multiplier process, the initial increase in spending would be equal to the tax cut times the MPC.

With the increase in government purchases, however, every penny of the increase is an addition to total desired spending in the first round of the multiplier process. Therefore, the government purchases increase required in order to close the recessionary gap, would be equal to the MPC times the tax cut required. Since the MPC is only a fraction, the tax cut would have to be larger than the purchases increase to achieve the same total increase in equilibrium GDP.

The essential ingredient in this successful answer is the explanation of why the multiplier effect for a tax cut is smaller than the multiplier effect for an equal dollar amount of increase in government purchases. The answer then utilizes this information to establish that closing a given recessionary gap would require a tax cut that is larger than the government purchases increase that would accomplish the same objective. The analysis of the question requires an understanding that, while an increase in government purchases adds to aggregate demand directly, a tax cut increases aggregate demand only indirectly, by increasing disposable income, and since part of the increase in disposable income is saved, the impact of the tax cut on aggregate demand is "watered down".

4. (25 points) Describe the economy's self-correcting mechanism, which will eventually eliminate an inflationary gap automatically.

ANSWER

An inflationary gap is a situation in which the equilibrium GDP is greater than the economy's normal full-employment level of output. It is called an inflationary gap because, when it occurs, the tight labor market that accompanies the high level of output tends to lead to an increase in wages. This increase in production costs shifts the aggregate supply curve upward and prices rise, i.e., inflation occurs. But since aggregate demand varies inversely with the general price level, the higher prices bring a decrease in consumption and net export spending and, therefore, a reduction in the size of the inflationary gap. However, as long as the inflationary gap remains, the tight labor market will continue to push wages up, and the process will continue. When prices have risen enough for the aggregate demand to fall to the level of normal full-employment output, the inflationary gap will be eliminated and the adjustment process will come to an end, since there will then be no further upward pressure on wages. The economy will have reached a long-run equilibrium.

A successful answer requires an explanation of how the self-correcting mechanism operates, i.e., it requires a statement of the chain of events that will be spawned by an inflationary gap and that will eventually eliminate that gap.

The strategy here is to start with a statement of what an inflationary gap is, and then to describe the scenario in which it will automatically be eliminated. An aggregate supply–aggregate demand diagram might both aid in making sure none of the steps are left out in the verbal description of the process and strengthen the answer in its own right.

FINAL EXAM

Use the textbook graphs as a way of reviewing key analytical points, and be sure you understand them well enough to explain them to your roommate who has never taken economics. Also, be able to give definitions of all terms in each chapter, and be able to explain these terms in your own words."

1. (15 points) What is the principle of increasing costs? What bearing does this principle have on the production possibilities frontier? What is the explanation for increasing costs?

ANSWER

The principle of increasing costs is the principle that the opportunity cost of producing an additional unit of a good tends to rise as the output of that good is increased.

Since the absolute slope of the production possibilities frontier is simply the opportunity cost of producing an additional unit of the good on the horizontal axis, the principle of increasing costs implies that this absolute slope is increasing as one moves to the right along the frontier. In other words, the principle of increasing costs implies that the production possibilities frontier is bowed outward (concave to the origin). The explanation for increasing opportunity costs is that many productive resources tend to be specialized and more productive in one production activity than in another. When the output of a good is low, an increase can be achieved by shifting those resources that are highly suited to producing the good whose output is being expanded and not at all suitable for producing the other good. But as the output of the good rises to a higher and higher level, the only resources still being used to produce the other good are those that are highly productive there and not very suited to production of the first good. Shifting these resources to expand the output of the first good, therefore, requires the sacrifice of a relatively large amount of the other good.

A successful answer requires both a familiarity with the principle of increasing costs and its explanation, and an understanding of how the concept of opportunity cost is manifested in the production possibilities frontier diagram. For an essay question like this one, which is a composite of several shorter questions, a good strategy is to organize your answer by simply answering the individual questions in sequence, being sure not to skip any.

2a. (10 points) What causes recessions?

ANSWER

A recession is a situation in which real output and employment are at levels below those they reach at normal full employment. One possible cause of a recession is a drop in one or more of the components of aggregate demand. With an upward-sloping aggregate supply curve, this drop in demand will cause prices to fall to some extent, but it will also cause output and employment to fall, as producers cut production to avoid unwanted increases in their inventories. The other possible cause of a recession is a supply-side shock, such as an increase in world oil prices, which raises production costs and, therefore, shifts the aggregate supply curve upward. The resulting higher prices reduce the real wealth of consumers, reduce net exports, and reduce investment spending because of the accompanying increase in interest rates. Aggregate demand therefore falls as the economy moves up along its aggregate demand curve, and output and employment therefore fall as producers respond to this drop in demand. Thus the economy finds itself in a recession. In this case, however, the recession is accompanied by inflation, i.e., we get "stagflation" from the supply shock.

This is a very basic question that, in some sense, the entire course has been devoted to answering. The question tests whether the student has fully absorbed the answer. The logical place to start is with the definition of *recession*. Once that situation has been defined, a little mental review should bring back the two scenarios that would open a recessionary gap: a drop in aggregate demand on the demand side, or an adverse supply shock on the supply side.

2b. (10 points) In the absence of any government policy measures, would the economy ever find its way out of a recession? Explain how this might come about.

ANSWER

The economy does have a self-correcting mechanism, which, given enough time, would eventually end a recessionary gap. The abnormally high unemployment and the scarcity of jobs in a recession may eventually cause wages to fall. This decrease in production costs will then shift the aggregate supply curve downward. Prices will fall, bringing an increase in consumption, net exports, and investment as the economy moves down along its aggregate demand curve. This deflation and resulting boost in desired spending will gradually eliminate the recessionary gap. However, given our economy's resistance to wage cuts, this self-adjusting process could take a very long time.

> The question is essentially asking whether the economy has a self-correcting mechanism, which will automatically eliminate a recessionary gap. A successful answer requires remembering that such a self-correcting mechanism is a possibility and describing the chain of events through which it would operate.

2c. (10 points) What fiscal policy measures might a government take to end a recession, and how would they work?

ANSWER

Since a recession is a situation in which aggregate demand is insufficient to call forth the full-employment level of output, the fiscal measures which would end a recession would be those that would stimulate an increase in aggregate demand. One possibility would be an increase in government purchases of goods and services. Each dollar of the additional government purchases would add directly to aggregate demand and would ignite a multiplier process, which would cause consumption spending to increase as well, as output and employment increased. Another possibility would be a reduction in taxes or an increase in government transfer payments (negative taxes). Both measures would increase the disposable income of households, and would therefore induce households to spend a fraction of the income increase on consumption and save the remainder. This increase in consumption spending would then start a multiplier process that would bring further increases in aggregate demand, output, and employment.

The limited impact of the 1968 surtax is a reminder, however, that tax changes that the public considers more or less permanent or long-term will have a much greater impact than those that the public considers temporary.

> This is a basic question about fiscal policy tools and how they would be expected to operate. A significant part of the course has been devoted to the analysis of fiscal policy and its effects and limitations, so a successful answer here requires merely summarizing that analysis. The answer must include the three types of fiscal policy actions and a brief summary of the impact they would have on output and employment, including an explanation of the differences in the way they operate.

3. (20 points) If the Federal Open Market Committee decides to move toward a more contractionary monetary policy, what specifically would the Fed do to bring this about? What would the economic consequences be?

ANSWER

To contract the money supply, the Federal Open Market Committee would need to reach the decision to sell U.S. government securities in the open market. When these securities are paid for with money, the nation's money supply will decrease. Although this result could be reinforced with an increase in banks' required reserve ratio and an increase in the discount rate, the predominant means that would be used today would be the open-market sale of government securities. The consequence would be that the public would find itself holding more securities and less cash balances than it would like to be holding, given the current interest rate and national income level. But as the public attempts to adjust the composition of its portfolios by trading securities for cash, they will bid up the interest rate on securities. The higher interest rate will then reduce investment spending and other interest-sensitive components of aggregate demand, shifting the aggregate demand curve to the left. This would bring a decrease in both real output and the general price level (or inflation rate), which were presumably the Fed's objectives in moving toward a contractionary monetary policy.

This answer describes in specific terms the actions the Fed would take to implement a contractionary monetary policy. This answer requires knowledge of the mechanics of open-market operations. It also requires an understanding of the channel through which monetary policy affects the goods market.

4. (15 points) Comment on the following statement: "Increasing the national debt through deficit spending paves the way to disaster. If we keep it up, our nation will soon exceed its borrowing capacity and go bankrupt. Even if things don't go that far, the future generation as a whole will be weighted down by high interest payments."

ANSWER

Whether a government deficit is disastrous or not depends on the macroeconomic circumstances. Deficits when the economy is at full employment or beyond tend to raise interest rates and therefore crowd out investment and other interest-sensitive components of spending. As a result, the economy will end up with a lower capital stock than it would have had otherwise. However, when the deficits occur during a recession, they will stimulate an expansion in output that will tend to bring an increase in investment spending: a crowding-in effect. The argument that the government has a limited borrowing capacity and faces bankruptcy if it exceeds this capacity is groundless. A government with the power to tax and the power to print the dollars that its debt obligates it to pay will never face bankruptcy. Moreover, to the extent that the debt is held by domestic residents, future interest payments simply represent transfers from all future Americans as taxpayers to some future Americans who are debt holders. These transfers may not have a desirable effect on the distribution of wealth, but they do not represent a burden on the future generation as a whole. On the other hand, the portion of the debt that is owed to foreigners does represent a burden on the future generation.

In general, deficits incurred for the purpose of fighting a recession can usually be very helpful, but deficits incurred in a full-employment economy are undesirable because of the crowding out they cause.

A good answer to this question requires both pointing out the holes in the groundless arguments against deficits in the quotation and clarifying the circumstances in which deficits really will have harmful effects and those in which they will have beneficial effects."

5. (20 points) If interest rates increase in the United States, but remain constant in Taiwan, what impact would this have on the exchange rate for the Taiwan dollar? How would this affect the Taiwan economy? Explain.

ANSWER

The relative increase in U.S. interest rates would attract capital out of Taiwan and into the U.S. This would increase foreign demand for U.S. securities, and, therefore, for U.S. dollars to buy these securities, and decrease demand for Taiwan securities, and, therefore, for the Taiwan dollar. Therefore, the Taiwan dollar would tend to depreciate relative to the U.S. dollar in the foreign exchange market. This depreciation would make Taiwan goods relatively cheaper to Americans and U.S. goods relatively more expensive to the Taiwanese, so Taiwan's net exports would tend to rise. This would raise Taiwan's aggregate demand. However, the depreciation would raise the cost of any imported inputs that Taiwan uses in production, and would therefore lower its aggregate supply.

This means that Taiwan's price level would definitely rise, and since the aggregate demand shifts that result from depreciation are generally larger than the aggregate supply shifts, Taiwan's real GDP would be likely to increase.

A successful answer must describe both the impact that interest rate movements have on exchange rates and the impact that exchange rate movements have on real GDP and the price level. A good answer should utilize the tools of aggregate supply and demand to analyze this second set of impacts.

CHAPTER 23

FRANKLIN AND MARSHALL COLLEGE

ECONOMICS 101: INTRODUCTION TO MACROECONOMICS

William E. Whitesell, Mary B. and Henry P. Stager Professor of Economics

THREE EXAMS ARE GIVEN DURING THIS COURSE, TWO "MIDTERMS" AND A FINAL. ONE midterm and a final are included here. All are essay exams.

The course is designed to introduce students to the history, organization, and functions of capitalism. Elementary supply and demand and its applications introduce students to fundamental concepts of how markets work. I emphasize problems of growth and stability, particularly the possible trade-offs between full employment and price stability. Topics include national income and the price level, money and banking, interest rates and the role of financial intermediaries, fiscal and monetary policy, and inflation and unemployment. The course also covers the elements of comparative advantage and international trade. Fundamentally, the course is designed to introduce students to key concepts of an economic system and elements of public policy evaluation in order that they may be informed voters and citizens who can function effectively in a market-oriented society.

Students should develop an ability to use fundamental economics concepts to attack a variety of problems and resolve fundamental questions. This means application of concepts such as opportunity cost, cost-benefit analysis, and similar basic economic ideas and approaches. Students have to develop basic ideas about supply and demand and the forces that affect the shape and position as well as the movement of each curve. Students also have to develop and use basic macroeconomic models such as the Keynesian cross and an integrating four-quadrant diagram that connects the so-called goods and financial sectors of the economy. They use the models as part of their analysis of how particular economic stimuli may affect economic activity in general and, sometimes, specific markets. Having a good command of the elementary models should then enable students to attack other questions and issues when they leave the course and as they function in their roles as citizens and participants in the economy.

The emphasis of the course is on the importance of careful analysis to determine the consequences as well as the causes of various economic phenomena.

MIDTERM EXAM

A midterm carries a weight of 17.5 percent of the total grade, and the final exam is weighted as 35 percent of the total grade. The real importance of the midterm often lies in helping students understand what areas need more study and attention in their own preparation. The midterm, especially, also enables students to see how well they are mastering the requisite skills and information for the course.

Generally, I advise students to follow the preview, view, and review method of study—whether it is for a test or for an initial reading of materials. One asks questions about what one expects to find; one does the reading; and one then asks what one has read. In terms of studying for tests per se, this strategy becomes one of asking what questions one might ask and answer about the materials, checking the materials to assure that one can in fact develop adequate responses to these and similar questions, and then quickly reviewing what one has just studied.

I also urge students to organize materials by asking first what they consider to be the big topics are and then breaking these big topics into component parts. For example, one might ask why prices are what they are. One might then respond that prices are what they are because demand is what it is and supply is what it is. The next question is why demand is what it is followed by another question that asks why supply is what it is. This approach to the dissection of issues into elemental parts enables students to see how particular phenomena or particular changes may affect other things that are related."

Each of the two questions carries equal weight and should receive equal time. Use about 5 minutes to plan your answer and 20 minutes to write each response.

1. Use the model of perfect competition (industry and firm) to explain how the price system works to enlarge, decrease, or keep stable the supply of a particular good or service in a market. (*Hint:* Start by showing the contribution of a single firm. Explain what you have depicted. Extend the argument.)

Answer: In perfect competition, all firms are price takers, meaning that they must sell their goods at the market price. If the firm lowers its price, its competitors will follow, and if the firm raises its price, it will lose business and eventually exit the market (consumers will purchase cheaper goods from other firms).

This portion of the answer needs some expansion or correction, since firms are price takers, not price makers.

Most firms in perfect competition will operate with regular profits. The firm operates at point *A*, where marginal revenue equals marginal cost. Cost per unit is shown by the rectangle *ABCD*.

The graphs in these samples are actual student work, illustrating the level of legibility and detail expected in the exam setting.

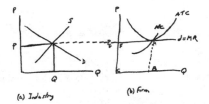

Here the student has a properly constructed pair of graphs, G1a and b, with industry supply and demand setting price = marginal revenue = demand for the firm, and average total cost and marginal cost curves for the firm correctly drawn.

If the firm was operating with supranormal profits, as seen below, it would have curves similar to those shown below— with the average total cost curve below where the firm operates at point *B* (where MR = MC). The total cost for the firm is shown by the rectangle *OKLM*, and the firm's supranormal profits by the rectangle *MLRT*.

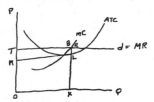

In perfect competition, since each firm is a price taker, as other firms move into the market, the supply curve is pushed down and to the right, lowering the market equilibrium price, and therefore the price at which the firm must sell its goods, eliminating the supranormal profits.

Graphs G3a and b, showing industry and firm, come to the conclusion just mentioned.

If a firm operates below its average total cost curve (MR = MC at a point below the ATC curve), it is suffering losses and will eventually exit the market, pushing the supply curve up and to the left, increasing the equilibrium price.

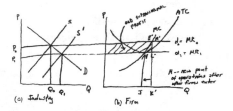

The student should have noted that the change in the supply curve requires *many* firms to leave the market.

In perfect competition, since firms are price takers, they must operate and sell their goods at the market price or exit the market.

Nonsense. Why would a firm exit if it were making supranormal profits? What did the student really mean?

Higher prices within the market will entice firms to produce more and new firms to enter the market, because at a higher price they will receive greater returns for the production of their good. The higher price will enlarge the supply of that good within the market.

Why? The response is a bit garbled here and needs clarification.

Lower prices may force some firms to exit the market, therefore decreasing the supply of that particular good within the market. If firms are producing with normal profits, and the price for the good remains steady with the market, the supply of that good within the market will remain stable.

The student has packed into a short answer all the essentials for understanding what happens in a typical market under perfect competition. The response is logically organized. Major points are illustrated with appropriate graphs. The language is clear and precise, for the most part, although there are a couple of places where one might wish for less vagueness. Organization, development, and mechanics are all generally good here.

A generally successful response, such as this one, should indicate the relative nature of supply and demand in the case of the industry and the firm in the industry, i.e. the relationships that exist between them. The answer should contain an indication of the forces that might cause a shift in the curves that would produce a subsequent change in the quantities supplied where this would be the case. There should be in the response a statement about the conditions under which we would expect no change in quantity in the market. Students should be careful to tie the price signals to what subsequently happens in competitive markets.

2. Use macroeconomic theory to explain how public-sector (governmental) policies might be employed to achieve any one of the three goals of macroeconomic policy. (*Hint:* State what the goal is. Next, tell how macroeconomic policy might be used to achieve the goal you have selected. At this point in the course, you should reflect knowledge of the broad outline rather than particularized detail of how specific policies work.)

Answer: Public-sector policies can be used to achieve any of the three macroeconomic goals: less unemployment and inflation and more growth. I discuss how the government can help reduce unemployment.

Before we see how the government can reduce unemployment, it is important to see how unemployment is created. Unemployment is the result of sticky wages and decreased aggregate demand. A reduction in aggregate demand would initiate a drop in the production of goods and services in the economy. This in turn leads to a decrease in the demand for labor in the labor market. If wages were fully adjustable, we would see a decrease in the wage level from W_0 to W_1, without any change in the quantity of labor employed.

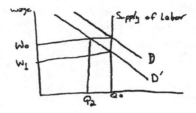

But since wages are sticky, they remain at W_0 level, where producers demand and employ less labor (Q_1) than households are willing to supply (Q_0). Thus there is unemployment.

Now, we know that the government cannot force workers to take wage cuts. Thus the only other alternative it has is to increase aggregate demand. An increase in aggregate demand would lead to an increase in the demand for labor and thus would reduce unemployment.

Aggregate demand has four components: consumption, investment, government expenditure, and net exports (= exports - imports). Through its policies, the government can try and increase any of the above to increase aggregate demand and reduce unemployment.

The government can increase (private) consumption by reducing taxes as a fiscal policy measure. This would increase the disposable income of the households and thus increase their demand for goods and services, thus increasing aggregate demand.

In order to increase investment [*sic*], the government must increase the money supply. This can be done by reducing interest rates and making credit easily available. This would spark investment and thus increase aggregate demand.

The government can also increase its own demand for goods and services. In other words, it can increase its expenditures. One way of doing this would be to give unemployment doles, subsidies, and other types of transfer payments. The government could also consume more goods by increasing expenditures on defense, public services, etc. All these measures would increase aggregate demand and thus decrease unemployment.

The government cannot really determine exports or imports, as they are based partly on decisions made by foreign economies. However by expanding trade policy and removing restrictions on trade, it could increase exports and thus increase net exports. This would again increase aggregate demand.

Thus we see that by increasing any or all of the components of aggregate demand, government can bridge the gap between the demand for and the supply of labor and thus reduce unemployment.

The student has given the essentials of the response. At this point in the course, students are not expected to know all the details, but they are expected to have a firm grasp of the essential nature of policies the government might undertake. Notice that the student goes directly to the components of aggregate demand when describing what might be done. The alternative actions are immediately followed by a brief description of the expected results of the action(s). Taking each of the elements of aggregate demand in turn results in a good organization of the response and provides clear focus for comments.

The student emphasizes the major point in the first part of the essay with a graph, but fails to furnish an aggregate supply and aggregate demand graph for the second part of the essay. An aggregate supply and aggregate demand graph would have added to the response, even though the language is generally clear and precise.

Organization, development, and mechanics are all generally good here, just as they were in the first question. Always be sure that there is a logical structure to the response that will deal with the various aspects of the question. Be careful to explain connections in a clear, precise manner. Use of graphs at key points is generally a good approach in thinking about how to build an answer because the graphs frequently remind one of the essential items one should emphasize in discussions of the phenomenon or phenomena in question.

FINAL EXAM

Ideally, the examinations test the students' abilities to deal with economic issues. I sometimes give students actual data and ask them to analyze them. At other times, I present actual or hypothetical actions by consumers, businesses, or governmental entities and ask the students to work through the likely effects. Ergo, the design is to ask students to demonstrate that they have the analytical skills as well as the basic information to perform effective and accurate analysis.

I ask students to spend two hours of preparation outside of class for each hour in class. I also encourage them to read *The New York Times*, *The Wall Street Journal*, and other papers, journals, and magazines to become acquainted with economic issues and how various entities are handling them, being affected by them, or affecting them.

Part I. *Mostly Microeconomics. Choices as indicated. 36 min. each, 20 points each*

Microeconomics has numerous uses. One of these is *explanation*. Another is *prediction*. Demonstrate your mastery of microeconomics by responding to 1 *or* 2 (not both).

   1. (Explanation) Price has changed. Why might this have happened?

   2. (Prediction) Forecast the effect(s) of each of the following:

   a. A change in tariff levels
   b. A change in beverage preference from coffee to tea
   c. A change in demand from a factor of production

Answers: (Student A's response to option #1)

1. Price is determined by supply and demand in the market for that product it produces. A consumer's demand function looks like the following:

As the price of a good falls, the quantity demanded will increase. The supply curve for a market looks as follows:

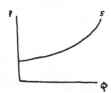

As price rises, the producers want to produce more, so quantity will increase. The intersection of demand and supply will determine the equilibrium point with the equilibrium quantity and price.

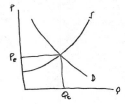

P_c and Q_c represent the equilibrium price and the equilibrium quantity. These two things will change with any change in either demand or supply. Remember, the whole curve must shift to change the price. Demand could shift because the cost of comparable goods or substitute goods has gone up, population changes, income changes, wealth changes, or changes in expectations or other factors. Supply could have changed because the price of inputs has gone up or any other factor it has to account for to produce the good.

The last sentence is vague and the thought incomplete.

Now let's look at the question. First, I will take the simple approach to this question. Price could have changed with a change in supply. Supply could have increased with a new technology.

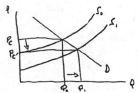

P_c to P_{c_1} represents a change in price that is caused by an increase in supply.

Another way to see a change in price is to look at the demand curve. If the price of coffee goes up, consumers will demand more tea, thus raising the price of tea. P_c to P_{c_1} represents a rise in the price of the tea resulting from a change in the demand for tea.

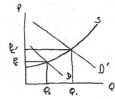

This is the simple way to show a change in price for a supply and demand function. Since demand and supply determine price, let's shift to a perfectly competitive firm that has price changes.

A perfectly competitive firm is characterized as being efficient, operating as an atomistic unit, and facing free entry and exit. The perfectly competitive firm is a price taker and makes only normal profits in the long run.

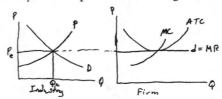

This is what the normal perfect competitor would look like in the long run. The firm receives its price from the market intersection of the $S = D$ curve. Then it will produce where MC = MR and, in the graph above, make normal profits.

However, if prices change, then the firm will not be making normal profits. The graph below shows the scenario (action shown as completed) that could have caused the price change.

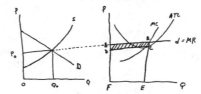

The S and D of the market have determined the price that the firm will charge. However, momentarily the price is above the point where we have long-run efficiency; the intersection of MC and MR is above the ATC curve. The MC curve will always intersect the ATC curve at its lowest point because the ATC curve will always fall until the MC curve is equal to or above it. Keep in mind that the firm will always operate where MC = MR.

In this case, the price the firm will charge is above the point of long-run efficiency. *PCBA* represents the box of supranormal or supernormal profits the firm will make in this case. Costs will consist of only *FECD*. This will not last long, as other firms will begin to realize that this perfect competitor is making supernormal profits. In the long run, more firms will decide to enter the industry. Now the supply curve will shift to the right, causing prices to fall and pushing the firm to making normal profits.

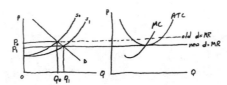

The old D = MR curve is driven down to a point where just the costs (including, of course, a normal profit) will be covered and supernormal profits will no longer be made. Now the price has decreased for the maker because other firms have entered the market. This increase in supply decreases the price, and this could be the reason why the price has changed.

This could have also worked the other way with a firm making losses and then having to shut down. As more and more firms shut down, this could have caused the price to increase. The supply curve would then have shifted to the left instead of to the right because of the decrease in the number of firms in the industry. Now the price would be restored to equilibrium.

Another reason why the price could have changed would be change in the ATC and MC curves:

ATC and MC could have shifted to ATC' and MC' because of a change in labor costs. As labor prices go up, the marginal cost to produce and ATC to produce would have increased, thus the price could ultimately have been forced to change.

> **More detail is needed here.**

Let's face it: This world does not consist only of perfectly competitive firms. A change in the price could have come from an industry changing from oligopoly to monopoly or from a dominant firm changing its prices for a variety of reasons. In these cases, firms could have had a direct control over the price change. A monopolist is able to charge the price it wants to, subject to the constraint of the demand curve, so it could have calculated the need to change the price.

To close, in microeconomics there are many ways to change a price; and I have laid out the basic ways in which prices are depicted and changed. Of course, this is not the only way, but supply and demand ultimately are the tools by which prices are set.

> The student has given the essentials of the response. When there is sufficient time, one expects students to develop complete responses. When there is not time for a complete exposition, one looks for indications that the student has the essentials and could develop them further if given more time. This is a general rule for all questions.
>
> In this question, the student has given the basic notions surrounding the determination of price

by the interaction of supply and demand. The student then demonstrates that she or he knows what will move each curve and notes the results in each case. Graphs illustrate the points and help to develop a more nearly complete response to the question. One always looks for graphs or mathematical statements that indicate understanding or that help to illustrate descriptions in the prose or even that can introduce appropriate prose. Again, this is a general expectation in viewing responses to questions.

Notice that the student attempts to build some appreciation of the cost basis of supply curves. If this were a microeconomics course, one would expect to see a similar demonstration regarding demand theory but there is not sufficient time for a more nearly complete development of supply and demand concepts in an introductory *macroeconomics* course. The stress here is on fundamentals and how they are used.

It is often a good idea to begin with a general statement of the overall principle(s) and then proceed to refine one's response with detail and examples.

Organization, development, and mechanics are all generally good here. These elements are always important.

Even a quick reading of the response indicates that the student has focused on the essentials of supply, demand, and what underlies the curves. This means that one needs some discussion regarding shifts and what may cause shifts in supply and demand curves, along with the expected effects.

Overall, the most effective approach to most essay questions is to begin with the fundamentals that demonstrate understanding of guiding principles. Elaborate as time permits. Illustrate whenever possible. Graphs and symbolic formulations frequently can be used appropriately to establish points, to illustrate, and, in some cases, to elaborate. Use mathematical statements whenever possible but if you cannot supply the more formal mathematics, use simple geometry and algebra as appropriate.

Think initially of establishing the central theme or point of the essay or response. Elaborate as you are able. Note how the response to this question and to others uses a common approach that follows this essential outline.

(Student B's response to option 2)

2. (Prediction) Forecast the effect(s) of each of the following:

a. A change in tariff levels
b. A change in beverage preference from coffee to tea
c. A change in demand from a factor of production

a. A change in tariff levels.

A tariff is an amount of money that is added to the price of a foreign-produced good.

This is vague and imprecise.

The purchaser of the foreign-produced good pays this extra amount.

Again, vague and imprecise.

However, this increase in the price of a foreign-produced good is a detriment for domestic consumers. The government (of the domestic country) usually places tariffs on goods that foreigners produce in a certain industry that the government wants to protect. For instance, if the U.S. government lowers or eliminates the tariff on good X that is produced in a foreign country, the price of good X will be more attractive to domestic consumers —i.e., a decrease in the tariff lowers the purchase price of that foreign good. Therefore, more domestic consumers will purchase good X, especially if the price of good X is now lower than its domestic counterpart. The lowering of the tariff decreases the demand for the domestic counterpart of good X and thus opens the domestic producers of this counterpart to industrial competition.

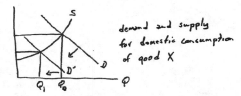

This lowering of the tariff causes the price of the counterpart to be bid down and the quantity of the counterpart sold to be lower. The opposite is true if the tariff is increased—i.e., the price increases and the quantity sold increases because the demand for this counterpart shifts right, not left.

The student should note clearly that the rightward demand shift is for the domestically produced good if the price of a substitute, foreign-produced good is in fact increased because of a new tariff. As written, it appears that a price increase causes the demand for the foreign-produced good to shift to the right; that is incorrect.

b. A change in beverage preference from coffee to tea

If people now prefer tea to coffee, the price of coffee will increase and so will the quantity of coffee sold. This is because when coffee is highly demanded, the price gets bid up because of the rightward shift of the demand curve. Suppliers and entrepreneurs see the high price of coffee and enter into the market and bid the price down again.

Note the error here. Suppliers enter the market only when the price has been bid high enough for them to cover their costs of production. Entry is shown on the supply curve by a movement along the supply curve—not by a rightward shift of the supply curve. A rightward shift of the curve would imply that costs have somehow been lowered. They have not.

This is a long-run effect.

An instructor will be sure to note the error here. Be sure to keep in mind that the student assumes that there will be a rightward shift of the supply curve in the long run, but there is no apparent reason why this would be true. We have no information about any fundamental change in the factors of supply that would justify such a shift.

Assuming that coffee and tea are substitutes, the price of tea is lowered as a result of the shift in the demand curve (see graphs) for tea to the left. The quantity of tea sold is also lower than the quantity sold before the preference change.

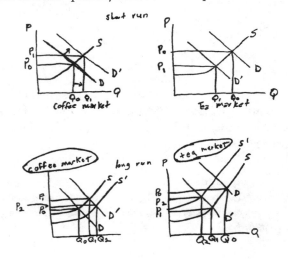

Notice that in the long run the price of coffee is P_c, which is lower than P_1 (where the new suppliers had not yet entered the market). The quantity of coffee sold is greater than the quantity before and directly after the change in fad to favor coffee.

What should be obvious by this time is that the student does not have a firm grasp of what may change supply and what may change quantity supplied, what may change demand and what may change quantity demanded.

An analogous long-run effect will occur in the tea market. The price of tea will get bid back up as some suppliers exit the market for tea.

It is unlikely that this will be the case.

Yet the quantity of tea sold (Q_1) is lower through the short-run change in quantity supplied of tea.

This is far too vague and imprecise. The student should have noted that the demand curve moved along the supply curve, producing a reduction in both quantity and price.

c. A change in demand from a factor of production.

A factor of production is one of the inputs that gets incorporated into the finished product that is then marketed. If there is an increase in demand for a factor of production such as input Z, the price of the finished product is increased.

Why?

Since the demand for input Z has increased, the price of input Z has increased to C_e. This occurs because the demand curve for input Z shifts left.

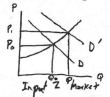

Because of the increased costs of inputs, the ATC curve for the firm has increased or shifted up. Similarly, the MC curve has shifted to the left.

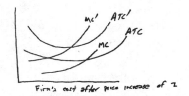

If a perfectly competitive market is assumed, the price P [in the industry] still determines the price of the good [for the individual firm] because price level P is where the supply and demand [curves] for the market intersect. Some firms, such as the one in the example, will not be able to stay in business because the price of input Z has increased the cost of producing a good to beyond the price that the firm can get for the good. As firms close down, the supply for the finished good shifts to the left for the market, which bids the equilibrium price for the finished good up. Therefore, some firms in danger of closing and efficient firms remain open and sell their product at a new price *P*.

> The student has given the essentials of the response. When there is sufficient time, one expects students to develop complete responses. When there is not time for a complete exposition, one looks for indications that the student has the essentials and could develop them further if given more time. This is a general rule for all questions.
>
> In the instant question, Part a, the student has attempted to define what a tariff is and has produced a too-vague response. However, the student correctly identifies what will happen in terms of demand and supply effects. Note the emphasis on substitution effects and the demand curve shifting effects produced in the market for a substitute good in cases of both increasing and decreasing tariffs. Notice, too, the emphasis on tariffs as part of the supply considerations in the market, an increase causing an upward and leftward shift of the supply curve and a decrease causing the opposite.
>
> Part b is designed to test whether or not the student recognizes one of the fundamental determinants of demand for a consumer good or service. Again, one looks for the correct shifting. Note that the student became confused when he or she began to try to explain market reaction. The student should have been content to shift the demand curves in each case but began to think of entering and exiting firms as somehow producing a whole new set of additional curves. This will not happen.
>
> Part c finds the student back on track with a change in demand for a factor of production. One finds only minor errors here or requirements for amplification and clarification.
>
> Organization, development, and mechanics are all generally good. These elements are always important.

Part II. *Mostly Macroeconomics. Respond to the following. 36 minutes each, 20 points each.*

3. "It is sometimes said that inadequate demand to sustain the economy at a high level of employment is the result of too much saving. However, this cannot be true because what is saved is always invested." Discuss.

4. Homer Hardcrust, chairman of the Council of Economic Advisers, proposes that because of the economic situation, the government should prepare an austerity program and cut down government expenditures to set an example for private households. Under what economic conditions might Hardcrust's advice make sense? Under what economic conditions would it worsen the economic situation? Discuss.

5. What, if any, relationship(s) exist(s) between the classical model of economic aggre-

gates, namely full employment, including but not limited to wages, and current theory about these same aggregates? (*Hint:* Recall the classical model I developed in class and the extensive notes I provided to accompany that discussion.)

Answers:

3. "It is sometimes said that inadequate demand to sustain the economy at a high level of employment is the result of too much saving. However, this cannot be true because what is saved is always invested." Discuss.

Inadequate demand to sustain the economy at a high level of employment because of too much saving is a real possibility. If one looks at Japan's current economic problems, one can see that the people of Japan are high savers; the economy has relatively low levels of employment [in relation to the levels customarily seen in Japan], and the economy is in a recession.

What is saved is not always invested.

> I have marked this as an error. What the student means to say is that what is saved is not always what is willingly invested. Unwanted inventory accumulation is, indeed, investment. It is unintended investment, but still an investment.

The people who save are not the same ones who invest. Those who save are the people who work in the economy and receive a salary, for example. Whatever they do not consume, they save by purchasing common stocks and bonds; or they may simply hold cash in savings accounts. Those who invest are the people who receive those savings and then start new business ventures, such as a new company, that they believe will bring them profits.

When a worker receives his paycheck, he can do two things with the money he receives. He can either spend the money (which is consumption) or save the money. When the amount of saving is high, the amount of consumption will be low; and there will not be money going back into the economy that can be used to grow or help expand the economy.

> Imprecise.

The spending multiplier shows how a change in one of the components of GDP will affect the income of the economy. The equation is, $\Delta Y = \Delta X \left[1/(MPS + MP_{tax} = MP_{imp}) \right]$. ΔY stands for the change in income, ΔX stands for a change in a component of GDP, MPS stands for the marginal propensity to save, MP_{tax} stands for the marginal propensity to tax, and MP_{imp} stands for the marginal propensity to import. These three elements constitute the denominator portion of the fraction.

For example, say consumption (which is a component of GDP) is $100 billion.

Also assume that MPS is 1/4, MP_{tax} is 1/8, and MP_{imp} is 1/8. If savings went up dramatically and consumption went down, there would be a change in income. If consumption decreased by $10 billion, then income would decrease by $20 billion. This is what happens when savings increases, consumption decreases, and none of the other components of GDP change to make up for the decrease in consumption. The economy slows down and the living standard lowers.

When looking at a Keynesian cross as shown in Fig. 1, it can be seen that the amount of intended investment does always equal the amount of actual investment. If the economy is not at equilibrium, where the aggregate expenditures equal output, there is either an accumulation of inventories or a depletion of inventories.

(Fig. 1)

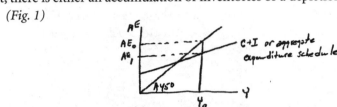

When the economy is producing at a level to the right of the equilibrium, as at point *W*, the economy is producing at a level [where total expenditures would have to be] AE_0 [for the economy to be in equilibrium at this level of output], but the economy is only consuming at a level of AE_1. When producers see those inventory accumulations building up, they will begin to cut production until the economy is back at equilibrium [where aggregate expenditures cut the 45-degree line]. The aggregate expenditures schedule might be so low because investors and consumers are worried about the possible future condition of the economy. For example, people do not want to invest when they believe that the prospects for their investments paying off look poor.

(Fig. 2)

As shown in Fig. 2, the economy is not producing at full capacity. The aggregate demand curve does not cut the aggregate supply curve at the full employment level (Nf), even though employment may be at a very high level.

Note that the student initially goes to the heart of the issue: the question of whether or not so-called inadequate demand can cause problems in an economy. The student also notes why problems may arise: The individuals who do real investment are not usually the same ones who save. Alas, the student then makes a fundamental error by failing to differentiate between intended and actual investment.

The student then goes through the multiplier effects of changed spending in terms of its total impact on economic activity. This may be a good way to introduce what occurs when one of the factors that make up aggregate demand (C, I, G, or NX) changes. Graphs are then used to illustrate not only what unwanted inventory accumulation may look like, but the multiplier effects as well. Once again we see effective use of graphs to illustrate main points.

One might have used some simple mathematical statements here, but this illustrated response demonstrates how one may express fundamental ideas without complicated presentations.

Organization, development, and mechanics are all generally good here. The elements are always important.

4. Homer Hardcrust, Chairman of the Council of Economic Advisers, proposes that because of the economic situation the government should prepare an austerity program and cut down government expenditures to set an example for private households. Under what economic conditions might Hardcrust's advice make sense? Under what economic conditions would it worsen the economic situation? Discuss.

The advice that the government should cut back on spending in order to set an example for society could make sense when the economy seems to be expanding too fast and there is the fear of inflation setting in. His advice probably wouldn't make sense when the economy was in a recession, and levels of investment and expenditures were low.

The current situation in the United States is that the economy is overheating because the aggregate supply cannot keep up with the aggregate demand and that soon inflation could set in if demand does not slow down. If the government cut back on its expenditures but did not cut back on taxes, it would be [doing what, if it were consumers we were discussing, would be called] increasing its savings and decreasing its consumption. The spending multiplier can be used to show how the government's drop in spending will lower the income of the entire economy. With lower incomes, consumers will demand less, which will relieve pressures of inflation. A $100 billion decrease in government spending on "trivial" expenses would decrease income in the economy by $200 billion if the multiplier were 2. Similarly, if households cut their consumption by $100 billion, there would be another $200 billion decrease in income if the same multiplier were used. Combined, this would make for a $400 billion decrease in income, which would decrease the amount of money households had available to spend. This way they would have to buy what was necessary first and then spend what they had left over on less important items.

In Figure A, I have shown the economy as a point where aggregate demand is very high and an increase [in aggregate demand] would lead to inflation.

(Figure A)

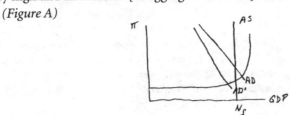

If AD were to shift to the left, as AD' shows, then fears about inflation would be diminished, since the AS curve is not able to shift out to the right fast enough for AD to continue to increase at the previous level.

The student means that the AD curve is now on the horizontal portion of the AS curve, implying no increase in price levels. Over time, the AS curve will shift to the right as the economy grows, further diminishing the inflationary pressures.

If the government were to decrease its spending during a time of recession, it would only be hurting the economy, because of the same example with the spending multiplier. Less consumption leads to lower income, which will lead to a lower level of demand. Finally, as there is less demand, producers will cut back on the amount they supply, and the economy will contract. When the economy is in a recession, the government must increase spending so that income will increase. AD will shift to the right, and producers will begin to supply more. With higher income, there will be more savings. More savings will push interest rates down and increase the level of investment in the economy, as shown in Figure B.

(Figure B)

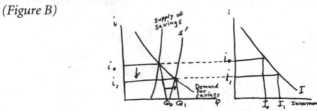

An increase in investment will also be factored into the spending multiplier. The increased investment will lead to a higher level of income in the economy, and this will lead to a higher living standard. This can be achieved by the government's increasing its expenditures, without increasing its taxes. If the government increased taxes as much as expenditures the people would not be able to spend as much [even though there are still the balanced budget multiplier effects]; and, therefore, the effects of the increase in government spending would be diminished [in relation to what they would have been without any increase in taxes].

> The question here has probably been around since the introduction of Keynesian concepts into economics classes. The question deals with the issue of inadequate aggregate demand and a Keynesian response to it. Other economic traditions will have different responses, but a conventional response is shown above.
>
> The main issues to be addressed are the possibilities of excessive demand in the economy and what government might do and the possibilities of inadequate demand in the economy and what government might do.
>
> The basic approach is one of considering how government might restrain aggregate demand when the economy cannot produce supply growth that is sufficient to absorb the excess purchasing power somehow extant in the economy. The student employs without elaboration the use of the multiplier. If there were more time, one would expect him or her to develop the elements of the multiplier, but, given the time constraints, it is acceptable here not to have these as part of the answer. The key is the question of possible excess or deficient demand in relation to the full-employment level in the economy.
>
> The student could have made this a better response by providing more detail and elaboration (development of ideas), but the basic concepts are here. Organization, development, and mechanics are all generally good here.

5. What, if any, relationship(s) exist(s) between the classical model of economic aggregates, namely full employment, including but not limited to wages, and current theory about these same aggregates. (*Hint:* Recall the classical model I developed in class and the extensive notes I provided to accompany that discussion.)

The classical model of economic aggregates implies that the natural state of the economy is at full employment. The classical economists believed that the economy should always be at full employment.

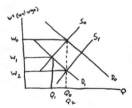

The classical economists believed that if the demand for labor falls from D_0 to D_1, wages would fall to W_1, from W_0. W_0 was a subsistence wage rate, and W_1 is a sub-subsistence wage rate. At this point, workers are unemployed and are willing to take their old jobs back at an even lower wage. This would increase supply and shift the supply curve to S_1, from S_0. At this point, consumers feel that goods are cheaper, and they have more wealth because they have a pool of savings, which they had acquired when they were getting paid at wage rate W_0.

The student neglected to say that workers now spend more, according to Pigou.

As a result of this, the demand for labor increases, and the demand curve shifts back to D_0. When workers see that the demand for their labor is high once again, they ask for higher wages, and this shifts the supply curve back to S_0. At this point we are at equilibrium.

The student really should have described the change in wage rates as a bidding up of wages rather than suggesting that it is workers asking for higher wages that drives up the wage rate.

This is the classical theory.

It is *not* the classical theory, but it does describe the part of the classical position central to the question.

Current theory is somewhat different. Keynesians believe that the economy does not have to be at full employment in order to function. If the demand for labor falls, wages do not necessarily have to fall. This brings me to the concept of sticky wages, which modern economists have recognized.

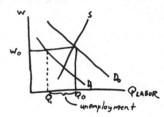

In our society today, wages do not generally fluctuate according to the demand for labor. Employers often prefer to lay off workers rather than reduce wages.

There are several reasons why wages are sticky. They include such considerations as union contracts and explicit wages, implicit contracts, the insider-outsider theory, and minimum wages.

Union contracts cause sticky wages because employees sign a contract that states the length of employment and wages to be paid.

Rather imprecise here.

These contracts are written documentation and are legal and binding. They are also called explicit contracts, and employers cannot deviate significantly from their contents. Sometimes unions fight for higher wages, and they might agree to accept lower wages in times of recession, but, ultimately, once a contract is signed, the wages are sticky until the contract expires.

Implicit contracts are not documented [in a similar way]. They may be implied verbal agreements and understandings between employers and employees. The employers agree to pay a fixed wage. Employees do not have any guaranteed benefits in this case, but they can be assured that their wages are fixed.

> **The last sentence is imprecisely expressed.**

As a result of the insider-outsider theory, wages are also sticky. Workers on the inside may demand that outsiders get paid the same wages and get the same benefits as they do. This is [in part] because the insiders have to train the outsiders; and if the outsiders get lower pay, the bargaining power of the insiders is reduced. The jobs of the insiders will no longer be secure because they could be threatened with replacement by the outsiders. Because of this, wages tend to be sticky.

The government has also established a minimum wage rate, and wages cannot go below it. Some people might also not feel compelled to work at a wage rate below minimum wage.

> **It is not clear what the student has in mind with the last sentence.**

As we can see from the above statements, the economy is not always at full employment because wages tend to be sticky. This results in unemployment.

Keynesians would call for government intervention to alleviate the situation—to help raise the demand for labor and also help create new jobs.

> The question allows a good deal of room for students to explore and explain some basic concepts. One can imagine quite a different response from another student with a different point of view or from one who wished to emphasize a somewhat different approach.
>
> This particular response briefly explains the classical model and what classical economists suggested might happen, with a bit of Pigou's contribution added to bring the model a bit closer to the current century.
>
> During the 1980s, a basic approach to unemployment in the United States actually seemed to be a government-led policy to lower the general level of wages on the theory that this would help to restore the economy to full employment. Other countries pursued other policies, such as the enhancement of skills and general abilities of workers to increase their value-added contribution. The idea here was that increased worker productivity would ultimately result in increased demand

for labor. A bidding down of wages was an attempt to do the same thing—lower labor costs in relation to value added. One may debate which approach is better, but that is not the focus of the question

The question permits one to simply compare classical approaches to wage determination to some current views about why wages might or might not adjust if aggregate demand were to fall. The question also can be used, as here, to comment briefly on minimum wage policies. In short, a student has some freedom in how he or she might approach the question. However, the essential elements of the responses are the same. One must explain in sufficient detail whatever one chooses to explain. The answer the student proffers above is not very detailed, nor does it elaborate very much on any of the points. It is adequate, though, to suggest to the instructor that the student would be able to write more or to develop the ideas if time permitted.

In this question, one might have used a different approach and gone on to describe the Keynesian idea that an economy could find demand shifting and the establishment of equilibrium at less than full employment. One could then compare and contrast the classical view of what might happen with the Keynesian ideas surrounding the proper role of government in adding to aggregate demand to push the economy back toward full employment. One could, of course, use this as the door to discussing the whole concept of whether or not government participation in the economy in that way is desirable. In short, the question permits students to respond "correctly" in a variety of ways. Only one approach is developed in the model answer.

Organization, development, and mechanics are all generally good here.

Part III. *No choice. Respond to the following question. 36 minutes, 20 pts.*

6. The Federal Reserve is widely reported to be considering pushing up interest rates.
   a. Why might the Fed currently want to do this?
   b. Why might the Fed currently not want to do this?

This question essentially asks for the pro and con arguments related to the proposed move.

Answer: If the federal reserve wishes to push up interest rates, this is a clear sign that the Fed feels that investment should be lowered.

Actually, this may not be true. It may indicate other things, but one should at least note the possibility that perhaps consumption (in the C + I + G + NX model) is too robust.

The only way the Fed can push up interest rates is to limit the money supply.

I would rather the student say that the conventional approach to pushing up interest rates is a decrease or at least a slowing in the rate of growth of the money supply."

By pushing up interest rates, the Fed is trying to push the AD curve back.

> This is imprecise. The Fed may want to keep the economy from growing too fast; this is not the same thing as pushing the AD curve back.

This would be a good move if currently the economy is facing a threat of inflation. This is one of the ways in which the Fed tries to lower inflation.

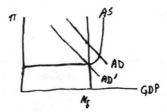

Currently the economy is reaching a point where the Fed does not know when inflation will occur or if it will occur at all. The Asian crisis has probably caused the AD curve to shift back and to the left, but the Fed feels that it has not pushed us back far enough. At first the Fed was not worried about the situation because it felt that the Asian crisis would save us from a too-rapidly-rightward-shifting AD curve. So far the United States is fine with the unemployment rate approaching 4.5 percent. But how far can it go down before the Fed needs to take action? The Fed can't wait too long because there are so many lags that exist with the use of monetary policy. The Fed does not want to get caught up in a period of high inflation because it failed to act when it should have. This is why the Fed must act now. The risks are too great otherwise. It will not hurt to slow the economy down a bit. What if inflation hits, and the lag to Fed action is a possible 23 months? Failure to act now would be a lot worse. The Fed must weigh a lot of things in deciding what to do in the current situation. Does it do something when nothing really has to be done yet? How long will the lag be between a Federal Reserve monetary action and a change in economic activity? When will inflation kick in?

These are the essential questions that the Fed must answer in deciding how to act in response to the current situation. Let's look at what would happen if the Fed does nothing. Two obvious things could happen: Either inflation would occur, or there would be no inflation. Everything is fine if there is no inflation because the economy will be strong, but how long will this last? Inflation could hit at any day. The unemployment level can only go so low before the Fed needs to take action. If the Fed does nothing and inflation occurs, then people will blame the Fed for not recognizing the need for action, and they will lose their trust in the Fed.

The Fed is stuck in a tight situation here because there is really no right answer in the eyes of the people. Some people will understand that the Fed did what it did because it had to, while others see no need for action when no inflation is currently occurring.

The Fed will raise interest rates in order to avoid the problems that will occur if it waits too long to do something. Another reason it will do it is because inflation is coming eventually with unemployment dropping. The Fed does not want the lag to be in effect when the action needs to be taking place [in terms of impact on the economy]. The Fed is saved and needs reassurance because, let's face it, when was the last time we had unemployment at 4.5 percent and no inflation?

> I have no idea what the student means by this last comment. It is vague and imprecise. It does not fit well with what the student has written above. I think the student means that the Fed is safe in acting to slow the rate of growth of economic activity because the economy cannot continue to grow as it has without inflation. However, I cannot be sure. Thus, the student loses points here for vagueness and a lack of clear direction in the essay.

The Fed might not want to do this because it will put a halt to the growth that has been occurring in the nation. AD has been pushed outward to the point where we "think" it will eventually intersect the AS curve in the upward position. The problem here is that this is what we think—not what we know. By raising interest rates, the Fed could stall an economy that was growing without inflation. No one knows where full employment is.

> The statement is unnecessarily vague and imprecise. What does the student really mean?

We thought it was at 6 percent, but now it may be as low as 4 percent. It is the belief that the Fed should act only if we are below this full employment point, but now we do not even know where that is.

> The student has the right idea here, but the statement is not precise and clear.

The Fed must make a decision as to what is best for an economy in the current situation. Right now, no one can tell if what it does is the right thing to do, but in a year we will clearly know the results of what it has done. The Fed does not want to be known for either causing inflation by not acting or stalling a growing economy, but it must decide which of these things it would not want to affect the economy the most.

> The student again has the correct idea but has missed an opportunity to summarize and conclude with a clear, cogent statement that restates the issues and concludes the arguments.

This is one of those answers that is basically correct but imprecisely argued and is rather unrefined in its approach. It could have been a superior essay if the student had taken a little more care to lay out each point more precisely. The use of an AD, AS graph is appropriate in this situation. One might have included some discussion of the question of how rapidly aggregate supply may be expanding in relation to changes in AD, and one might have asked the relevant questions related to the exact shape of the AS curve.

This question clearly requires students to demonstrate some knowledge of current economic data. A course in macroeconomics is fairly easy to relate to current economic conditions, and the question requires (1) that students reflect in their responses that they are aware of current economic conditions and (2) that they understand the possible macroeconomic effects of a given Federal Reserve action.

What specifically one writes depends in part upon the particular macroeconomic model that one selects. But this is an elementary course. The instructor does not expect students to demonstrate the same sophistication in handling theory that an instructor may expect in upper-level courses. At this point, it is usually sufficient to demonstrate a firm grasp of received theory. (I use this term mindful of the debates surrounding just exactly the issue of what received theory is or ought to be.) The instructor wants to see if the student can tell a little story about current economic conditions, tell what the current conditions suggest regarding possible appropriate Federal Reserve policy, and predict what might happen if the Fed engaged in a particular kind of behavior. A successful answer then will engage the issues directly, present an appropriate model to provide the setting, and describe the expected effects of Federal Reserve actions to push up interest rates.

Organization, development, and mechanics are all generally good here.

CHAPTER 24

E202: INTRODUCTION TO MACROECONOMICS

Willard E. Witte, Associate Professor

OURSE OBJECTIVES ARE TO GIVE STUDENTS AN AWARENESS OF BASIC STYLIZED FACTS concerning the macroeconomy, to provide an understanding of the basic trade-offs that underlie macroeconomic outcomes and policy decisions, and to provide a framework for understanding the macroeconomic effects of policy and other disturbances.

The two midterm exams and one final are designed to assess the student's ability to understand and interpret macroeconomic data, ability to think about macroeconomic questions in a systematic cause-and-effect fashion, and ability to see the long-run implications of policy, especially when they are inconsistent with short-run effects.

I am most interested in having students develop the capability to approach questions from an economic point of view—for example, thinking in terms of opportunity cost, costs vs. benefits, and cause and effect (within a systematic framework). I am less interested in a demonstration of knowledge of specific details.

MIDTERM EXAMINATION

Each of the two midterm exams counts for 20 percent of the final course grade. Students have two hours to complete the exam, but most are able to do it in 60 to 75 minutes. Generally speaking, students should plan on spending about 20 minutes on the multiple-choice questions, 12 minutes on the numerical problem (Question II), 20 minutes on the short-answer section (Question III), and a little over 20 minutes on the essay question (Question IV).

Success on the examinations requires a sound approach to the course. You need to understand that many terms are used in economics in specific ways that differ from their vernacular use. You must pay careful attention to the definition of the terms used.

You need to learn to think about the issues raised using the framework of economics, not your common sense or your own personal opinions.

You must work at learning this material. It isn't enough to simply read through the notes and text-book. You need to be able to apply the material.

As for the exams: Read the questions carefully, then answer the question that is asked. You will not get credit for comments that are off the point, only for material that responds to the question.

Use analysis from the course. You won't get much (if any) credit for personal opinion or common sense. In many cases, opinion and common sense are likely to be analytically incorrect and will count against you.

Begin by understanding the answers to the basic questions for this section of the course: What determines the level of output in the long run? What are the causes of economic growth?

Learn the terminology introduced in the course. Pay special attention to terms that are used with specific meanings different from their meanings in everyday usage.

You must learn (memorize) certain basic relationships (for example, those relating to the National Income and Product Accounts), but you also need to understand the logic of these relationships.

I. *(60 points) Multiple choice. Select the best answer.*

1. Over the past 125 years the growth of real output in the United States has averaged:
   a. less than 1 percent per year
   b. between 1 and 2 percent per year
   c. between 2 and 3 percent per year
   d. more than 3 percent per year
Answer: d

A correct response here requires factual knowledge.

2. Which of the following describes the activities of the firm sector?
   a. Buyer in goods, factor, and asset markets
   b. Seller in goods, factor, and asset markets
   c. Buyer in asset markets, and seller in goods and factor markets
   d. Buyer in goods and factor markets, and seller in goods and asset markets
Answer: d

If you encounter difficulty answering multiple choice questions, try to determine why some of the choices are incorrect. For example, if you think a is the right answer, try to convince yourself that b, c, and d are correct. Of course, you may need to modify this strategy if you are running out of time. This particular answer requires an understanding of the activities of the sectors of the economy.

3. Suppose that a country with balanced trade (exports = imports) is running a government surplus. Which of the following is true?

    a. For this country, net investment will exceed personal saving.

    b. For this country, borrowing from foreigners will finance part of the government deficit.

    c. For this country, personal saving will exceed net investment.

    d. A country with a government surplus must also have a trade surplus.

Answer: a

> You will need to understand the saving-investment identity from the NIPA in order to answer this question.

4. Which of the following functional relationships depicts the situation illustrated?

    a. $X = f(Y, Z)$
             $+$ $+$

    b. $X = f(Y, Z)$
             $+$ $-$

    c. $X = f(Y, Z)$
             $-$ $+$

    d. $X = f(Y, Z)$

Answer: a

> This response requires an understanding of the relationship of algebraic representation and graphic presentation of theoretical relationships.

5. If all prices have doubled in the past ten years but quantities have not changed, then

    a. both nominal and real GDP will have doubled.

    b. nominal GDP will have doubled and real GDP will be unchanged.

    c. real GDP will have doubled and nominal GDP will be unchanged.

    d. the GDP deflator will be unchanged.

Answer: b

> To answer this correctly, you must understand and be able to calculate nominal and real aggregates.

6. Which of the following would *not* be counted as investment in the NIPA?

　　a. The construction of a new house
　　b. Purchase of 500 shares of IBM common stock
　　c. An increase in General Motors' inventory of new cars
　　d. Construction of a new engine factory by Cummins Engine

Answer: b

This question tests understanding of the definition of investment.

7. Transfer payments are

　　a. an outlay for the foreign sector and a receipt for firms.
　　b. an outlay for the government sector and a receipt for households.
　　c. an outlay for firms and a receipt for the government sector.
　　d. an outlay for the financial sector and a receipt for households.

Answer::b

Here an understanding of the definition of transfer payments is required.

8. If the natural rate of unemployment for the economy is 5 percent and the current unemployment rate is 7 percent, which of the following is true?

　　a. The economy is at full employment and is experiencing a recession.
　　b. There is an excess of structural unemployment in the economy.
　　c. The economy is above full employment and is experiencing a boom.
　　d. The economy is below full employment and is experiencing a recession.

Answer: d

This question calls on the student's understanding of the relationship among actual unemployment, the natural unemployment rate, and the business cycle.

9. The largest category of factor income in our national income is

　　a. personal consumption expenditures.
　　b. employee compensation.
　　c. transfer payments.
　　d. corporate profits.

Answer: b

A question requiring factual knowledge.

10. Suppose that the U.S. labor force grows by 3 percent, the capital stock grows by 1.5 percent, and technology improves 1 percent. This will lead to growth in potential output of about

    a. 1.8 percent.
    b. 3.0 percent.
    c. 3.5 percent.
    d. 5.5 percent.

Answer: c

Apply the output growth decomposition equation.

11. Suppose that in the course of a year, a business experienced the changes shown in its balance sheet.

Cash	−$5000
Machinery	+$40,000
Other assets	+$15,000
Bank loans	+$30,000
Other debt	+$30,000

As a result, its net worth has

    a. increased by $5000.
    b. decreased by $10,000.
    c. increased by $50,000.
    d. decreased by $5000.

Answer: b

This answer requires an understanding of balance sheet relationships.

12. Suppose that a young couple puts away $10,000 when a new child is born. They estimate that they will need $80,000 to cover college expenses in 18 years. What annual rate of return will they need to earn in order to reach this goal?

    a. 4 percent
    b. 8 percent
    c. 12 percent
    d. 16 percent

Answer: c

This answer requires use of the Rule of 72.

II. *(40 points) Provide numerical answers to the following questions. You may receive partial credit if your work is shown in legible fashion.*

> These questions are largely a matter of knowing and applying national income and product identities. I organize numerical questions in the order in which they should be answered. In some cases, earlier answers are used in later questions. Here, for example, the answer to Question 1 is required for Question 2.

The following table is a partial list of entries from the 1995 NIPA of a small economy. Figures are in current dollars except where indicated. You may assume that business taxes and retained earnings are zero.

Consumption	15,000	Rental income	1000
Employee compensation	16,000	Net interest	2000
Government expenditures	5000	Net investment	8000
Corporate profits	3000	Proprietors' income	5000
Exports	5000	Imports	6000
Taxes	9000	Transfer payments	4000
Depreciation	4000	Real GDP (1990 $)	24,000

Calculate:
1. Gross domestic product (1995 $)
2. GDP deflator for 1995 (1990 = 100)
3. National income (1995 $)
4. Personal saving (1995 $)
5. Government surplus/deficit (indicate which)

Answers:
1. GDP = C + net I + depreciation + G + EX - IM   31,000
2. P = (nominal GDP/real GDP) × 100   129.2
3. Y = WRiPP = GDP - depreciation   27,000
4. Personal saving = Y + transfer payments - taxes - C   7,000
5. Government surplus = taxes - transfer payments - G   0 (balanced budget)

III. *(50 points) Answer both of the following questions.*

Describe the budget constraint of the household sector and relate it to the activities of households in the various markets of the economy.

ANSWER

Budget constraints restrict a sector's receipts relative to its outlays. For the household sector, receipts are income (Y) from the sale of factors of production (supply in the factor markets) and transfer payments (TRF) from the government (a nonmarket item). Outlays are for consumption (C) (demand in the goods market) and for taxes (TX) paid to the government (another nonmarket item). With the surplus left out of income plus transfers after consumption and tax payments, households are buyers of financial assets (demand in the asset markets). This surplus is called saving (S). The budget constraint is S = Y + TRF – C – TX.

This question is intended to demonstrate mastery of the basic framework used in macro. It is important that the answer be complete: Mention each of the items in the household budget, identify its relationship to the markets of the economy, and show understanding of budget items' relationships to one another. A successful answer requires a correct (and complete) statement of the household budget constraint and the relationship of budget items to relevant macro markets.

A student must first understand the notion of a sector budget constraint. She must then apply it to the household sector.

Notice that the answer begins by defining what a budget constraint is. This kind of basic information indicates mastery, and also provides organization to the answer. Note also that the question asks for both a description of the budget constraint and its relationship to the economy's markets. A full answer requires both of these.

IV. *(50 points) Answer the following question.*

Suppose the U.S. government is successful in eliminating its deficit and achieving a balanced budget.

   (i) Describe how this will affect the situation in the world and U.S. financial markets.

   (ii) Discuss the implications for U.S. economic growth.

Be concise and use the concepts developed in the course. Mere statement of opinion will not count for much.

This question requires application of the long-run theoretical analysis used in the course. The analysis required for this question was touched on in lectures and reading, but was not presented in full. The student must consequently extend what he has studied to a new situation. In this type of question, I am more interested in how the question is approached than in the student's coming up with the "right" final conclusion.

ANSWER

The budget deficit shows the imbalance between the outlays and receipts of the government. Outlays are expenditures on goods and services (G) and transfer payments to households (TRF). Receipts come from tax payments (TX). The deficit is the amount by which the former exceed the latter.

(i) A government budget deficit reduces the level of national saving (the sum of household saving and the government surplus). When the government has a deficit (negative surplus), some of household saving (supply of funds) must go to finance this deficit. The rest is available to finance the investment of firms (demand for funds). If investment exceeds the funds available domestically, the excess will be financed by international borrowing. Foreigners acquire the funds as a result of a domestic trade balance deficit. If the budget moves from deficit to balance, this will increase the amount of saving available domestically. The portion of household saving that is now going to the government will become available to firms. This will reduce the extent to which firms must borrow abroad, implying a reduction in the U.S. trade deficit. In the world financial market, the outcome depends on the extent to which the decline in the U.S. government deficit affects world saving. If the increase in U.S. national saving amounts to a significant increase in world saving, then interest rates worldwide will tend to decline.

(ii) Reducing the deficit might affect growth in a variety of ways. The labor supply could be affected through changes in the participation rate, but offsetting pressures could arise. Cuts in transfer payments might induce people who lose benefits to enter the labor force. This could occur if welfare is cut and might also occur if social security benefits were reduced. At the same time, if tax rates are raised, the incentive to work might be reduced, leading to lower participation.

Cuts in government spending could fall in part on education and training programs and on spending on research activities. If so, there could be a negative effect on technological advance and on worker quality, with adverse effects on growth.

Balancing the budget could also affect the capital stock through its effects on investment. As explained above, reducing the deficit will produce an increase in national saving. If the world market is not affected, the main impact will be on the U.S. demand for foreign funds (and its mirror image, the trade deficit). But if the deficit reduction is enough to affect the world market, an increase in world saving will lower interest rates. This in turn will tend to raise investment, leading to a larger capital stock and more rapid growth.

An answer should include a statement of the government deficit and what is involved in moving into balance (from deficit).

Part i of the question requires a relatively straightforward discussion of the effect of the deficit on the saving/investment situation in an open economy. A really good answer would probably include a diagrammatic depiction of the loanable funds market.

In part ii, I am looking for an organized discussion of the elements that determine economic growth (the labor supply, the capital stock, the level of productivity).

The best approach to the question is to first explain the deficit and its components, even though this is not explicitly asked for. Then, for part i, you should describe the effect of a reduced deficit on the financial markets. This discussion should be in analytic terms—that is, in terms of supply and demand.

In part ii it is important that you organize your answer. You also need to avoid falling back on common sense or opinion. The question asks about the effects on economic growth, not on the short-run cyclical course of the economy.

Be aware that a complete answer will include definitions for terms used—especially the deficit. The question says to use concepts from the course. This means that you should use the supply–demand approach to financial markets and the labor, capital, productivity approach to economic growth."

FINAL EXAM

The final exam accounts for 30 percent of the total course grade. Students have two hours to complete the exam, which should be ample, although time management is important. In general, expect to devote about 30 minutes to the multiple choice questions, 12 minutes to the numerical problem (Question II), 20 minutes to the short-answer question (Question III), somewhat over 20 minutes to Question IV, and 25 minutes to Question V.

In terms of grade on the exam, the points distribution indicated is definitive. Subjectively, I consider performance on essay-type questions the best indicator of a student's learning in the course. Numerical problems give an indication of problem-solving ability, but, in my opinion, indicate almost nothing about economic understanding. Multiple-choice questions are adequate on average, but often poor indicators at both extremes. There are some students whose understanding is poor, but who do quite well on multiple choice; there are other students whose understanding is adequate, but who do miserably on multiple choice.

I. *(90 points) Multiple choice. Select the best answer.*

1. Which of the following would result in structural unemployment?

    a. A woman taking a leave to have a baby

    b. A factory relocating overseas

    c. An amusement park closing down for the winter

    d. A factory closing down due to a recession

Answer: b

You need to understand the definition of structural unemployment.

2. Suppose that your salary rose from $40,000 in 1990 to $60,000 in 1996, and that the value of the GDP deflator (1992 = 100) was 90 in 1990 and 115 in 1996. What happened to your real income (in 1992 $)?

   a. It rose by about $7,700.
   b. It was unchanged.
   c. It rose by $20,000.
   d. It rose by about $15,600.

Answer: a

A correct response requires converting nominal to real using the price index.

3. In the U.S. national income and product accounts, which of the following would raise both national income and disposable income?

   a. An increase in transfer payments
   b. An increase in personal income taxes
   c. A cut in personal income taxes
   d. An increase in corporate profits

Answer: d

The correct answer requires an understanding of income identities from the NIPA.

4. Suppose that in a country with a population of 200 million, there are 90 million employed and 10 million unemployed. What is the unemployment rate?

   a. 5 percent
   b. 8 percent
   c. 10 percent
   d. 11 percent

Answer: c

You need to understand the calculation of the unemployment rate.

5. The life-cycle theory of consumption predicts that

   a. households will spend most of a one-time increase in income.
   b. based on projected future income, households will adjust spending and savings to achieve a relatively smooth consumption path.
   c. consumption will start low, increase steeply, and then decline rapidly over a household's lifetime.

    d. consumption will never exceed disposable income.

Answer: b

This question requires understanding of the basic logic of the life-cycle model.

6. An increase in foreign income implies

    a. a decrease in net exports, leading to a decrease in aggregate demand.

    b. an increase in net exports, leading to an increase in aggregate demand.

    c. a positive effect on investment, leading to an increase in aggregate demand.

    d. offsetting effects on imports and exports, with no net effect on aggregate demand.

Answer: b

This requires understanding of the determinants of net exports.

7. In the short run, a decrease in the real interest rate will

    a. increase investment and decrease consumption, leading to an ambiguous effect on equilibrium output.

    b. decrease both investment and consumption, leading to a decrease in equilibrium output.

    c. decrease investment and increase consumption, leading to an ambiguous effect on equilibrium output.

    d. increase both investment and consumption, leading to an increase in equilibrium output.

Answer: d

This question requires an understanding of the effects of interest rates on the components of aggregate demand.

8. Which of the following can shift the long-run aggregate supply curve?

    I.   A change in the labor supply

    II.   A change in the money supply

    III.   A change in productivity

    a. I only.

    b. I and III only.

    c. I, II, and III.

    d. None of the above; the long-run aggregate supply curve is permanently fixed.

Answer: b

A successful answer requires an understanding of the sources of economic growth.

9. A decrease in the tax rate will cause
   a. an increase in autonomous expenditures.
   b. an increase in induced expenditures.
   c. an decrease in household saving.
   d. a decrease in the multiplier effect.

Answer: b

The question calls for an understanding of the multiplier process.

10. Suppose that the government wants to increase aggregate demand by $50 billion, and that it estimates the autonomous expenditure multiplier to be 2.0. By how much should the government increase its spending on goods and services?
   a. $25 billion
   b. $40 billion
   c. $50 billion
   d. $100 billion

Answer: a

This question requires application of the multiplier equation.

11. A high level of cyclical unemployment
   a. will be inflationary, since it means that output is low, causing shortages.
   b. will lead to rising wages as a result of excess demand for labor.
   c. will reduce inflationary pressure as a result of downward pressure on wages.
   d. is to be expected when output is rising.

Answer: c

The answer calls for an understanding of the determinants of price change.

12. Suppose that a worker who is anticipating inflation of 5 percent wants to increase her *real* wage by 3 percent. To do this, she should
   a. negotiate a contract which lowers her wages by 2 percent.
   b. negotiate a contract which raises her wages by 3 percent.
   c. negotiate a contract which raises her wages by 5 percent.

    d. negotiate a contract which raises her wages by 8 percent.

Answer: d

> To answer successfully, you will need to understand the relationship between changes in real and nominal variables.

13. Rising prices
    a. exert an expansionary effect on aggregate demand via higher interest rates and higher terms of trade.
    b. exert a contractionary effect on aggregate demand via lower interest rates.
    c. exert an expansionary effect on aggregate demand by causing real wages to rise.
    d. exert a contractionary effect on aggregate demand via higher interest rates and higher terms of trade.

Answer: d

> The question requires understanding of the causes of the downward-sloping aggregate demand curve.

14. During the past 30 years, the source of federal government revenues which has grown most sharply is
    a. the corporate income tax.
    b. the personal income tax.
    c. tariff receipts on imports.
    d. the payroll tax for social security.

Answer: d

> This question requires factual knowledge.

15. Suppose that government spending (G) increases in an economy with an income tax. As a result,
    a. the government deficit increases by the amount of the rise in G.
    b. the government deficit is reduced by the amount of the rise in G.
    c. the government deficit increases, but by less than the rise in G.
    d. the government deficit increases by more than the rise in G.

Answer: c

> The question requires an understanding of induced changes in taxes.

16. The real wage is

    a. the nominal wage divided by the price level.

    b. the nominal wage minus the interest rate.

    c. the nominal wage minus the inflation rate.

    d. inversely related to the purchasing power of labor income.

Answer: a

The question tests understanding of the definition of real wage.

17. During a recession,

    a. the GDP gap rises and the unemployment rate falls.

    b. the GDP gap becomes negative and the unemployment rate falls.

    c. the GDP gap becomes positive and the unemployment rate rises.

    d. the GDP gap becomes negative and the unemployment rate rises.

Answer: d

The question calls for understanding of the concept of the GDP gap and the cyclical behavior of the gap and unemployment.

18. The level of investment tends to

    a. fall when technology advances.

    b. increase when firms expect higher future sales.

    c. increase during periods of economic stress.

    d. increase when interest rates rise.

Answer: b

This question requires an understanding of the determinants of investment.

II. *(50 points) Provide numerical answers to the following questions. You may receive partial credit if your work is shown in legible fashion.*

A small open economy has the following characteristics:

◆ The net tax rate on total income is 20 percent.

◆ An increase in disposable income of $1000 causes consumption to rise by $900.

◆ 12 percent of domestic income is spent on imports.

◆ Exports are $8000.

◆ Investment expenditures are $8000
◆ Government expenditures are $24,000

Using this information, calculate:

1. The level of output in short-run equilibrium
2. The government surplus/deficit in equilibrium (indicate which)
3. The level of *net* exports in equilibrium
4. The level of consumption in equilibrium

Suppose that government expenditures are reduced to $20,000. Calculate:

5. The government surplus/deficit in the new equilibrium (indicate which)

I organize numerical questions in the order in which they should be answered. In some cases, earlier answers are used in later questions. Here, for example, the answer to Question 1 is required for Questions 2 to 4. Question 5 requires recognition that a change in G will induce a change in income, which affects the tax side of the budget.

The first step in this question is to organize the given information. This requires calculating (a) the multiplier from the information on tax rates (tr), saving rate (tps), and import rate (mpm), and (b) autonomous spending (= EX + I + G). These then allow the determination of equilibrium Q. This answer is then used in Questions 2 through 4.

My approach to the multiplier model is nonstandard. It ignores unimportant trivia (such as the marginal propensity to consume, autonomous consumption, and autonomous taxes), but includes such elements as income taxes.

Answer:

1. Q = (multiplier) (autonomous spending) = 100,000
2. D = G – tr Y = 4000 (deficit)
3. X = EX – mpm Y = –4000
4. C = Y - T - S = Y - tps Y - tr Y = 72,000
5. D = G – tr Y = 2000 (deficit)

III. *(50 points) Answer the following questions.*

First define each of the following and describe how it is calculated. Then explain briefly how and why an increase in each would affect aggregate expenditures. The "how" part of your answer should describe the direction of the effect and the component(s) of expenditure affected. The "why" should explain the economic logic of the effect.

1. The terms of trade
2. The real interest rate

> This question asks for four related but different items: Define the term, explain its calculation, state its effect on aggregate expenditures, and explain the causal logic of its expenditure effect. Each must be addressed in a good answer.

Answer:

1. The terms of trade are the relative price of domestically produced goods compared to that of foreign products. Formally, $T = EP/P^*$, where T is the terms of trade, E is the foreign exchange value of the domestic currency (the exchange rate), P is the price level of domestic goods measured in domestic currency, and P^* is the price of foreign goods measured in foreign currency. This means that EP is the price of domestic goods in foreign currency. The relative price EP/P^* will influence purchases of domestic vs. foreign goods (i.e., exports and imports). If T increases, this means that domestic goods are getting more expensive compared to foreign goods. As a result, purchases of domestic goods by foreigners (exports) should drop, while domestic purchases of foreign goods (imports) should rise. As a result, aggregate expenditures on domestic goods will decline.

2. The real interest rate is the nominal (market) rate adjusted for inflation. That is, $r = i - \pi$, where r is the real rate, i is the nominal rate, and π is the inflation rate. The real rate represents the cost (return) to a borrower (lender) after adjustment for the loss of purchasing power of the funds borrowed (lent). Since households and firms are ultimately concerned with the real level of their borrowing/lending costs or returns, it is the real interest rate that should determine behavior. For a household, a higher real rate means a higher return on its saving. If saving is increased, consumption will decrease, thus lowering aggregate expenditures. For firms, a rise in the real rate raises the cost of financing investment. This will lead to lower investment spending and lower aggregate expenditures.

> This question is partly about the basic definition of the two concepts. It also concerns the determinants of consumption, investment, and net exports. A good answer must show awareness of the economic logic underlying the effects of T on exports and imports, and of r on consumption and investment. I am looking for correct definition of the terms, using both verbal and symbolic exposition. This should include some identification of the variables required to calculate T and r. And I am looking for a discussion of the impact of changes in T and r on components of aggregate expenditure. This discussion should indicate understanding of the economic mechanisms at work, not merely memorization of a formula relationship.
>
> It is important to learn the meaning of basic variables such as the terms of trade and the real interest rate. In studying behavioral relationships such as the consumption function, you should focus on the economic behavior involved, rather than trying to memorize relationships.

IV. *(55 points) Answer the following question.*

Explain the mechanism of the multiplier process. Include in your answer an explanation of the factors that determine the strength of the process. Explain how a tax cut would affect the strength of the process.

> This question asks for three related but different items: a description of the multiplier process, a discussion of the factors that determine its strength, and an analysis of the effect of a tax rate change. Each must be addressed in a good answer.

Answer: The multiplier effect results from the induced spending that occurs when higher output raises income in the economy. Following an initial autonomous stimulus to aggregate demand, output and income will rise. Some of the income will go to taxes, some will be saved, and some will be used to purchase imports, but the rest will be spent on domestic goods. This induced consumption will lead to further output increases, starting the next round of the process.

The strength of the multiplier effect depends directly on the amount of induced spending per dollar of additional income. This means that it depends inversely on the amount of income that is not spent domestically. In an open economy, there are three main "leakages" from the income stream: taxes, imports, and saving. Consequently, a high income tax rate, a high marginal propensity to import, or a high saving propensity will yield a low multiplier.

For example, if the tax rate is cut, households will have a larger proportion of their total income available as disposable income. The tax leakage will be smaller. Some of this additional disposable income will be used for (induced) consumption, producing a stronger multiplier effect.

> This question asks about the multiplier process, not simply for a mathematical exposition. An answer must demonstrate an understanding of the behavioral basis of the multiplier effect. The answer could be related to the multiplier formula, but this is less important than showing an understanding of the process. I am looking for an explanation of the source of the multiplier effect. This could involve introduction of the concepts of induced vs. autonomous spending. I am also looking for identification of the factors that contribute to the strength of the multiplier—and an explanation of their effects. Finally, I want to see a discussion of the specific effects of a tax cut.
>
> You must recognize the difference between autonomous and induced spending and the effects of the latter on the expenditure adjustment process. You need to think in terms of cause and effect, but within the structure of the circular flow. You need to be prepared to analyze the effect of policy changes (like a change in the tax rate) and also behavioral effects (like an increase in consumer confidence)."

V. *(55 points) Answer the following question.*

Earlier this week, the Federal Reserve was widely expected to raise interest rates in an effort to head off inflation.

    a. Explain why the Fed might be concerned about inflation even though, currently, prices are not rising much. That is, explain what there is about the current situation that could lead to inflation.

    b. Explain how an increase in interest rates could lessen the danger of inflation's becoming a problem. That is, explain how higher interest rates can lead to lower inflation.

Be concise and use the concepts developed in the course. Mere statements of opinion will not count for much.

This question requires integration of material from the entire course, including some knowledge of the current state of the economy. Organization is important to a good answer. It is also important that the answer utilize ideas and analysis from the course, not merely common sense or opinion.

Answer: a. Inflation can arise when expansion of aggregate demand causes output to rise beyond its full employment level (potential GDP). Rising output will raise the demand for labor as firms hire additional workers, forcing unemployment below its natural rate and producing upward pressure on wages. (In the labor market the demand curve will shift right.) In other factor markets, demand will also rise, putting upward pressure on the prices of nonlabor inputs. These increases in costs will put pressure on goods prices, causing them to rise. In the goods market, capacity utilization will rise, possibly allowing firms to increase their profit margins by raising prices beyond cost increases. The Fed is worried that the U.S. economy is close to this situation. Output has been growing rapidly, and the unemployment rate is close to the natural rate. Capacity utilization is relatively high. Since any action it takes will require time to have any effect, the Fed cannot wait until inflation actually begins to be apparent if it wants prevent a serious problem.

b. Higher interest rates will have an adverse effect on investment expenditures by firms and on consumption by households. Households will consume less, since higher rates make saving more attractive; firms will invest less, since the cost of borrowing to finance investment will be higher. This impact is intended to slow the growth in aggregate demand to a rate that is consistent with the growth in the labor supply (preventing further tightening of the labor market situation) and in productive capacity (easing pressure on capacity utilization). In the goods market the aggregate demand curve will shift back to the left. If interest rates are raised to an appropriate degree, this will lower output to the level of potential.

> To answer this question, you must have absorbed some basic knowledge of the current situation, but even more important is an ability to see the broader interconnections between the short-run situation and the long-run course of the economy. Finally, you must also understand the basic nature of monetary policy and its effects. The question itself gives you a lot of clues about the correct answer. You are told that the Fed might raise interest rates, and that the problem is potential inflation. The question also says to use concepts from the course. What has been said in the course about the causes of inflation? About the effects of higher interest rates?
>
> I am looking for a discussion of the current situation and its possible implications for inflation. This will involve some discussion of the causes of inflation (using analysis from the course). I am also looking for a discussion of the transmission mechanism of monetary policy, including its effects on components of aggregate demand, and the resulting implications for prices and inflation.

CHAPTER 25

THE UNIVERSITY OF IOWA

06E:002: PRINCIPLES OF MICROECONOMICS

William P. Albrecht, Professor

PRINCIPLES OF MICROECONOMICS INCLUDES A MIDTERM AND A FINAL EXAM, BOTH of which are in essay format. Professor Albrecht points out that both exams are very important in determining the student's grade for the course.

My course objectives are to teach the basic tools of microeconomics, to acquaint the students with some important microeconomic policy issues, and to show how to apply the tools to these issues. I expect students to develop an understanding of supply and demand, opportunity cost, elasticity, fungibility, and the incentive and rationing function of prices

To prepare for the exams, review all reading assignments and lectures, and determine what concepts are emphasized in both. Also practice drawing and applying the major graphs, and practice answering workbook and end-of-chapter questions. It is expected that students will answer all the questions within the time allotted.

Read assignments before class; read about current issues in newspapers and magazines; practice using the concepts presented in the course.

MIDTERM

The midterm accounts for 30 percent of the course grade.

1. Explain why the price elasticity of demand is different at different points on a linear demand curve. Be sure to define price elasticity of demand in your answer.

Answer: The price elasticity of demand expresses the responsiveness of quantity demanded to a change in price. Arithmetically, it is the percentage change in quantity divided by the percentage change in price. Given a linear demand curve, this number declines as price falls because the percentage change in price increases for a given price change and the percentage change in quantity decreases for a given price change.

> A successful answer must show that the student understands the concept of elasticity. Answering the two parts of the question correctly indicates that the student has this understanding.

2. **Is the price elasticity of supply for crude oil higher in the short run or in the long run? Explain.**

Answer: It is higher in the long run, because new wells can be developed or old wells can be brought into operation in response to an increase in the price of oil. Similarly, wells can be shut down in response to a fall in the price of oil. In the short run, there is much less opportunity to change the quantity of oil supplied in response to a change in the price of oil.

> A successful answer shows that the student understands elasticity of supply and why it typically is higher in the long run than in the short run; therefore, reference should be made to price and quantity supplied and to why this relationship depends upon the period of time being considered.

3. **Use a production possibilities frontier (PPF) with increasing costs to illustrate the concept of opportunity cost. Be sure to show the opportunity cost of one good at some point on the curve.**

> In addition to answering textbook end-of-chapter questions and practicing drawing the major graphs before the midterm, Professor Albrecht suggests reviewing materials with other students, perhaps even forming study groups.

Answer:

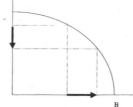

The outward-bending curve shows the production possibilities for an economy that can produce two goods, A and B. The downward-pointing arrow on the vertical axis shows the amount of A that must be given up to get the amount of B shown by the rightward-pointing arrow on the horizontal axis. Thus, at this point on the PPF, the opportunity cost of the increase in B shown by this arrow is the amount of A shown by the downward-pointing arrow.

To answer this question, the student must be able to draw a PPF and use it to illustrate the concept of opportunity cost.

4. Draw hypothetical supply and demand curves for rental housing in a city. Label the curves S_0 and D_0, respectively. Show the equilibrium price and quantity. Label them P_0 and Q_0.

Answer:

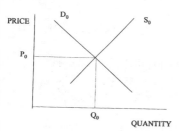

The purpose of this question is to test students' ability to do this basic exercise. I find that a surprisingly large number make mistakes in drawing and labeling the diagram.

5. Redraw the diagram from Question 4. Now assume that there is a sudden, large increase in the population of the city. Show the impact of this, if any, on supply, demand, price, and quantity in the short run. Briefly explain.

Answer:

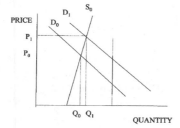

The increase in demand creates a shortage at the existing price. In response to this, the price of rental housing increases. This, in turn, leads to a small increase in quantity supplied, as some people decide, for example, to rent out spare rooms.

A good answer contains the correctly drawn diagram and shows the ability to distinguish between movement along a curve and shifts of the curve. A large number of students always incorrectly insist on shifting the supply curve in response to a demand curve shift.

6. If each firm in a perfectly competitive industry has annual accounting profits of $5,000,000 and an investment of $100,000,000 is required to enter the industry, would you expect firms to enter the industry? To exit it? Explain.

Answer: The annual opportunity cost of the $100,000,000 investment would be the forgone interest on the investment plus depreciation. Given that a safe investment, such as a government bond, pays about 6 percent, the opportunity cost of the $100,000,000 is more than $6,000,000 per year. This means that economic profits are negative. Therefore, firms would exit rather than enter the industry.

A good answer shows an understanding of the opportunity cost of capital (both conceptually and with respect to actual interest rates), of the difference between economic profit and accounting profit, and of the effect of profits on entry and exit.

7. Assume that a perfectly competitive industry is in long-run equilibrium. Show this graphically for both the industry and a firm. Be sure to include industry supply and demand curves, the demand curve for an individual firm's product, and the firm's marginal cost and short-run average total cost curves. Briefly explain.

Answer:

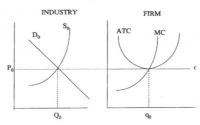

The intersection of the industry D and S curves determines the price. The firm, as a price taker, has to determine the profit-maximizing quantity at this price. This is the quantity at which MR = MC. Since MR = MC in perfect competition, the firm produces the Q at which P = MC. In long-run equilibrium, there are no economic profits, and thus P = ATC. In long-run equilibrium, then, P = MC = ATC. The firm is therefore operating at the lowest point on the ATC curve.

The correct answer shows the relationship between industry S and D and the firm's perfectly elastic demand curve, the relationship between MC and ATC, and the profit conditions of LR equilibrium.
To prepare for this type of question, students not only must work on understanding these relationships but should also practice drawing the curves.

8. Redraw the graph from Question 7. Now show the short-run impact of an increase in demand for the product. Briefly explain.

Answer:

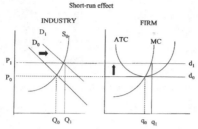

The increase in demand is shown by the new industry demand curve D_1. This leads to an increase in P, which causes quantity supplied to rise as each firm increases output until P = MC at Q_1. Now P > ATC, and each firm is earning economic profits.

9. Redraw the diagram from Question 8 showing the short-run impact of the demand increase. Now show the long-run impact. Assume that the industry is a constant-cost industry. Briefly explain.

Answer:

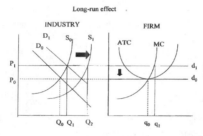

In the long run, the economic profits cause entry, and the industry supply curve shifts to the right to S_1. Price falls, and industry output increases to Q_2. Since this is a constant-cost industry, the ATC in the long-run equilibrium is the same as in the original equilibrium. Thus P returns to the original P; each firm is producing the same quantity as in the original equilibrium, but there are more firms in the industry, and so Q is higher. To sum up, the long-run effect of a demand increase in a perfectly competitive constant-cost industry is to increase Q but not P.

Good answers to questions 8 and 9 show an understanding of the impact of a demand increase and then the impact of positive economic profits. The best answers explain this with words *and* diagrams. Before the exam, students should practice showing all this with graphs.

The course final tests the student's understanding of different types of market structures, the determinants of factor demand, public choice theory, some important microeconomic policy issues, and the application of microeconomic tools to these issues. The final represents 30 percent of the course grade.

1. What is the relationship among price, marginal cost, and marginal revenue in a profit-maximizing monopoly? Explain in words and with a graph.

Practice answering workbook questions and end-of-chapter questions. Memorization of lists and definitions will not be enough to get a good grade.

Answer:

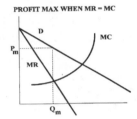

PROFIT MAX WHEN MR = MC

A monopoly, like other firms, maximizes profits when marginal cost (MC) = marginal revenue (MR). A monopoly faces a downward-sloping demand curve (the industry demand curve) for its product. Because of this, price (P) is greater than MR. So at the profit maximizing output,

P > MC = MR.

A good answer explains this relationship with words and graphs. Practice working with graphs and interpreting them for others.

2. Economic theory can be used to determine the equilibrium price and quantity in both perfect competition and monopoly. Can it determine the equilibrium price and quantity in an oligopoly? Explain.

Answer: In an oligopoly, each firm's revenues and profits are affected by what its rivals do. A firm does not know how many units of its product it can sell at a given price unless it knows what its rivals are doing. In other words, the firm does not know exactly what the demand curve for its product is unless it knows what its rivals will do. This is different from the situation in both perfect competition and monopoly. Thus there is no unique industry equilibrium because of the interdependence of the firms. Theory cannot predict the industry's price and quantity without making very specific assumptions about how each firm in the oligopoly will act and how it will react to its rivals' actions.

> A good answer explains the nature of the interdependence of firms in an oligopoly and why there is no single model of oligopoly behavior.

3. What is the purpose of antitrust laws? Give two examples to illustrate how antitrust can achieve this purpose. Discuss at least one criticism of U.S. antitrust law.

Answer: The purpose of antitrust laws is to keep markets reasonably competitive in order to avoid the loss in consumer welfare that comes from monopoly prices. One example is Section 1 of the Sherman Act, which outlaws restraints of trade such as price fixing. Without this prohibition, oligopolies would be more likely to collude and charge a price close to the monopoly price. Another example is Section 7 of the Clayton Act. It prohibits mergers that may lessen competition or create a monopoly. Again, the purpose is to prevent monopoly pricing. Another example is Section 2 of the Sherman Act. It outlaws monopolizing and attempts to monopolize—again with the intent of preventing monopoly pricing.

One criticism is that Section 7 of the Clayton Act sometimes prevents mergers that would lead to significant efficiencies in production and thus would help rather than hurt consumers. Another criticism is that the laws are often used to protect competitors rather than competition. For example, firms that expand their market share by lowering prices can be accused of monopolizing even though consumers benefit from the low prices.

> The answer should show an understanding of the basic thrust of U.S. antitrust law and of some problems that have arisen in implementing it.

4. Explain how a system of marketable licenses to pollute can be used to control pollution. Explain why such a system can be an efficient means of achieving a given level of pollution control or environmental quality. What other advantages are there to such a system?

Answer: Under such a system, each existing source of a certain type of pollution is granted a certain number of licenses to pollute. These licenses can be used or sold. Each license permits the owner to emit one unit of pollution. Thus the number of licenses determines the overall amount of pollution that will be allowed.

Since these licenses can be sold, the firms that have the lowest cost of reducing pollution will sell licenses to firms with the highest costs of reducing pollution. The low-cost firms will sell licenses for more than it costs them to reduce pollution, and the high-cost firms will buy them for less than it costs them to reduce pollution. Since the pollution reduction is done by the firms with the lowest costs, the system is efficient.

Other advantages are that the system provides incentives for firms to find cheaper ways of controlling pollution. As they become more efficient, firms can sell more licenses or buy fewer. The system also provides good information on what it costs to control pollution, since the price of licenses should reflect the marginal cost of reducing pollution. This will permit more informed choices concerning the allocation of resources to pollution control.

> A successful answer shows an understanding of efficiency and of how to use market incentives to achieve efficiency. This is a difficult question for many students, but it is a good test of their understanding of why market forces can bring about efficient outcomes.

5. Briefly explain the theory of public choice.

Answer: Public choice theory views governmental policy choices as the result of interactions in a political marketplace. The main actors are voters, politicians, and bureaucrats. Voters support policies and politicians that they believe will make them better off. Politicians behave in ways that will get them elected and reelected. Bureaucrats try to maximize their own utility. In short, public choice theory is based on the belief that self-interest plays a very important role in government decision making—just as it does in the market for goods and services. Public choice theory recognizes the possibility of government failure or government inefficiency.

> The answer should explain the major elements of public choice theory as well as the major conclusion of this theory.

6. A good welfare system provides adequate assistance to those who need it. A good welfare system also helps people become self-sufficient. Is there a conflict between the two goals? Explain.

Answer: In one sense, there is a conflict: If people are given money because they have low incomes, they have less incentive to work and to become self-sufficient. This is particularly true if welfare benefits are reduced sharply when they earn income. Also, the longer people are not working (unless they are in school), the harder it will be for them to become self-sufficient. They will not be developing the skills necessary to obtain employment that pays a decent wage. In another sense, there may be less conflict: If assistance takes the form of ensuring that people (especially children) have adequate education and medical care, they are more likely to be able to be self-sufficient.

A successful answer shows an understanding of the incentive effects of guaranteed incomes and high marginal tax rates. It also shows an understanding of some of the factors that affect the development of human capital. These concepts are important, regardless of the current policy issues in the area of welfare and welfare reform.

7. What determines the demand for labor? The demand for capital? Explain.

Answer: The demand for any factor of production depends upon its marginal revenue product (MRP). Thus the demand for labor is determined by the MRP of labor. The demand for capital is determined by the MRP of capital.

The MRP of a factor is the marginal product of the factor times the marginal revenue to the firm when it sells the product. For example, if the marginal product of a worker is 10 units of X per hour, the price of X is \$2, and the industry producing X is perfectly competitive, the MRP of the worker is \$20. The firm will pay up to \$20 per hour to hire the worker. The marginal product of labor depends upon the worker's skills, the amount of capital, and the technology used by the firm.

This is a straightforward question, but it is useful for seeing if students understand factor demand and that market forces determine both the demand for labor and the demand for capital."

CHAPTER 26

ECON 22060: PRINCIPLES OF MICROECONOMICS

Constantin Ogloblin, Teaching Fellow

T HREE EXAMS ARE GIVEN IN THE COURSE. ONE SAMPLE MIDTERM AND THE FINAL ARE included here. All exams require problem solving.

Primary course objectives are to help students learn the key principles of microeconomics, develop the economic way of thinking, and apply the power of economic analysis to real-world situations in order to be able to reach informed conclusions and make decisions.

The student should try to understand key concepts rather than memorize definitions, focus on learning how to use the tools of economic analysis, and make sure he or she can read and understand graphs, which help in visualizing many important economic relationships. Moreover, the student should do as many end-of-chapter and study guide problems as possible. The proverb "Practice makes perfect" is very true regarding studying economics.

MIDTERM EXAM

(30 points + 3 bonus points)

1. The company that you manage has invested $7 million in developing a new product, but the development is not quite finished. At a recent meeting, your salespeople report that the introduction of competing products has reduced the expected sales of your new product to $5 million.

    a. If it would cost $1 million to finish development, should you go ahead and do so? Why or why not? (3 points)

b. What is the most that you should pay (if any) to complete development? Explain. (2 points)

Answers:

a. Yes, I should finish the development. The expected marginal benefit of introducing the new product is $5 million, while the marginal cost is $1 million.

b. The amount I pay to complete development (my marginal cost) should be less than the amount I expect to receive from the sales of the new product (my expected marginal benefit). Thus I should complete development only if it costs me less than $5 million.

> The answer should unambiguously state the manager's decision and justify it concisely. It is important that students justify their answers. Responses that simply say "yes" and "$5 million" will receive only partial credit. In part b, full credit will be given if, instead of saying "less than $5 million," a student simply says "$5 million."
>
> The question calls for knowledge of the principles of rational decision making, marginal thinking, and opportunity cost. Making decisions requires comparing the costs and benefits of alternative courses of action. Recall that a key idea in economics is that a rational decision maker takes an action if and only if the marginal benefit (MB) of the action exceeds the marginal cost (MC). In this particular problem, the expected marginal benefit of completing the new product is what the firm expects to receive from its sales, or $5 million. The marginal cost is the *additional* cost required to complete the development project, or $1 million. Thus, MB > MC, and the firm should complete the product development. This principle also tells you that you should complete development only if it costs you less than $5 million.
>
> Notice that as soon as we use the principle of marginal thinking, the past investment in the project—however important it might seem—does not matter. That is, the $7 million already invested is irrelevant to your decision. If you still doubt it, consider the alternatives in part a from the total cost perspective. If you continue the project, you lose $3 million (7 + 1 - 5), but if you don't, you lose even more, since, in the latter case, the $7 million you invested will bring no return.
>
> To answer this question successfully, students need to understand and be able to apply to a practical situation one of the key principles of economics: Rational people think at the margin. Alternatively, the concept of opportunity cost may be used. In this case, a successful variant of answers would be (a) "Yes, I should finish the development. The opportunity cost of not doing this is the $5 million of sales that I lose, which is greater than the $1 million that I pay to finish the product development." and (b) "The amount I pay to complete development should be less than my opportunity cost ($5 million of potentially lost sales); that is, I should complete development only if it costs me less than $5 million."

2. Suppose that there are 10 million workers in Canada, and each of these workers can produce either 2 cars or 30 bushels of wheat a year.
   a. What is the opportunity cost of producing a car in Canada? (2 points)
   b. Draw Canada's production possibilities frontier with cars on the vertical axis. If Canada chooses to consume 10 million cars, how much wheat can it consume

without trade? Label this point on the production possibilities frontier. (3 points)

c. Now suppose that the United States offers to buy 10 million cars from Canada in exchange for 20 bushels of wheat per car. If Canada continues to consume 10 million cars, how much wheat does this deal allow Canada to consume? Label this point on your diagram. Should Canada accept the deal? Why or why not? (3 points)

Answers:

a. 15 bushels of wheat

b. 150 million bushels (point A)

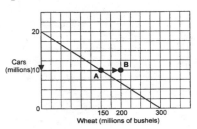

c. 200 million bushels of wheat (point B). Canada should accept the deal, since it makes the country better off. Canada's opportunity cost of producing 10 million additional cars is 150 million bushels of wheat. That is, by giving up 150 bushels of wheat, Canada can produce 10 million additional cars, exchange them with the United States for 200 million bushels of wheat, and end up consuming 10 million cars and 200 million bushels of wheat (50 million bushels more than without trade).

The problem deals with opportunity cost, the production possibilities frontier (PPF) and its graphic representation and interpretation, and gains from trade. The response is successful because it gives correct, complete, and concise answers to each part of the question. In part a, although no explanation is needed, it's important to specify the units in which the opportunity cost of a car is measured (bushels of wheat). In parts b and c, the axis and points on the graph should be properly labeled. A brief explanation of why Canada should accept the deal is needed in part c.

"The opportunity cost of a good is what you give up to get it. If a worker in Canada produces 2 cars, he or she does not produce 30 bushels of wheat. Thus, the opportunity cost of producing 2 cars is 30 bushels of wheat, which means that the opportunity cost of producing 1 car is 15 bushels of wheat. The easiest way to draw Canada's PPF is to graph the two extremes, where only one good is produced. If all 10 million workers produce cars, 20 million cars and no wheat will be produced. If all 10 million workers produce wheat, the economy will produce 300 million bushels of wheat and no cars. Connecting these to points on the graph gives us the PPF. The point on the PPF corresponding to 10 million cars on the vertical axis shows the quantity of wheat consumed without trade on the horizontal axis. Now, since the opportunity cost of producing 10 million cars in Canada is 150 bushels of wheat (15 × 10), by giving up 150 bushels of wheat produced domestically, Canada can produce 10 million additional cars and get for them 200 bushels of wheat from the United States."

Understanding (and being able to apply) the concept of opportunity cost, the ability to draw and read the PPF graph, and basic numerical, analytical, and graphical skills are required for a successful response to this question."

3. An article in *The New York Times* (Oct. 18, 1990) described a successful marketing campaign by the French champagne industry. The article also noted that "many executives felt giddy about the stratospheric champagne prices. But they also feared that such sharp price increases would cause demand to decline, which would then cause prices to plunge." What mistake are the executives making in their analysis of the situation? Illustrate your answer with a graph. (3 points)

Answer: A price increase cannot cause the *demand* to decline. It causes the *quantity demanded* to decline, *ceteris paribus*. However, this is not the case in the situation in question, where the price increase is due to a rightward shift in the demand curve, which resulted from a successful marketing campaign.

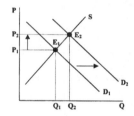

Supply and demand analysis, shifts in the demand curve vs. movements along the curve, and factors influencing demand are the principles and concepts involved in answering this question. The response is successful because it gives a correct, complete, and concise answer to the question, illustrating it with a self-explanatory graph.

It is helpful to use the supply and demand diagram to see what happened in the market. As soon as the marketing campaign affected consumers' preferences, the whole demand schedule shifted to the right, causing the price to increase.

The response demonstrates an understanding of supply and demand analysis, the ability to apply the *ceteris paribus* principle and to distinguish between shifts in a curve and movements along a curve, the ability to draw and read the supply and demand diagram properly, and basic analytical and graphical skills.

4. Because bagels and cream cheese are often eaten together, they are complements. We observe that the equilibrium *price* of cream cheese and the equilibrium *quantity* of bagels have risen. What could be responsible for this pattern—a fall in the price of milk or a fall in the price of flour? Illustrate and explain your answer. (5 points)

Answer: A fall in the price of milk (an input for the production of cream cheese) would shift the supply curve for cream cheese to the right, causing the equilibrium price of cream cheese to fall (see Fig. 1). This is not what we observe.

A fall in the price of flour (an input for the production of bagels) will shift the supply curve for bagels to the right, causing the equilibrium quantity of bagels to rise (see Fig. 2). This is what we observe.

As shown in Fig. 2, the price of bagels falls as a result of the increased supply. Because bagels and cream cheese are complements, this causes the demand for cream cheese to increase (Fig. 3). As a result, the equilibrium price of cream cheese rises. This explains our observation. Thus, the factor responsible for the increase in the equilibrium price of cream cheese and the equilibrium quantity of bagels is a fall in the price of flour.

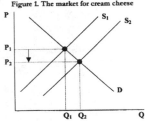

Figure 1. The market for cream cheese

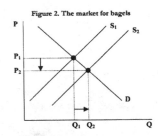

Figure 2. The market for bagels

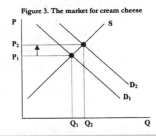

Figure 3. The market for cream cheese

Concepts that figure in this question include supply and demand analysis, the influence of input prices on supply, and the influence of prices of related goods on demand. The response is successful because it gives a correct, complete, concise, and logically consistent answer to the question, illustrating it with graphs that demonstrate understanding of and ability to apply the supply and demand diagrams.

The best way to approach the problem is to examine, in turn, the possible influence of each of the two factors on the equilibrium price of cream cheese and the equilibrium quantity of bagels. First, ask yourself which market and which curve is directly affected by the fall in the price of milk and in which direction the curve shifts. Then draw a supply and demand diagram to see how the shift changes the equilibrium. You will see that the price of cream cheese should fall as a result of the fall in the price of milk. Thus a fall in the price of milk could not be responsible for the observed increase in the price of cream cheese. Repeat the same steps to examine what happens if the price of flour falls. You'll see that the equilibrium quantity of bagels increases. Notice also that the equilibrium price of bagels falls. Because bagels and cream cheese are complements, this causes the demand for cream cheese to increase and the equilibrium price of cream cheese to fall.

Required for a successful response are an understanding of supply and demand comparative statics, knowledge of the factors influencing supply and demand, the ability to draw and read the supply and demand diagram, and basic analytical skills.

5. *The New York Times* (Feb. 17, 1996) reported that subway ridership declined after a fare increase: "There were nearly four million fewer riders in December 1995, the first full month after the price of a token increased 25 cents to $1.50, than in the previous December, a 4.3 percent decline."

   a. Use these data to estimate the price elasticity of demand for subway rides. (Show your work.) (3 points)

   b. According to your estimate, what happens to the Transit Authority's revenue when the fare rises? Explain. (3 points)

   c. Why might your estimate of the elasticity be unreliable? (2 points)

Answers:

a. $E_p = \Delta\%Q/\Delta\%P$; $\Delta\%Q = 4.3\%$; $\Delta\%P = 0.25/1.25 \times 100\% = 20\%$; $E_p = 4.3/20 = 0.215$

b. The revenue increases. Since the demand is price inelastic ($0.215 < 1$), the effect of the price increase is greater than the effect of the decline in quantity.

c. The estimate of the elasticity might be unreliable because it assumes that other factors hold constant, whereas in reality they might change.

The principal concepts here are the price elasticity of demand and its relationship to the total revenue. The response is successful because it gives a correct, complete, and concise answer to the question. Since part a of the question says "show your work," showing how the elasticity is calculated is essential for full credit. Most likely, the percentage change in quantity given in the article was calculated using the standard method (by dividing the change by the initial level). For the sake of consistency, the same method is used to calculate the percentage change in price; however, the midpoint method for calculating the percentage change in price ($0.25/1.375 = 0.18$) is also acceptable and yields essentially the same result.

If you remember that with inelastic demand, an increase in price causes the total revenue to rise, the elasticity calculated in part a tells you the answer to part b. However, you don't have to memorize this relationship. Simply notice that the rise in price increases the revenue, while the fall in quantity decreases it. If the price increased by 20 percent, and this led to only about a 4.3 percent fall in the quantity, the effect of price prevails and the revenue increases. Your estimate of the price elasticity of demand may be unreliable, however, since the observed change in the number of riders may be a result of factors other than price. For example, an increase in population could shift the market demand curve to the right, which would partly offset the effect of the price increase on the quantity demanded. In this case, the price elasticity of demand would be underestimated.

Essential to a correct answer are understanding the price elasticity of demand, having the ability to apply the concept of elasticity to real-world situations, having knowledge of the factors influencing supply and demand, and using general analytical skills.

6. Two drivers—Tom and Jerry—each drive up to a gas station. Before looking at the price, each places an order. Tom says, "I'd like 10 gallons of gas." Jerry says, "I'd like $10 of gas." What is each driver's price elasticity of demand? (3 bonus points)

Answer: Tom's price elasticity of demand is zero. Jerry's price elasticity of demand is 1.

The key concept here is special cases of the price elasticity of demand. Tom wants 10 gallons of gas no matter what the price is. That is, regardless of the price, his quantity demanded stays the same, which means a zero elasticity. Jerry wants to spend $10, regardless of the price. For example, if the price is $1 per gallon, Jerry will buy 10 gallons of gas; if the price is $1.25, Jerry will buy 8 gallons. Thus, a higher price will always be offset by a smaller quantity demanded, and a lower price will be offset by a greater quantity demanded. In other words, to keep the amount spent constant, the percentage change in price should be equal to the percentage change in quantity demanded, which means unit elasticity.

To answer this question correctly, the student must understand the price elasticity of demand and be able to apply the concept of elasticity to analyses of real-world situations. Also required are knowledge of the special cases of the price elasticity of demand and general analytical skills.

FINAL EXAM

(40 points +6 bonus points)

The three course exams are very important to the final grade, with each "midterm" accounting for 30 percent of the grade and the final, for 40 percent.

Even if you are taking this course only because it's required, try to get interested in economics, study it as though you really wanted to learn it and to use it in your everyday life, not just to pass the exams; think of this course as an intellectual adventure. Also remember: "Anything worth doing is worth doing well." Aim high and you'll hit the target.

1. Larry, Curly, and Moe run the only saloon in town. Larry wants to sell as many drinks as possible without losing money. Curly wants the saloon to bring in as much revenue as possible. Moe wants to make the largest possible profits. Using a single diagram of the saloon's demand curve and cost curves, show the price and quantity combination favored by each of the three partners. Explain. (6 points)

Answer: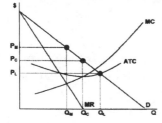

Larry favors Q_L, the maximum quantity where the average total cost does not exceed the price P_L. Curly would sell Q_C, at the point where the marginal revenue is zero— that is, the total revenue is maximized. This corresponds to P_C on the demand curve. Moe wants to sell Q_M, where the marginal cost equals the marginal revenue and the profit is maximized. According to the demand curve, this quantity can be sold at P_M.

> The response is successful because it gives a correct and concise answer with clear explanations illustrated with a correctly drawn graph. Concepts demonstrated are the demand curve faced by a monopoly, the cost curves, the marginal revenue curve, total revenue maximization, and profit maximization.
>
> First, notice that since Larry, Curly, and Moe run the only saloon in town, their firm is a monopoly. Therefore, to answer this question, you should use a diagram illustrating how a monopoly determines the quantity to produce and the price to charge. Draw such a diagram. To determine the quantity favored by Larry, simply find the rightmost point of intersection of the demand curve with the ATC curve. For Curly, who wants the maximum total revenue, the optimal point is where the marginal revenue is zero. For Moe, the profit is maximized where the marginal cost is equal to the marginal revenue.
>
> A successful response calls for an ability to recognize a monopolistic market and to draw and properly read a diagram illustrating a monopolist's production and pricing decisions. It also requires an understanding of the demand curve faced by a monopolist, the marginal revenue curve, and the cost curves, as well as basic analytical skills."

2. Johnny Rockability has just finished recording his latest CD. His record company's marketing department determines that the demand for the CD is as follows:

Price	Number of CDs	MR
$20	10,000	
18	20,000	
16	30,000	
14	40,000	

12	50,000
10	60,000

The company can produce the CD with no fixed cost and a variable cost of $4 per CD.

a. Find the marginal revenue for each 10,000 increase in the quantity sold. (2 points)

b. What quantity of CDs would maximize profit? What would the price be? What would the profit be? (4 points)

c. If you were Johnny's agent, what recording fee would you advise Johnny to demand from the record company? Why? (3 bonus points)

Answers:

(a)

Price	Number of CDs	MR
$20	10,000	
		$16
18	20,000	
		12
16	30,000	
		8
14	40,000	
		4
12	50,000	
		0
10	60,000	

b. $Q_{opt} = 45,000$; $P_{opt} = \$13$; profit = $405,000.

c. $405,000. To receive economic profits, the record company needs a unique resource—Johnny's ability to produce his special music. Since Johnny owns this key resource, he should demand the economic profit received from the sales of his CD.

The response is successful because it gives correct and concise answers. An explanation is needed only in part c. Basic concepts addressed here include the causes of monopoly, the demand curve faced by a monopoly, special cases of cost curves, and production and pricing decisions made by monopolists.

The marginal revenue for the first 10,000 increase in the quantity sold may be found as follows:

$$18 \times 20,000 - (20 \times 10,000)/10,000 = \$16$$

Similarly, the marginal revenues may be found for each 10,000 increase in the quantity sold. As there is no fixed cost, ATC = AVC = $4, and since the AVC is constant, MC = AVC = $4. [Since MC = $\Delta TVC/\Delta Q$ and TVC = AVC × Q = $4, MC = $\Delta(\$4 \times Q)/\Delta Q = \$4 \times (\Delta Q/\Delta Q) = \$4$.] The profit is maximized if MC = MR. This corresponds to Q = 45,000 and P = 13. The TC then is $4 × 45,000 = $180,000, TR = $13 × 45,000 = $585,000, and the profit is $585,000 − $180,000 = $405,000. Sketching a diagram (see below) helps visualize all these relationships.

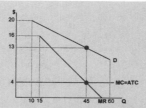

To answer part c, first, notice that the actual product in question is Johnny's music on CDs, not the CDs themselves. Since this product is unique, the demand curve for Johnny's CDs slopes downward and the record company can control the price and make economic profits. To be able to do this, however, the company needs a unique resource—Johnny's ability to produce his special music. Since Johnny owns this key resource, he is the real monopolist, not the record company. Thus he should demand the economic profit received from the sales of his CD.

Required for a successful answer: understanding of a monopoly firm and its profit-maximizing decisions, understanding of the cost curves and their special cases (constant average variable cost), and basic analytical skills.

3. A large share of the world supply of diamonds comes from Russia and South Africa. Suppose that the marginal cost of mining diamonds is $1000 per diamond, there is no fixed cost, and the demand for diamonds is described by the following schedule:

Price	Quantity
$8,000	5,000
7,000	6,000
6,000	7,000
5,000	8,000
4,000	9,000
3,000	10,000
2,000	11,000
1,000	12,000

a. If there were many suppliers of diamonds, what would be the price and quantity? (2 points)

b. If there were only one supplier of diamonds, what would be the price and quantity? (2 points)

c. If Russia and South Africa formed a cartel, what would be the price and quantity? If the countries split the market evenly, what would be South Africa's production and profit? What would happen to South Africa's profit if it increased its production by 1000 while Russia stuck to the cartel agreement? (4 points)

Answers:

a. $P = \$1000$; $Q = 12,000$.

b. $P = \$7000$; $Q = 6000$.

c. $P = \$7000$; $Q = 6000$.

If the countries split the market evenly, South Africa's production would be 3000 and its profit would be $18 million. If South Africa increased its production by 1000 while Russia stuck to the cartel agreement, South Africa would produce 4000 diamonds, the total quantity produced would be 7000, and South Africa's profit would be $20 million.

> The response is successful because it gives correct numerical answers. No explanation is needed.
>
> Correct responses require an understanding of production and pricing decisions made by perfectly competitive firms, monopolies, and cartels; also required is an understanding of special cases of cost curves. Further, the student needs to understand how perfectly competitive firms, monopolies, and cartels make their profit-maximizing decisions and how cartels work.
>
> If there were many suppliers of diamonds, the market would be perfectly competitive—that is, the firms would maximize their profits at the production levels where P = MC = $1000. If there were only one supplier of diamonds—that is, a monopoly—it would maximize the profit if its MC = MR, where MR < P. Calculate marginal revenues using the same technique as in the previous question. Then you can see that MR = MC corresponds to Q = 6000 and P = $7000. This would be unchanged if Russia and South Africa formed a cartel, since the market is in effect served by a monopoly. If the countries split the market evenly, they would produce 3000 diamonds each. As there is no fixed cost, ATC = MC = $1000 (see the comments for the previous question). Thus the per-unit profit would be $6000, and each country will receive a total profit of $18 million. If South Africa increased its production by 1000, while Russia stuck to the cartel agreement, the total quantity produced would be $7000, and, according to the market demand schedule, the price would be $6000. This means that the per unit profit would be $5000, and South Africa would get a total profit of $20 million.

4. The makers of Tylenol pain reliever do a lot of advertising and have very loyal customers. In contrast, the makers of generic acetaminophen do no advertising, and their customers shop only for the lowest price. Assume that the marginal cost of Tylenol and that of generic acetaminophen are the same and constant.

   a. Draw a diagram showing Tylenol's demand, marginal revenue, and marginal cost curves. Label Tylenol's price and markup over marginal cost. (4 points)

   b. Repeat part a for a producer of generic acetaminophen. How do the diagrams differ? Which company has the bigger markup? Explain. (4 points)

   c. Which company has the bigger incentive for careful quality control? Why? (2 points)

Answers:

a.

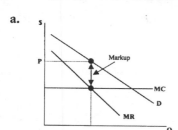

b.

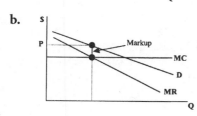

Tylenol's demand curve is steeper; that is the demand for Tylenol is less price, elastic than that for generic acetaminophen. The reason is a higher degree of product differentiation created by the brand name. This allows Tylenol to have the bigger markup.

c. Tylenol has the bigger incentive for careful quality control. The company's competitive advantage and profits depend to a large degree on maintaining the reputation of its brand name. If Tylenol does not maintain quality, it may easily lose the product's reputation for which consumers pay a higher price.

> The response is successful if the diagrams are drawn correctly, all curves and axes are labeled properly, and the explanations are correct and concise. Required are an understanding of how monopolistically competitive firms work and make their profit-maximizing decisions, and an understanding of the demand curve faced by a monopolistically competitive firm and of the role of brand names in a monopolistically competitive market.
>
> The market for pain relievers has the defining characteristics of monopolistic competition: many sellers, product differentiation, easy entry and exit. The slope of the demand curve faced by a monopolistically competitive seller and the price elasticity of demand for its product depend on the degree of product differentiation, which is greater for Tylenol than for generic acetaminophen because of the brand name of the former. This is also the reason why Tylenol has the bigger incentive for careful quality control. Consumers pay a higher price for Tylenol (as shown in the diagrams) because they believe that Tylenol works better than generic acetaminophen. In contrast, the lower price of generic acetaminophen, not higher quality, is the main factor in its competitive advantage. Hence, quality control is less important for generic acetaminophen than for Tylenol.

5. Your enterprising uncle opens a sandwich shop that employs 7 people. The employees are paid $6 per hour, and a sandwich sells for $3. If your uncle is maximizing his

profit, what is the value of the marginal product of the last worker he hired? What is that worker's marginal product? (4 points)

Answer:

The value of the MP = $6 per hour, and the MP = 2 sandwiches per hour.

This question requires only numerical answers. No explanation is needed. A successful response requires an understanding of how a profit-maximizing firm makes its hiring decisions, an understanding of the demand curve faced by a monopolistically competitive firm, and an understanding of the marginal product of labor and the value of the marginal product.

Recall that a competitive, profit-maximizing firm hires workers up to the point where the value of the marginal product of labor (MP)—that is, the value of the product of the last worker hired—equals the wage. Thus, if the wage is $6 per hour, then the value of the marginal product of labor (VMP) = $6. Since the VMP is equal to the MP times the price of the product (P), the MP is 2 sandwiches per hour (MP = MPV/P = $6/$3 = 2).

6. A company is considering building a bridge across a river. The bridge would cost $2 million to build and nothing to maintain. The following table shows the company's anticipated demand over the lifetime of the bridge

Price per Crossing	Number of Crossings, in Thousands (Q)
$8	0
7	100
6	200
5	300
4	400
3	500
2	600
1	700
0	800

a. If the company were to build the bridge, what would be its profit-maximizing price? Would that be the efficient level of output? Why or why not? (4 points)

b. If the company is interested in maximizing profit, should it build the bridge? Why or why not? What would be the profit or loss? (2 points)

c. If the government were to build the bridge, what price should it charge? Why? (3 bonus points)

Answers:

a. The profit-maximizing price would be $4. This would not be the efficient level of output, since P > MC.

b. The company should not build the bridge. The loss would be $400,000.

c. If the government were to build the bridge, it should not charge anything for crossing it. In this case the marginal benefit would be equal to the marginal cost, and society's welfare would be maximized.

A successful response requires correct and complete answers with clear and concise explanations. Needed is an understanding of natural monopoly and the demand curve faced by a monopoly. Also required: an understanding of special cases of the cost curves, production and pricing decisions made by monopolies, the inefficiency of monopoly, society's marginal benefits being measured by the consumer surplus, and socially efficient production and pricing decisions.

Recall that a firm maximizes its profit if MC = MR. In this particular case, MC = 0. Thus, the profit is maximized where MR = 0. The table below shows the necessary calculations. As soon as MC = 0, ATC = AFC. Then MR = 0 if Q = 400, which corresponds to P = $4. At this point, the ATC = $5, that is, the company loses ($5 – $4) × 400,000 = $400,000. Sketching a diagram (see below) helps visualize these relationships.

P	Q	MR	ATC
$8	0		—
		700	
7	100		20.0
		500	
6	200		10.0
		300	
5	300		6.7
		100	
4	400		5.0
		-100	
3	500		4.0
		-300	
2	600		3.3
		-500	
1	700		2.9
		-700	
0	800		2.5

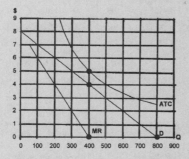

If the government were to build the bridge, its goal would be to maximize social welfare, rather than profit. This is achieved at the point where the society's marginal benefit from the bridge is equal to the marginal cost. Since the marginal benefit is reflected by the demand curve—which shows the value of the good to consumers measured by their willingness to pay for it—and MC = 0, the socially optimal point corresponds to a zero price and a quantity equal to 800,000. Now, if the government builds the bridge and allows free crossing, the total benefit—the consumer surplus, represented by the area under the demand curve—will be $3.2 million ($8 × 800,000/2), while the total cost is $2 million. That is, society's net benefit from the bridge will be $1.2 million.

CHAPTER 27

LOYOLA UNIVERSITY OF CHICAGO

ECONOMICS 201: INTRODUCTION TO MICROECONOMICS

David Augustin, Instructor

THE MAIN OBJECTIVES OF THIS COURSE ARE TO GIVE THE STUDENTS AN INTRODUCtion to the science of economics, show them how basic economic theory relates to real-world phenomena, and prepare them to take more advanced coursework in economics.

Key competencies and skills that students need to acquire and develop in the course include an understanding of the jargon (or "economic fluency"), a knowledge of basic definitions, the ability to analyze simple market changes, an exposure to advanced theories, and a basic understanding of the policy issues raised by economics.

Two exams are given in the course, a midterm consisting of multiple-choice questions and a final consisting of multiple-choice and short essay questions.

MIDTERM EXAM

To complete the course successfully, be sure to read the recommended chapters *before* the lectures. Do assigned problems *before* you're given the solutions. This requires some discipline, but it will improve your comprehension enormously. Obviously, economics is not the only subject this advice applies to, but economics lectures rely on understanding of specialized models and their logic, which is difficult for most students to achieve instantly."

1. Which of the following is correct? Positive economics

   a. deals with economic theories that stress the positive rather than the negative aspects of humanity's prospects.

    b. deals with economic laws that have been established without doubt.

    c. describes what is rather than what ought to be.

    d. describes what ought to be rather than what is.

    e. is practiced by a school of economists known as positivists.

Answer: c

The key concept here is positive versus normative economics.

2. When the variable held constant for a particular curve changes,

    a. the curve itself will shift.

    b. there will be a movement along the curve.

    c. the curve will become steeper.

    d. the curve will become flatter.

Answer: a

The question calls for an understanding of movement along a curve versus movement of a curve.

3. The production possibilities frontier between ale and bread will shift upward if

    a. more ale is produced.

    b. less ale is produced.

    c. more bread is produced.

    d. less bread is produced.

    e. none of the above is true.

Answer: e

The main concept tested is growth in an economy.

4. The production possibilities frontier will shift upward if

    a. more labor, land, or capital becomes available.

    b. more consumer goods are produced.

    c. unemployment is reduced.

    d. the law of diminishing returns operates.

    e. unemployment is increased.

Answer: a

Again, growth in an economy is the concept central to this question.

5. When the relative price of beef rises, the consumption of

    a. pork will fall and consumption of chicken will rise.

    b. pork will tend to fall.

    c. chicken will tend to fall.

    d. pork and chicken will tend to rise.

    e. pork and chicken will fall only if their absolute prices don't change.

Answer: d

> The relevant concept here is substitutes.

6. Assume that Betty and Ann live on a desert island. With a day's labor, Ann can produce 8 fish or 3 coconuts; Betty can produce 4 fish or 1 coconut. Ann has

    a. an absolute disadvantage in both fish and coconuts.

    b. a comparative advantage in fish.

    c. a comparative advantage in coconuts.

    d. a comparative advantage in both fish and coconuts.

    e. none of the above.

Answer: c

> Comparative advantage is the concept tested by this question.

7. Shortages and surpluses vanish when the invisible hand

    a. uses its monopoly power.

    b. sets equilibrium prices.

    c. uses price controls.

    d. uses government.

    e. does none of the above.

Answer: b

> The point here is an understanding of competitive equilibrium.

8. A decrease in the quantity demanded of a product occurs when

    a. the price of the product rises.

    b. the price of a substitute for the product rises.

    c. the price of a complement for the product falls.

    d. the price of the product falls.

    e. income increases.

Answer: a

The question focuses on change in demand versus change in quantity demanded.

9. If the demand for automobiles falls as a result of a drop in consumer income, and if, at the same time, increases in factor prices cause the supply of automobiles to fall, the price of automobiles will

   a. rise.
   b. fall.
   c. remain the same.
   d. be impossible to forecast from the information given.

Answer: d

A correct answer requires an understanding of comparative statics.

10. Where the demand curve intersects the supply curve

   a. the price and quantity are in equilibrium.
   b. consumers are willing to buy what sellers are willing to sell.
   c. there is no shortage of the good.
   d. the price will neither rise nor fall until something else changes.
   e. all of the above are true.

Answer: e

The key concept is competitive equilibrium.

11. Whenever prices are prevented from reaching their equilibrium level by government rules and regulations,

   a. shortages or surpluses can result.
   b. resources are not allocated entirely by prices.
   c. the quantity supplied will not necessarily equal the quantity demanded.
   d. price is not set at the intersection of the supply and demand curves.
   e. all of the above are true.

Answer: e

Knowledge of two concepts is tested here: competitive equilibrium and price controls.

12. Factors held constant along the supply curve include

   a. technology only.

b. technology and factor prices.

c. other prices and the number of buyers only.

d. the number of sellers and consumer incomes.

Answer: b

Key to this question is the concept of supply determinants.

13. If the demand for crackers goes up when the price of cheese goes down, crackers and cheese are

a. inferior goods.

b. substitutes.

c. both substitutes and complements.

d. complements.

e. normal goods.

Answer: d

This requires knowledge of substitutes.

14. Bad harvests often cause prices to rise because

a. supply creates its own demand.

b. the supply curve shifts to the right.

c. the supply curve shifts to the left.

d. the demand curve shifts.

e. the quantity supplied falls.

Answer: c

The concept that is important here is competitive equilibrium.

15. The effect of an increase in student incomes and an increase in the cost of ink on the equilibrium price and quantity of *new* textbooks is

a. indeterminate with respect to price, while quantity increases.

b. indeterminate with respect to price, while quantity decreases.

c. to decrease price, while quantity is indeterminate.

d. to increase price, while quantity is indeterminate.

Answer: d

An understanding of the concept of comparative statics is tested here.

16. Which of the following is correct? The marginal cost curve
    a. intersects the average variable cost curve at its minimum after it intersects the average total cost curve at its minimum.
    b. intersects the average variable cost curve at its minimum before it intersects the average total cost curve at its minimum.
    c. must be between average variable costs and average total costs.
    d. is above the average total cost curve when the average total cost is falling.
    e. is usually the same as the average variable cost curve.

Answer: b

A correct answer requires a knowledge of cost curves.

17. The incidence of taxation is
    a. who actually collects a tax.
    b. the distribution of the burden of the tax before prices adjust to the tax.
    c. the distribution of taxes between income and sales taxes.
    d. how often in the year sales taxes are collected.
    e. the distribution of the burden after higher prices are taken into account.

Answer: e

This question requires familiarity with competitive equilibrium and taxation concepts.

18. The price elasticity of demand is the
    a. percentage fall in quantity demanded associated with a 1 dollar rise in price.
    b. percentage fall in quantity demanded divided by the percentage rise in price.
    c. percentage fall in price divided by the percentage rise in quantity demanded.
    d. percentage fall in price when it is less than the percentage increase in quantity demanded.
    e. change in demand divided by the change in price.

Answer: b

Elasticity is the key concept in this question.

19. When demand is price-inelastic,
    a. a higher price lowers total revenue.
    b. a lower price raises total revenue.
    c. price and revenue change in the same direction.

d. price and revenue change in different directions.

e. a higher price raises total revenue only if consumers purchase more of the good.

Answer: c

20. **Demand will tend to be more price-elastic for a product that**

a. is a small portion of the budget.

b. is a necessity.

c. has many substitutes.

d. has very few substitutes.

Answer: c

21. **If airline revenues rise as a consequence of discount fares, the demand for airline travel must be**

a. income-elastic.

b. price-inelastic.

c. unitary price-elastic.

d. price-elastic.

e. perfectly price-elastic.

Answer: d

22. **The tax burden of a good will**

a. be borne by the consumer if the good is scarce.

b. be borne by the producer if it is a perfect competitor.

c. be borne by only the producer if demand is perfectly inelastic.

d. be borne by only the consumer if demand is perfectly inelastic.

Answer: d

23. **The demand for personal computers is**

a. more inelastic than the demand for the IBM personal computer.

b. as elastic as the demand for the IBM personal computer.

c. unitary-elastic, as is the demand for the IBM personal computer.

d. less elastic than the demand for table salt.

Answer: a

This question requires an understanding of the determinants of elasticity.

24. Perfectly inelastic demand

a. is illustrated by a vertical demand curve.

b. is the case in which quantity demanded is least responsive to price.

c. usually occurs within some range of prices.

d. is all of the above.

Answer: d

This requires knowledge of elasticity.

25. Preferences are

a. people's evaluations of goods once they have considered their budget.

b. what people buy at a given income level.

c. what people buy at a given price.

d. the same as demand.

e. none of the above.

Answer: e

The relevant concept is consumer theory.

26. The consumer is in equilibrium if

a. utility is being maximized by the proper allocation of expenditure.

b. all income is spent on goods in such a way that the marginal utility of an extra penny spent on the good is the same for each good.

c. total utility falls whenever spending is reallocated.

d. the utility lost by spending a penny less on one good just equals the utility gained by spending a penny more on an alternative good.

e. all of the above are true.

Answer: e

Consumer theory is the central issue in this question.

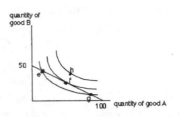

27. Use the figure above to answer this question. The consumer maximizes his or her satisfaction at point
    a. *e.*
    b. *f.*
    c. *g.*
    d. *h.*

Answer: b

28. Use the figure to answer this question. The price of good A divided by the price of good B is
    a. 50.
    b. 100.
    c. 1/2.
    d. 2.

Answer: c

29. Use the figure to answer this question. In equilibrium, the marginal rate of substitution (MRS) is
    a. 100.
    b. 50.
    c. 2.
    d. 0.5.
    e. impossible to calculate.

Answer: d

30. Use the figure to answer this question. Points *e* and *g*

    a. give the consumer the same amount of utility.

    b. cost the same.

    c. do not maximize utility.

    d. are not as good as point *f*.

    e. do all of the above.

Answer: e

Consumer theory.

31. From the shareholder's point of view, the main advantage of the corporation is

    a. that liability is limited.

    b. that corporations pay dividends.

    c. management by professional managers.

    d. that corporations can retain undistributed profits.

    e. that corporations can raise large amounts of capital by issuing new stock.

Answer: a

This tests understanding of types of firms and the concept of limited liability.

32. The major advantage(s) of a single proprietorship is (are)

    a. limited liability and the ability to plow back profits.

    b. that the owner has full control of the business and that it is simple to set up.

    c. that the owner must personally raise capital.

    d. that the owner can issue shares to partners.

    e. that the owner can raise more financial capital than the corporation.

Answer: b

This requires knowledge of types of firms.

33. The principal/agent problem refers to the fact that

    a. partnerships tend to be very large.

    b. the principal and the principal's agent have different goals and objectives.

    c. corporations can raise more capital than other business forms.

    d. agents are the eyes and ears of the principal.

    e. principals do not carry out the orders of their agents.

Answer: b

Relevant concepts are types of firms and principal/agent problems.

34. That corporations exist in spite of double taxation suggests that
    a. corporations illegally avoid taxes.
    b. the other advantages of corporations outweigh the disadvantages of double taxation.
    c. dividends are not important to stockholders anyway.
    d. corporations do not seek to maximize after-tax profits.
    e. many stockholders are in relatively low income tax brackets, so double taxation isn't very significant.

Answer: b

The question calls for an understanding of types of firms and the concept of double taxation."

35. Costs that do not vary with output are called
    a. variable costs.
    b. opportunity costs.
    c. total costs.
    d. average costs.
    e. fixed costs.

Answer: e

A correct answer requires an understanding of fixed versus variable costs.

FINAL EXAM

Multiple Choice

The easier questions test the basic knowledge that every student should master in order to pass the class. The more difficult questions and essays test advanced knowledge that a student should gain at this level in order to prepare for more advanced classes. Mediocre grades suggest at this level that the student should question whether he or she should continue in economics.

Always ask yourself what the question is asking. Don't just leap to an answer that looks good. Try to answer the question before looking at the possible answers. Given time, try to determine why each alternative is incorrect.

1. If goods X and Y have a positive cross-elasticity of demand, we know that
    a. they are both inferior goods.

b. they are substitutes.

c. they are complements.

d. they both have price elasticities greater than 1.

Answer: b

This requires an understanding of the concept of cross-price elasticity.

2. All of the following statements about price floors are true except:

a. There will be a surplus of a commodity when a price floor is set above the equilibrium price.

b. The government may have to set up a storage system to handle the excess supply when a price floor is set above the equilibrium price.

c. If the price floor is set below the equilibrium price, the intervention will have no effect on the market.

d. If the price floor is set below the equilibrium price, the price must be reduced.

Answer: d

This tests knowledge of the price floor concept.

3. The demand curves for inferior goods

a. cannot be anything but downward-sloping.

b. are always upward-sloping.

c. will be upward-sloping only if the negative substitution effect is strong enough to offset the income effect.

d. will be upward-sloping only if a negative income effect is strong enough to offset the substitution effect.

Answer: d

Concepts relevant to the question are income and substitution effects and Giffen goods.

4. Sunk costs

a. should have no influence on the decision on what is currently the most profitable thing to do.

b. must be considered when a decision is made on what is the most profitable thing to do.

c. are another term for opportunity cost.

d. indicate that bygones are never really bygones.

Answer: a

This question requires an understanding of sunk as well as fixed costs.

5. New firms will enter a perfectly competitive industry whenever
   a. P > minimum AVC.
   b. P > minimum ATC.
   c. P > MC.
   d. MR > MC.

Answer: b

A correct response requires an understanding of positive profits in a competitive industry.

6. The profit-maximizing monopolist will usually set a price
   a. in the elastic portion of the demand curve.
   b. where the demand has a price elasticity of 1.
   c. in the inelastic portion of the demand curve.
   d. equal to marginal revenue.

Answer: a

Monopoly pricing and the elasticity-revenue relationship are the concepts relevant to answering this question.

7. Economists would be willing to say that price discrimination is more efficient than single-price monopoly pricing if it results in
   a. higher total revenue for the firm.
   b. an increase in the available sum of producer and consumer surplus.
   c. the producer's capturing some of the consumer surplus.
   d. some consumers paying lower prices than under a single-price monopoly.

Answer: b

Understanding of three concepts is relevant to a correct answer: price discrimination, social surplus, and efficiency.

8. A zero-profit equilibrium for a monopolistically competitive firm occurs at an output
   a. less than the one at which average total cost is at a minimum.
   b. at which average total cost is at a minimum.
   c. at which price equals marginal cost and average total cost.

d. greater than the one at which average total cost is at a minimum.

Answer: a

A correct response requires knowing the excess capacity theorem.

9. If an agency regulating a natural monopoly were to set a price equal to marginal cost, all of the following would be true except:

   a. The firm would be losing money.
   b. The output would be greater than if the firm were unregulated.
   c. The price would be less than if the firm were unregulated.
   d. The firm would be operating at capacity.

Answer: d

Natural monopoly and economies of scale are the relevant concepts here.

10. The imposition of an excise tax will reduce output of the product unless

    a. demand is relatively inelastic.
    b. supply is perfectly elastic.
    c. supply is relatively inelastic.
    d. demand is perfectly inelastic.

Answer: d

This question requires familiarity with tax policy and elasticity.

11. The additional revenue earned by a firm when one additional unit of labor is employed is called the

    a. marginal product of labor.
    b. marginal physical product of labor.
    c. marginal revenue product of labor.
    d. marginal cost product.

Answer: c

This draws on knowledge of labor costs and MRP.

12. Which of the following cannot eliminate the deadweight loss due to monopoly?

    a. An excise subsidy
    b. A price ceiling set below the monopoly price

c. Zero-profit regulation

d. Perfect price discrimination

Answer: c

13. Only about 10 percent of the viewers of public television contribute to help pay for the costs of operation. This is an example of

a. the Coase theorem.

b. the principal/agent problem.

c. incomplete property rights.

d. the free rider problem.

Answer: d

14. A horizontal merger occurs when two firms merge that are

a. in the same line of business.

b. in a supplier/buyer relationship.

c. major operators in the same state or locality.

d. in different lines of business.

Answer: a

15. A four-firm concentration ratio indicates the

a. exact degree of oligopoly in an industry.

b. number of firms in a particular industry.

c. percentage of industry sales accounted for by the largest 4 percent of firms in the industry.

d. dollar value of industry sales.

e. percentage of industry output accounted for by the top 4 firms.

Answer: e

16. A conglomerate merger is one in which

a. a company takes over a firm that supplies it with materials.

b. a company takes over another company that markets its products.

c. a vertical merger occurs.

d. a horizontal merger occurs.

e. a company takes over another company in a different line of business.

Answer: e

To answer correctly, the student must understand merger concepts and concentration.

17. In comparing monopoly and perfect competition, which of the following statements is true?

a. Monopolies automatically earn profits; perfectly competitive firms do not.

b. Competitive profits will disappear in the long run as new firms enter the industry; monopoly profits will be protected in the long run by barriers to entry.

c. In the long run, both monopoly and perfect competition produce at minimum average cost.

d. In the short run, both monopoly and perfect competition attempt to minimize average fixed costs.

Answer: b

The key concept set here is barriers to entry.

18. In order to maximize profits, any firm (whether competitive or monopolistic) must follow which of the following rules?

a. If average revenue is less than ATC, the firm should shut down.

b. If average revenue is greater than AVC, the firm should shut down.

c. If the firm should not shut down, it should produce that quantity of output at which MR = MC.

d. If the firm should not shut down, the firm should produce that quantity at which AVC is at a minimum.

Answer: c

The chief concept is profit maximization.

19. At any firm's profit-maximizing output, which of the following *cannot* be true?

a. Price equals average cost.

b. Profits are negative.

c. Price is greater than marginal revenue.

d. Marginal revenue is less than marginal cost.

Answer: d

> Profit maximization is the essential concept in this question.

20. There is economic efficiency whenever

a. a reallocation of resources that helps one person hurts somebody else.

b. resources are adequate to meet society's needs.

c. a reallocation of resources could in principle make everyone better off.

d. a reallocation of resources can make someone better off without hurting someone else.

e. resources are allocated to their lowest-valued uses.

Answer: a

> The correct response requires understanding of Pareto efficiency.

Short Essays: True, False, or Uncertain

> Use sample questions to help you study. Ask what the topic (or the point) of the question is. Ask yourself what other related questions might be asked. On multiple choice questions, don't study the correct answer. Instead, study why the other answers are incorrect and why they are given as plausible alternatives.

1. In a world with no transaction costs, all monopolists would produce like competitors.

Answer: True, if the monopolist is then able to perfectly price-discriminate. With no transaction costs, a firm would be able to satisfy the requirements for successful price discrimination: identification of customers and prevention of resale between markets. With no costs, the firm could identify the willingness to pay for each unit sold and would be able to withhold sale unless the customer contracted not to resell the unit.

> The key point is to recognize that the verb *produce* implies the quantity produced, not the pricing policies. A successful response demonstrates knowledge of price discrimination, the causes of deadweight loss, and the efficiency results of the various market structures.

2. In order to maximize its short-run profits, a competitive firm should operate at the

minimum point on its short-run average cost curve.

Answer: False. A competitive firm should maximize profits by equating MC = P, so long as it covers its variable costs. In the long run, a competitive firm *will* produce at the minimum point of its average cost curve, but as a consequence of the entry of other firms bidding price to that level, not as an overt goal.

> This is a good response because it recognizes that this is not the method for maximizing short-run profits. An even better answer would recognize that this statement is wrong for the long-run case as well. The student demonstrates a clear understanding of competitive profit maximization and the possibility that the competitive equilibrium is not a firm's conscious decision.

3. A monopolist is best off operating on the inelastic portion of the demand curve, where he can charge high prices without losing many customers.

Answer: False. A monopolist maximizes profits by producing on the elastic portion of the demand curve when MC = MR. If the firm were on the inelastic portion, it could increase revenues and decrease costs by producing less, and thus it would not be maximizing profit there. (If the good has a negative marginal cost, then the statement would be true.)

> The first part of the response is the basic fact. The second statement is the simple logic of why this fact is true. The parenthetical expression is beyond what an instructor could expect from most students at this point.
>
> This response demonstrates basic knowledge of the output restrictions under monopoly and also demonstrates the relationship between elasticity and revenue.

4. Everyone wants to pay for public goods because she or he recognizes the public benefits these goods provide.

Answer: False. Individuals wish to free-ride because a public good is nonexcludable and nonrival. Because a public good is nonexcludable, individuals cannot be prevented from enjoying the benefits, whether they pay or not, and because the good is nonrival, they do not compete with others for its consumption. Thus they can enjoy the benefits of the good without contributing anything to its production.

> The response shows an understanding of the idea of free riding and why it occurs with public goods. It further demonstrates knowledge of public goods and their characteristics.

5. Robbery is simply a transfer of wealth from one individual to another, so, from the point of view of one who is interested only in maximizing social surplus, there is nothing wrong with it.

Answer: False. Transactions are always efficiency-improving only if they are voluntary. Like other transfer programs, robbery may improve the utility of the robber by more than the utility lost by the victim, but there is no logical reason why this should always be true. Further, the loss of utility by the victim is likely to greatly exceed the marginal utility of the money lost.

> The student giving this response knows that the question involves a transfer of utility, and understands that voluntary transactions are Pareto improvements, but involuntary ones are not. The response demonstrates knowledge of social surplus and various programs of improvement.

CHAPTER 28

UNIVERSITY OF NOTRE DAME

ECON 115/225: INTRODUCTORY ECONOMICS

Esther-Mirjam Sent, Professor

THREE EXAMS ARE GIVEN IN THIS COURSE, TWO "MIDTERMS" AND A FINAL. INCLUDED here are examples of the midterm exams. The exams are the most important part of the course grade, with each midterm accounting for roughly 27 percent of the grade, and the final (identical in form to the midterms, but longer) accounting for roughly 47 percent.

Professor Sent quotes from the course syllabus: "The methods of economic inquiry are perhaps best described as 'eclectic,' meaning that they are drawn from many sources and selected according to their usefulness to the subject matter. Economists borrow from all the social sciences in order to theorize about human behavior. They borrow from mathematics in order to express theories concisely. And, finally, they borrow from statistics in order to make inferences from real-world data about hypotheses suggested by economic theory.

"Economists are interested in understanding human behavior not only for its own sake, but also because of the policy implications of this knowledge. How can we know what to expect as a result of public policy changes or business decisions unless we understand why people behave the way they do?

"As in other scientific disciplines, theory in economics is an abstraction, or simplification, of innumerable complex relationships in the real world. When thinking about some aspects of behavior, economists will build a model that attempts to explain the behavior under examination. The elements of the model are derived from economic theory. Economists study the model to see what hypotheses, or predictions, are suggested by the model. These can then be checked against real-world data.

"Economists clearly believe that they can make a significant contribution to the discussion and resolution of many important social issues. It is hoped that by the time you finish this course, you will agree with this belief."

Professor Sent hopes to develop in students economic intuition instead of memorization, enabling creative application of the tools learned in class to real-world situations. Accordingly, true/false exam answers are graded for all steps in the reasoning process to stress understanding instead of memorization. Essay questions encourage students to apply economic models. Don't fall behind; don't memorize; apply the learned material whenever possible; focus on intuition and reasoning.

MIDTERM EXAM 1

You have 50 minutes to complete this 50-point examination; allocate your time accordingly. Please be as precise and concise as possible, as statements that are either wrong or irrelevant (or both) will decrease your grade.

Please choose a total of *seven* statements from Parts I and II. If you have chosen *three* statements in Part I, you need to choose *four* statements in Part II. If you have chosen *four* statements in Part I, you need to choose *three* statements in Part II.

Good luck!

I. (15 or 20 points) *Choose* three *or* four *(only) of the following four statements (for a combined total of* seven *statements for Parts I and II) and indicate whether they are "true," "false" or "uncertain."* Please provide the reasons for your answer. Each is worth 5 points credit.

1. **The opportunity cost of going to an ND football game is only the fact that you could have sold your ticket and spent the money on buying a television. (Explain in detail.)**
Answer: False.
The opportunity cost of going to an ND football game is the best alternative use of the money spent on the ticket and the time spent at the game. For some people, the best alternative use of the money is buying a television; for others, it's something else.

> 2 points are awarded for mentioning the best alternative use of money; 2 points for mentioning the best alternative use of time; and 1 point for mentioning that these best alternatives are different for different people.

2. **Since the cross-elasticity of the demand for tapes with respect to the price of CDs is positive, the price of tapes will increase in response to an increase in the price of**

CDs. (Use a graph in your explanation.)

Answer: True.

The cross-elasticity of the demand for tapes with respect to the price of CDs is positive because tapes and CDs are substitutes. The magnitude of the cross-elasticity tells us the magnitude of the shift in demand. An increase in the price of CDs causes people to buy fewer CDs and more tapes, thereby shifting the demand curve for tapes to the right. This causes an increase in the price of tapes. Specifically, when the P for CDs increases, the demand curve for tapes will shift out from D_1 to D_2. After equilibrium is restored in the market for tapes, the price of tapes will be higher, at P(B).

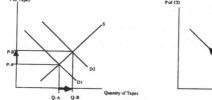

1 point is awarded for mentioning (and briefly explaining) that tapes and CDs are substitutes, 1 point for mentioning that the cross-elasticity of demand is positive for substitutes, 2 points for a correct graph (only 1 point if there's no supply curve), and 1 point for a correct explanation of the graph (points are deducted if the axes are not labeled or are incorrectly labeled).

3. Suppose that a leftward shift of the supply curve of ND T-shirts, caused by the UPS strike, decreases the total revenue of the bookstore. You could conclude that the demand for ND T-shirts is elastic. (Use one graph with relatively inelastic demand and one graph with relatively elastic demand in your explanation.)

Answer: True

The answer requires one graph with inelastic demand (steep) and one graph with elastic demand (flat) in which S shifts to the left. Graphs should illustrate that total revenue (P × Q) increases with inelastic demand and decreases with elastic demand. When price and quantity change, the total revenue (TR) will go down (up) in the elastic (inelastic) case.

Answer:

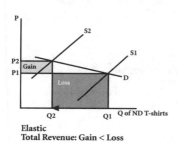

Elastic
Total Revenue: Gain < Loss

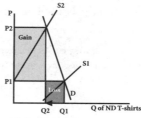

Inelastic
Total Revenue: Gain > Loss

1 point (each) is awarded for *D* curves with the correct slope, 1 point (each) for illustrating revenue change in each graph, and 1 point for a correct explanation of the graph (points are deducted if the axes are not labeled or incorrectly labeled).

4. Since U.S. workers lose their jobs when the United States buys cars from Japan or shoes from Brazil, these industries should be protected. (Explain in detail who benefits and who loses from protection.)

Answer: False (uncertain).

Car and shoe workers and firms benefit from protection; they keep their jobs. Consumers of cars and shoes lose from protection because they have to buy cars and shoes at higher domestic prices. The case against protection is the comparative advantage argument: Countries benefit from trading according to their comparative advantage.

2 points are awarded for explaining who benefits and why, 2 points for explaining who loses and why, and 1 point for explaining why protection, in general, isn't a good idea.

II. (15 or 20 points) *Choose three or four (only) of the following four statements (for a combined total of seven statements for Parts I and II) and indicate whether they are "true," "false," or "it depends." Please provide the reasons for your answer. Each is worth 5 points credit.*

5. If the Netherlands excels at producing cheese and the United States excels at producing chocolate-chip cookies, the Netherlands should export cheese and the United States should export chocolate-chip cookies. (Use one graph for the Netherlands and one graph for the United States to show which trade pattern will emerge and why. You may assume constant opportunity cost.)

Answer: True.

Since the Netherlands has a comparative advantage in cheese and the United States has a comparative advantage in cookies, the Netherlands should export cheese and import cookies, and the United States should export cookies and import cheese.

The PPFs of the two countries must have different slopes and PPFs shift as a result of trade (illustrating that the two countries benefit when they start trading).

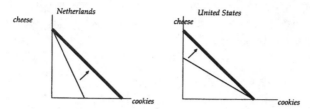

The PPFs of both countries shift with trade.

1 point is awarded for mentioning comparative advantage, 1 point (each) for correct slope in each graph, 1 point for correctly shifting each PPF as a result of trade, and 1 point for indicating that both countries therefore benefit from trade (points are deducted if the axes are not labeled or are incorrectly labeled).

6. A fall in the unemployment rate shifts the production possibility frontier outward. (Use a graph in your explanation.)

Answer: False.

The PPF gives efficient combinations of goods (those that are produced when all factors of production are used). Unemployment means that we're inside the PPF. A fall in the unemployment rate causes us to move closer to the PPF, but it doesn't move the PPF. The graph must illustrate this.

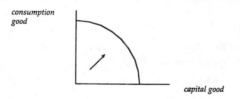

With a fall in unemployment, we go from a point inside PPF (inefficient) toward the frontier (efficient).

3 points are awarded for a correct graph (the PPF doesn't shift, but the point inside the PPF shifts), and 2 points for the correct explanation (the PPF is efficient, inside the PPF is inefficient).

7. Given what you know about the income elasticity of demand for cars, the demand curve for cars will shift to the right in response to an increase in income. (Use a graph in your explanation. Justify your assumption regarding the income elasticity of demand for cars.)

Answer: True.

Cars are a normal good, so they have a positive income elasticity of demand (when income goes up, demand for cars goes up). Therefore, an increase in income causes the demand curve for cars to shift to the right (demand increases for any price as a result of the income increase).

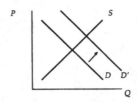

2 points are awarded for mentioning and explaining positive income elasticity, 2 points for a correct graph (*D* shifts right), and 1 point for the explanation of the graph (points are deducted if the axes are not labeled or are incorrectly labeled).

8. Katie and Esther-Mirjam are taking a ballet class that has a fixed number of spots, but Maiju had to join the waiting list. This surplus will cause the price of the class to increase. (Use a graph in your explanation. Go through the adjustment mechanism.)

Answer: False.

Yes. But *true* could be correct as well, depending on how the student interprets *surplus*. One could argue correctly that there's a *surplus of students*.

Since there's excess demand, there's a shortage, not a surplus. *Shortage* means a shortage of spots. The shortage (not a surplus) will indeed cause the price of the class to increase. The adjustment mechanism is that people who didn't make it into the class will offer to pay a higher price to get in, until the equilibrium price has been reached.

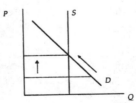

The supply curve is vertical because there is a fixed number of spots.

1 point is awarded for getting *shortage* right (excess demand is okay as well, and so is surplus of students), 1 point for drawing a vertical supply curve, 1 point for indicating that the price is below the equilibrium price, 1 point for showing in the graph that the price will increase (and that the curves do not shift!), and 1 point for explaining why the price will increase (points are deducted if the axes are not labeled or incorrectly labeled).

III. (15 points) *Turn in your take-home essay on Friday, September 26 at the start of your discussion class.*

Longer take-home essays are given in addition to the in-class exams. The material is not included here.

MIDTERM EXAM 2

How should you study economics? Not! Instead, you should practice. Active learning is the only way to learn the material. Do not waste valuable hours trying to remember masses of material. Do not become overwhelmed by the details. Instead, concentrate on the overall structure. The text has literally thousands of important details but only a dozen or so major themes.

Most students are generally much more interested in discussing current economic issues than in learning abstract economic theory and reasoning. To bring the course material to life, we will make an effort to relate economic theory to real-world events and incorporate a variety of interesting and relevant examples into class discussions.

People learn in a variety of different ways. In economics, some do best with a graphical approach, some like algebra, others find that computer simulation provides the sudden "Aha!" Try to fight any anxiety about mathematics or graphs that you might have. The text and the lectures provide a number of different paths to knowledge. Furthermore, you could consider buying the available computer software or the study guide.

Although lecture attendance is not generally recorded, you should recognize that performance in a course is usually positively correlated with attendance and that, from an economic perspective, it only makes sense to consume what you have paid for! Furthermore, part of your final grade is determined by class participation. Take the problem sets seriously. Study with a friend. Do not hesitate to come by during office hours or make an appointment if you have questions.

You have 50 minutes to complete this 50-point examination; allocate your time accordingly. Please be as precise and concise as possible, as statements that are either wrong or irrelevant (or both) will decrease your grade.

Please choose a total of *seven* statements from Parts I and II. If you have chosen *three* statements in Part I, you need to choose *four* statements in Part II. If you have chosen *four* statements in Part I, you need to choose *three* statements in Part II.

Good luck!

I. (15 or 20 points) *Choose* three *or* four *(only) of the following four statements (for a combined total of* seven *statements for Parts I and II) and indicate whether they are "true," "false" or "uncertain."* Please provide the reasons for your answer. Each is worth 5 points credit.

1. In moving from perfect competition to a single-price monopoly, all the surplus lost

by consumers is captured by the monopoly. (Use one graph for perfect competition and one graph for a single-price monopoly in your explanation. Make sure you label each relevant area in your graph.)

Answer: False.

While some of the surplus lost by consumers is captured by the single-price monopoly, some of the surplus will disappear into deadweight loss. In perfect competition, consumer surplus is simply the area between the equilibrium price and the demand curve. Conversely, producer surplus is the area between the equilibrium price and the supply (marginal cost) curve.

In a single-price monopoly, the producer limits output to the point determined by the intersection of the marginal revenue and marginal cost (supply) curves. This point has higher price and lower output. Some of the previous surplus goes to deadweight loss, and some is captured by the monopoly at the cost of the consumer. The deadweight loss is the surplus lost to society because the monopoly has restricted output to a less than socially efficient level.

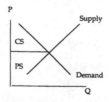

CS = consumer surplus
PS = producer surplus
d = deadweight loss

2 points are awarded for correct depiction of the consumer/producer surplus for perfect competition, 2 points for correct depiction of the consumer/producer surplus and deadweight loss for monopoly, and 1 point for the explanation of changes in consumer/producer surplus and deadweight loss (points are deducted if the axes/curves are not labeled or incorrectly labeled).

2. For normal goods, an increase in income causes a rightward shift of both the budget line and the demand curve. (Use one graph with a budget line and one with a demand curve in your explanation. Discuss the connection between the two graphs.)

Answer: True.

Since more of both goods can be purchased, an increase in income causes a parallel shift of the budget line. As a result, an indifference curve further away from the origin can be reached, and more of both goods, since we are assuming normal goods, will be demanded. Given the definition of normal goods, an increase in income causes an increase in the demand for normal goods. Since the demand for normal goods increases as a result of an increase in income, for any given price, this causes a rightward shift of the demand curve rather than a movement along the curve.

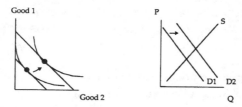

Parallel diagonals reflect budget lines.
Curves are indifference curves.

> 1 point is awarded for a correct rightward/parallel shift of the budget line, 1 point for a correct shift of indifference curve (tangent to the budget line), 1 point for a correct rightward shift of the demand curve, 1 point for the explanation of the shift of the budget line/indifference curve, and 1 point for the explanation of the shift of the demand curve (points are deducted if the axes/curves are not labeled or incorrectly labeled).

3. A perfectly competitive firm's supply curve is its entire marginal cost curve. (Use a graph in your explanation. Explain in detail how the supply curve is derived.)
Answer: False.
A perfectly competitive firm's supply curve is its marginal cost curve above the average variable cost curve, at least in the short run. It's the marginal cost curve because profit is maximized when $MR = MC$. Whenever MR changes, its new intersection with MC will determine how much the firm will supply. When MR is less than AVC, the firm will shut down. In the short run, it cannot influence its fixed cost, but it needs to make up at least its variable cost. That's why it won't produce when MR is less than AVC.

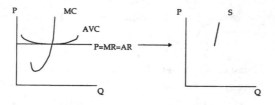

2 points are awarded for showing that the supply curve is the MC curve in the graph, 1 point for showing that the supply curve is above the AVC curve in the graph, 1 point for the explanation concerning profit maximization (MR = MC), and 1 point for the explanation of why firms operate with a loss in the short run (P > AVC, not necessarily P > ATC). (Points are deducted if the axes/curves are not labeled or incorrectly labeled; also, points deducted if curves do not have the proper shape/position, such as AVC not reaching its minimum at its intersection with MC.)

4. The fact that rubies are more expensive than milk reflects the fact that, for most consumers, the total utility from rubies exceeds that from milk. (Use an equation in your explanation of the mechanism responsible for this.)

Answer: False.

Rubies are more expensive than milk because, for most consumers, the *marginal* utility from rubies exceeds that from milk. Since people don't consume many rubies and do consume a lot of milk, the marginal utility from rubies is large and the marginal utility from milk is small. This follows from the law of diminishing marginal utility. The relevant equation that explains this further is

$$MU(\text{rubies})/P(\text{rubies}) = MU(\text{milk})/P(\text{milk})$$

With MU(rubies) high and MU(milk) low, it follows that P(rubies) is high and P(milk) is low.

1 point is awarded for mentioning that it's marginal utility, not total utility, that counts, 1 point for mention of the law of diminishing marginal utility, 1 point for the explanation of the law of diminishing marginal utility (low consumption → high MU, high consumption → low MU), 1 point for the equation, and 1 point for the explanation of the equation (low MU → low P, high MU → high P).

II. (15 or 20 points) *Choose* three *or* four *(only) of the following four statements (for a combined total of* seven *statements for Parts I and II) and indicate whether they are "true," "false" or "it depends."* Please provide the reasons for your answer. Each is worth 5 points credit.

5. From the perspective of allocative efficiency, it is better to tax liquor than to tax lemonade. (Use one graph for the market for liquor and one for the market for lemonade in your explanation. Focus on the relationship among excise tax, elasticity of demand, and allocative efficiency.)

Answer: True.

From the perspective of allocative efficiency, it is better to tax liquor rather than lemonade, because there is a *smaller deadweight loss*.

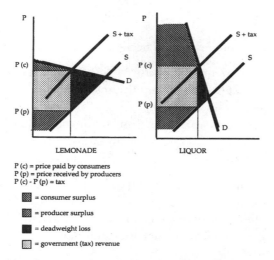

P (c) = price paid by consumers
P (p) = price received by producers
P (c) - P (p) = tax

▨ = consumer surplus

▨ = producer surplus

■ = deadweight loss

▦ = government (tax) revenue

Implementation of an excise tax shifts the supply curve to the *left* in both cases, increasing the price and decreasing the quantity demanded.

The demand curve for liquor is steeper than that for lemonade. The slopes of the demand curves reflect the elasticity of the good's demand. Since the demand for liquor is inelastic, the slope of its demand curve is steep, and since the demand for lemonade is elastic, the slope of its demand curve is relatively less steep.

In each case, imposing a tax creates a deadweight loss. However, the deadweight loss created by taxing liquor is less than that created by taxing lemonade. *Deadweight loss is an indication of allocative inefficiency*. Therefore, *from the perspective of allocative efficiency*, it is better to tax liquor.

---

1 point is awarded for graphing the shift of the supply curve to the left correctly in both graphs, 1 point for graphing the demand curves correctly in relation to each other (i.e., showing that the slope of the demand curve for liquor is steeper), 1 point for explaining in words the reason for the shift of the supply curve and the differences in the slopes of the demand curves, 1 point for correctly illustrating the deadweight losses in both graphs, and 1 point for explaining that the tax creates a smaller deadweight loss when taxing liquor than when taxing lemonade, and that, therefore, from the perspective of allocative efficiency, it is better to tax liquor than lemonade.

Note that giving an explanation that government taxes a good with more inelastic demand because this results in higher government revenue is considered *incorrect* in the context of the question. The question asks whether the statement is true *from the perspective of allocative efficiency*.

Using incorrect graphs, mislabeling or not labeling curves or axes, and making incorrect statements are penalized depending on the severity of the error.

---

6. An increase in normal profit causes an increase in economic profit. (Explain the difference between normal and economic profit. Make sure you include a discussion

of all components of firms' costs in your explanation.)

Answer: False.

An increase in normal profit results in a decrease in economic profit.

Economic profit = total revenue - opportunity cost (including normal profit)

Opportunity cost = explicit costs + implicit costs

Explicit costs = costs paid with money

Implicit costs = costs incurred by the firm, not directly paid with money, more specifically (1) cost of capital, (2) cost of inventories, and (3) cost of owners' resources (normal profit).

Normal profit = compensation the owner receives for supplying his or her entrepreneurial ability

Since normal profit is part of the opportunity cost of the firm, under the *ceteris paribus* (everything else staying constant) assumption, its increase will cause a decrease in economic profit.

> 1 point is awarded for defining economic profit correctly, 1 point for explaining clearly the difference between explicit and implicit costs, 1 point for discussing the three components of implicit costs, 1 point for defining normal profit correctly, and 1 point for explaining the difference/relationship between economic and normal profit.
> Making incorrect statements and giving incorrect definitions were penalized depending on the severity of the error.

7. When the interest rate increases, both the income effect and the substitution effect cause an increase in saving. (Explain in words.)

Answer: False.

Because the substitution and income effects work against each other, the impact of an increase in interest rate on savings is *uncertain*.

Increase in interest rate → (consumers decide between consumption and saving)

Substitution Effect: An interest rate increase causes an increase in saving, because the *opportunity cost* of not saving (consuming) increases along with the interest rate. Therefore, saving becomes a more attractive option.

Income Effect: An interest rate increase decreases saving, since, as a result of the higher return, not as much needs to be saved in order to end up with the same level of income.

The *net effect* of an interest rate increase on saving is uncertain, because in this case, the income and substitution effects work against each other.

> The following is not required for the answer, but is nonetheless relevant: Since the substitution effect generally outweighs the income effect, the likely effect of an interest rate increase is an increase in saving.
>
> 2 points are awarded for explaining the income effect correctly, 2 points for explaining the substitution effect correctly, and 1 point for discussing the net effect correctly.
>
> Partial credit is given for getting the *directions* of the substitution and income effects correctly. Making incorrect statements and giving incorrect definitions are penalized depending on the severity of the error.

8. Suppose the demand for diapers increases as a result of a baby boom. Over time, other firms will enter the diaper industry, so that both price and economic profits fall. (Use one graph for a firm and one graph for supply and demand in your explanation. Make sure you indicate economic profits in the graph for a firm.)

Answer: True.

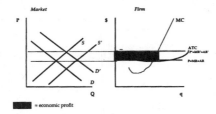

Short Run: The baby boom increases diaper demand, so that demand shifts from D to D', and causes firms to start earning economic profit. The demand shift increases market price, which at the firm level shifts the P = MR = AR curve upward to P'= MR' = AR'. As firms maximize their profits by equating MC = MR, a new short-run equilibrium point is found at MR'= MC, where economic profit is indicated by the shaded area.

Long Run: In a perfectly competitive industry, if a typical firm is earning economic profit, we would expect other firms to enter the market in the long run. Thus, the market supply curve will shift to the right, increasing industry output and driving down the market price. Since perfectly competitive firms are price takers (i.e., demand for the individual firm's output is perfectly elastic), the firm will see its horizontal demand/MR curve shift downward. In the long run, the entry of firms into the market will have driven down the price to the point at which the perfectly competitive firm earns only normal profit (i.e., zero economic profit). This point is long-run equilibrium, where MR = MC = ATC (at its minimum).

3 points are awarded for a correct and clear depiction of short-run and long-run equilibrium for the firm, showing economic profit in the short run and zero economic profit in the long run, 1 point for correct depiction of the demand and supply shifts for the market, and 1 point for a proper explanation of the shifts of the curves.

Points are deducted if the axes or curves are labeled incorrectly, or are not labeled, if curves do not have the proper shape/position, such as ATC not reaching its minimum at its intersection with MC, or if the wrong curves are shifted. Making incorrect statements, and giving incorrect definitions are penalized depending on the severity of the error."

III. (15 points) *Turn in your take-home essay on Friday, September 26 at the start of your discussion class.*

Students were required to create a take-home essay in addition to the in-class exam.

CHAPTER 29

ECON 202: MACROECONOMICS PRINCIPLES

Scott William Fausti, Associate Professor of Economics

THREE EXAMS ARE GIVEN IN THIS COURSE, TWO FIVE WEEKS APART AND A FINAL. THEY are all multiple-choice exams; on the two "midterm" exams, there are also true-or-false questions. One midterm and one final are included here.

The primary objectives of this course are to introduce the student to basic economic principles, to foster student understanding of how economic principles affect their everyday decisions, and to encourage students to think about selecting Economics as a major.

I try to encourage my students to think "outside the box," to look at their own lives and the decisions they make in the context of the basic economic principles I teach them, and to analyze issues and events occurring at the local, state, national, and global level. I want them to see the importance of identifying the economic forces that produce the issues and events that affect them, and then to think about the consequences of these events for their own lives and how they should adjust their behavior or plans, given a particular change in the economic environment around them.

EXAM 1

The first 15 questions are true/false questions. The final 30 questions are multiple-choice questions. Take your time, and good luck.

I try to frame my exam questions in the context of the topics I have discussed in class. I realize that it is difficult to design multiple-choice or true/false questions that are directly linked to a particular economic or political event. This is the shortcoming of these types of questions. Thus my questions focus on the basic concepts I have taught in class. Students should attend class, read the book, and ask questions about concepts that are not well understood.

1. An example of a positive economic issue would be the relationship between the price of pizza and the quantity of pizza demanded.
Answer: T

2. Economists consider the topic of inflation to be a macroeconomic issue.
Answer: T

3. Economists define extensive economic growth as the ability of a country to increase its output of final goods and services through technological innovation.
Answer: F

4. The relative price of a good or service is the monetary price of that good or service.
Answer: F

5. When a market supply curve shifts, economists say that this is caused by a change in demand.
Answer: F

6. If the government imposes a price ceiling in the market for corn, then we would expect a surplus of corn in the market for corn.
Answer: F

I tell my students that for this type of question, they should draw a diagram to find the correct answer.

7. The primary role of an economic system in society is to set prices for goods and services produced.
Answer: F

8. There is a positive relationship between a country's economic growth rate and its rate of saving.
Answer: T

9. With respect to exhaustive expenditures, state and local governments account for a larger share of total public spending than the federal government.
Answer: T

10. Transfer payments are simply transfers of goods and services from one income group to another in society.
Answer: F

11. Inflation is defined as an increase in the general price level.
Answer: T

12. Transactions costs are the costs associated with bringing buyers and sellers together in the market.
Answer: T

13. The largest source of household income in the United States is wages and salaries.
Answer: T

14. Sole proprietorships are the most common type of business organization in the United States.
Answer: T

15. The U.S. income tax is considered to be a regressive tax.
Answer: F

The final 30 questions are multiple-choice questions.

My class enrollment is well over 100 students per section. My midterm exams contain approximately two-thirds multiple-choice questions and one-third true/false questions. My final exam has 60 multiple-choice questions. I tell my students that they should read each exam question twice. If they are unsure of how to answer a particular question, then they should move on to the next question. They may return to the skipped questions when they have finished going through the exam for the first time.

16. When government revenues exceed government expenditures, economists say that the government is running
   a. a budget debt.
   b. a budget deficit.
   c. a budget surplus.

d. none of the above.

Answer: c

17. The absolute price of a good is its price in terms of

    a. units of money.
    b. ounces of gold.
    c. hours of labor.
    d. pounds of tobacco.

Answer: a

18. The price of an apple is $0.50 and the price of a jar of peanut butter is $2.00. The relative price of an apple is

    a. 1/5 jar of peanut butter.
    b. 1/4 jar of peanut butter.
    c. 1/3 jar of peanut butter.
    d. 1/2 jar of peanut butter.

Answer: b

19. If an increase in income results in a decrease in the demand for eggs, then eggs are

    a. a discretionary good.
    b. a luxury good.
    c. a normal good.
    d. an inferior good.

Answer: d

20. As the price of Express Mail rises, the demand for Federal Express rises, therefore Express Mail and Federal Express are

    a. complements.
    b. unrelated goods.
    c. substitutes.
    d. neutral goods.
    e. none of the above.

Answer: c

> I tell my students that for this type of question, they should draw a diagram to find the correct answer.

21. Suppose that in the market for blue-jeans, the supply of jeans has changed. This means that

a. at all prices, firms are now willing to supply a different quantity of jeans to the market.

b. at some prices, firms are now willing to purchase a different quantity of jeans than they previously were willing to purchase.

c. firms are producing more jeans.

d. firms are producing fewer jeans.

Answer: a

22. The law of demand states that price and quantity demanded are

a. inversely related, *ceteris paribus.*

b. directly related, *ceteris paribus.*

c. not related.

d. fixed.

Answer: a

23. The economic concept of "the invisible hand" was first discussed by:

a. James Buchanan

b. Adam Smith

c. David Ricardo

d. Alfred Marshall

Answer: b

24. The assumption(s) made concerning an economy that is positioned on its production possibility curve is (are)

a. that it's at full employment.

b. that it's producing at maximum efficiency.

c. that although its resources are fixed in supply, they can be used to produce a variety of different goods.

d. all of the above.

Answer: d

25. Consider two points on the production possibilities frontier: point *A*, at which there are 10 apples and 20 pears, and point *B*, at which there are 7 apples and 21 pears. If the economy is currently at point *B*, the opportunity cost of moving to point *A* is

a. 1 pear.

b. 7 apples.

c. 3 apples.

d. 21 pears.

Answer: a

I tell my students that for this type of question, they should draw a diagram to find the correct answer.

26. The upward and downward fluctuations in economic activity are usually referred to as
    a. business troughs.
    b. business cycles.
    c. economic recessions.
    d. business peaks.
Answer: b

27. The factors of production are
    a. labor, money, and land.
    b. labor, financial capital, and machinery.
    c. labor, land, and capital.
    d. labor, capital, and entrepreneurship.
    e. none of the above.
Answer: c

28. The government's macroeconomic role in the economy is most closely related to the goal of
    a. ensuring high employment and sustained economic growth.
    b. setting appropriate rules for business.
    c. providing public goods.
    d. controlling monopolies and collecting taxes.
Answer: a

29. The concept of a public good is best described by the following characteristic(s):
    a. nonrival
    b. highly profitable
    c. nonexclusive
    d. a and c
    e. b and c
Answer: d

30. Assume that the CPI was 90 in 1970 and 120 in 1987. What is the change in the general price level for the period from 1970 to 1987?
    a. Approximately 10 percent
    b. Approximately 15 percent

c. Approximately 20 percent

d. Approximately 25 percent

e. Approximately 33 percent

Answer: e

31. An unindexed progressive income tax structure combined with inflation can

a. push taxpayers into higher tax brackets even though their real income has remained constant.

b. pull taxpayers into lower tax brackets even though their real income has remained constant.

c. redistribute buying power away from taxpayers to government.

d. do both a and c.

e. do both b and c.

Answer: d

32. The Bureau of Labor Statistics would place a "discouraged worker" in the following category:

a. in the labor force

b. not in the labor force

c. employed

d. unemployed

Answer: b

33. Frictional unemployment is caused by

a. the business cycle.

b. workers' job skills becoming obsolete.

c. inflation.

d. voluntary job changes by workers.

Answer: b

34. If government tax policy is based on the "ability-to-pay principle," then government tax policy would be to levy only

a. proportional taxes.

b. progressive taxes.

c. regressive taxes.

d. fair taxes.

Answer: b

35. The U.S. unemployment rate equals

a. the number of employed persons divided by the number of unemployed persons.

b. the number of unemployed persons divided by the number of people in the labor force.

c. the number of unemployed persons divided by the number of people in the population.

d. the number of employed persons divided by the number of people in the labor force.

Answer: b

36. **Economic (business cycle) indicators that parallel the business cycle are known as**

a. coincident indicators.

b. lagging indicators.

c. leading indicators.

d. limping indicators.

Answer: a

37. **Which sector of the economy generates the largest proportion of employment in the U.S. economy?**

a. Household sector

b. Public sector

c. Government sector

d. Business sector

Answer: d

38. **The economic concept of "economies of scale" is most closely related to the economic concept of**

a. public goods.

b. economic systems.

c. supply and demand.

d. specialization.

Answer: d

Use these PPFs for Questions 39 to 41:

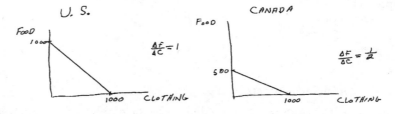

39. Assume that the PPF diagrams above represent the U.S. and Canada. Each country produces two goods, food and clothing. If the U.S. allocates all its resources to the production of only one good, it can produce 1000 units of food or 1000 units of clothing. If Canada allocates all its resources to the production of only one good, it can produce 500 units of food or 1000 units of clothing. According to David Ricardo, each country should specialize in the production of the good for which it has the lowest opportunity cost and then trade for the other good.

According to Ricardo's theory, _____ has an absolute advantage in food production and _____ has a comparative advantage in clothing production.

a. Canada, Canada
b. U.S., Canada
c. U.S., U.S.
d. Canada, U.S.

Answer: b

40. If the U.S. and Canada follow the advice of Ricardo, then the U.S. will produce _____ units of _____ and Canada will produce _____ units of _____.

a. 1000, food, 500, food
b. 1000, clothing, 500, food
c. 1000, clothing, 1000, clothing
d. 1000, food, 1000, clothing

Answer: d

41. In the above diagram, the opportunity cost in terms of food production when the U.S. increases clothing production is

a. constant.
b. decreasing.
c. increasing.
d. none of the above.

Answer: a

42. However, according to David Ricardo, the PPF of the U.S. is concave instead of linear. Therefore, Ricardo would argue that the opportunity cost in terms of food production when the U.S. increases clothing production should be:

a. constant.
b. decreasing.
c. increasing.
d. none of the above.

Answer: c

43. Ricardo credits the concave shape of the country's PPF to
   a. the law of comparative advantage.
   b. the law of demand.
   c. the principle of substitution.
   d. the law of diminishing returns.

Answer: d

The following table represents the market demand and supply schedules for butter in Canada (Questions 44 and 45).

Price ($)	Q_S (Pounds)	Q_D (Pounds)
0.50	110,000	190,000
1.00	150,000	150,000
1.50	190,000	110,000
2.00	210,000	70,000
2.50	250,000	40,000

44. The equilibrium price and quantity in the Canada butter market is $P_E=$_____ and $Q_E=$_____ .
   a. $1, 150,000
   b. $2, 70,000
   c. $0.50, 110,000
   d. $1.50, 190,000

Answer: a

45. The government decides that the equilibrium price of butter is too high and implements a price ceiling of $0.50 a pound to protect Canadian consumers. The effect of this policy will be to generate a _____ of _____ pounds of butter.
   a. shortage, 80,000
   b. surplus, 20,000
   c. shortage, 40,000
   d. surplus, 80,000
   e. surplus, 140,000

Answer: a

FINAL EXAM

I provide old exams. I encourage my students to work through the questions to sharpen their skills at answering abstract questions dealing with economic concepts.

1. The basic fact of economic life is that resources are scarce, people have unlimited wants, and thus choices must be made. This basic fact generates

   a. opportunity cost.
   b. unemployment.
   c. competition.
   d. monopolies.

   Answer: a

2. The law of supply is illustrated by a curve that is

   a. horizontal.
   b. downward sloping to the right.
   c. vertical.
   d. upward sloping to the right.

   Answer: d

3. In general, a market supply curve will not shift when

   a. the price of a good increases.
   b. rising input prices provide producers with the incentives needed to overcome rising opportunity costs.
   c. consumer income increases.
   d. technology improves over time, increasing the ability of firms to produce more at existing prices.

   Answer: a

4. A change in quantity demanded refers to

   a. a percentage increase in price in response to an increase in quantity demanded.
   b. the demand curve shifting.
   c. the maximum amount that consumers will pay for increased quantity.
   d. a movement along the demand curve.

   Answer: d

5. Economic growth is defined as an increase in

   a. nominal GDP.
   b. the factors of production.
   c. real GDP.
   d. the general price level.

   Answer: c

6. Gross domestic product is defined as

a. the total market value of all final goods and services produced annually within the borders of a country.

b. the total market value of all final and intermediate goods and services produced annually in an economy.

c. the total market value of all intermediate goods and services produced annually in an economy.

d. the total market value of all final goods and services produced by a country's factors of production over a one-year period.

Answer: a

7. Which of the following would be considered a macroeconomic topic?

a. The price of wheat

b. Government rent control for low-income housing

c. Price supports for agriculture

d. The budget of the federal government

Answer: d

8. That part of a person's income which is not consumed or paid out in taxes is his or her

a. saving.

b. profit.

c. surplus.

d. excess.

Answer: a

9. Which agency of the U.S. government is responsible for the production of U.S. paper currency?

a. The Federal Reserve

b. The U.S. Congress

c. The U.S. Mint

d. The U.S. Treasury

Answer: a

10. The purchasing power of money is determined by the

a. price of money.

b. interest rate.

c. general price level.

d. face value of money.

Answer: c

11. The factors of production are

    a. labor, money, and land

    b. labor, financial capital, and machinery

    c. labor, land, and capital

    d. labor, capital, and entrepreneurship

    e. none of the above.

Answer: c

12. Extensive economic growth is the result of an increase in

    a. factors of production.

    b. technology.

    c. factor productivity.

    d. international trade.

Answer: a

13. A budget deficit occurs when

    a. Aggregate demand is less than aggregate supply.

    b. potential output equals aggregate spending.

    c. planned investment exceeds planned saving.

    d. government spending exceeds tax revenue.

Answer: d

14. The consumer price index is a measure of the

    a. budget deficit.

    b. unemployment rate.

    c. economic growth rate.

    d. inflation rate.

Answer: d

15. The role of a country's economic system is to

    a. allocate scarce resources.

    b. produce goods and services.

    c. set government regulations.

    d. reduce business cycle fluctuations.

Answer: a

16. The definition of total bank reserves is

    a. money supply minus demand deposits.

    b. demand deposits times the legal reserve ratio.

c. excess reserves plus required reserves.

d. excess reserves minus required reserves.

e. assets minus liabilities.

Answer: c

17. A single bank in a multibank system is allowed by law to loan out its

a. customer demand deposits.

b. excess reserves.

c. required reserves.

d. net worth.

e. legal reserves.

Answer: b

18. If the required reserve ratio is 20 percent and Elmer Fudd deposits $5000 in Hicksville Bank, the maximum increase in loans that could be made by this bank would total

a. $4000.

b. $2000.

c. $1000.

d. $5000.

Answer: a

19. The face value of fiat money is

a. less than its intrinsic value as a commodity.

b. greater than its intrinsic value as a commodity.

c. equal to 100 times the money multiplier.

d. equal to its intrinsic value as a commodity.

Answer: b

20. The basic functions of money include serving as a

a. scoring system, relative price mechanism, and liability index.

b. standard of wealth, insurer of stability, and measure of productivity.

c. transfer payment, investment incentive, and interpersonal comparison.

d. measure of debt, interest premium, and exchange rate mechanism.

e. standard unit of account, medium of exchange, and store of value.

Answer: e

21. According to the "Vicious Cycle of Poverty Theory" and the Harrod-Domar model, the solution to Third World poverty is

a. international trade.

b. birth control.

c. democratic government.

d. foreign aid.

Answer: d

22. **If the required reserve ratio = 0.5, then the simple deposit multiplier is**

a. 50 percent

b. 2.

c. 1.

d. 4.

e. 3.

Answer: b

23. **Barter transactions**

a. involve exchanging goods directly for money.

b. hinder factor specialization.

c. are less costly than transactions involving money.

d. occur only in monetary economies.

Answer: b

24. **Which of the following is not included in (M1)?**

a. Coins and currency

b. Demand (transactions) deposits

c. Savings accounts in commercial banks

d. Traveler's checks

Answer: c

25. **The Fed can contract the money supply by**

a. cutting the discount rate.

b. lowering reserve requirements.

c. selling government securities to banks.

d. minting more U.S. coins.

Answer: c

26. **When the Fed expands the money supply,**

a. excess reserves are reduced.

b. total bank reserves decline.

c. interest rates tend to decrease.

   d. investment tends to decrease.

Answer: c

27. The Federal Reserve System was created in 1913. In the context of U.S. history, the Federal Reserve represents the _____ central bank of the United States.

   a. first
   b. second
   c. third
   d. fourth

Answer: c

28. The Federal Reserve requires all _____ to be members of the Federal Reserve System.

   a. state chartered banks
   b. national banks
   c. savings and loan institutions
   d. credit unions

Answer: b

29. The Fed changes the discount rate to

   a. maximize its rate of return on assets.
   b. balance the risk, liquidity, and return on its assets.
   c. signal a change in monetary policy to the financial markets.
   d. regulate the commercial banking sector.

Answer: c

30. Which of the following activities is *not* under the control of the Fed?

   a. Open-market operations
   b. The discount rate
   c. Setting reserve requirements
   d. Setting federal tax rates

Answer: d

31. The Fed signals the financial markets that it is increasing the money supply growth rate by

   a. conducting open-market operations.
   b. raising reserve requirements.
   c. increasing the level of government spending.
   d. lowering the discount rate.
   e. both b and d.

Answer: d

32. If the money supply is 2000 and nominal GNP is 6000, the income velocity of
     money is
     a. 1/3.
     b. 3.
     c. 5.
     d. 4.
Answer: b

33. Money demand
     a. varies inversely with the interest rate.
     b. varies directly with the interest rate.
     c. depends primarily upon variables other than income.
     d. must always be the same value as national income.
Answer: a

34. The chairman of the Federal Reserve System today is
     a. Paul Volcker.
     b. Alan Greenspan.
     c. John Maynard Keynes.
     d. Fred Tyson.
Answer: b

35. Which economist predicted that population growth rates will surpass economic
     growth rates, resulting in famine, war, and higher mortality rates among human
     populations?
     a. Adam Smith
     b. Karl Marx
     c. John Maynard Keynes
     d. Thomas Malthus
Answer: d

36. A decline in economic activity is usually referred to as
     a. a bear market.
     b. a business cycle.
     c. an economic recession.
     d. a business peak.
Answer: c

37. People demand money balances

a. for protection against inflation.

b. to pay their taxes.

c. for the purpose of collecting interest payments.

d. for transaction purposes.

Answer: d

38. Deflation is

a. an increase in the general level of prices.

b. an increase in the prices of oil, steel, and food.

c. an increase in the prices of services but not goods.

d. a decrease in the general level of prices.

Answer: d

39. The monetary policy committee of the Federal Reserve is referred to as

a. the Federal Reserve Open Market Committee.

b. the President's Council of Economic Advisors.

c. the Federal Reserve Board of Governors.

d. the Congressional Committee on Monetary Policy.

Answer: a

40. According to Keynesian economists, changes in monetary policy affect

a. potential GNP.

b. government spending.

c. investment spending.

d. aggregate supply.

Answer: c

41. A change in government spending levels would be considered to be a change in

a. supply-side policy.

b. automatic monetary policy.

c. fiscal policy.

d. monetary policy.

Answer: c

42. The Federal Reserve

a. is often called the "banker's banker."

b. regulates the commercial banking sector.

c. allows banks to borrow reserves from other banks.

d. was established by Congress in 1913.

e. is or does all of the above.

Answer: e

43. At full employment output, the equation of exchange (*ceteris paribus*) suggests that there is a relationship between the money stock and

a. the general price level.

b. real GNP.

c. the interest rate.

d. the unemployment rate.

Answer: a

44. The liquidity of an asset is inversely related to

a. differences between assets and liabilities.

b. the price of the asset.

c. the profitability of investing in stocks or bonds.

d. transaction costs incurred in converting an asset into money.

Answer: d

45. Which economist argued that capitalism was an exploitative and unstable economic system and was doomed to failure?

a. Adam Smith

b. Karl Marx

c. John Maynard Keynes

d. Thomas Malthus

Answer: b

46. The Federal Reserve Open Market Committee has _____ members.

a. five

b. twelve

c. seven

d. ten

Answer: b

47. When money is used to determine relative prices, it is acting as a

a. standard unit of account.

b. medium of exchange.

c. store of value.

d. standard of deferred payment.

Answer: a

48. Which of the following is *not* an institution of capitalism?

 a. Free markets
 b. Private property
 c. Moral incentives
 d. Individualism

Answer: c

49. As interest rates decline, people generally choose to hold

 a. more money and fewer nonmonetary assets.
 b. less money and fewer nonmonetary assets.
 c. more money and more nonmonetary assets.
 d. less money and more nonmonetary assets.

Answer: a

50. A decline in nominal national income would generally be expected to

 a. decrease money demand at every interest rate.
 b. increase money demand at every interest rate.
 c. have no effect on money demand.
 d. affect money demand only if interest rates are rising.

Answer: a

> I tell my students that for this type of question they should draw a diagram to find the correct answer.

51. Which of the following is *not* an institution of socialism?

 a. Private property
 b. Economic planning
 c. Communist Party rule
 d. Cooperation

Answer: a

52. If nominal national income remains constant and the money supply increases, the

 a. nominal interest rate will rise.
 b. nominal interest rate will fall.
 c. money demand curve will shift to the right.
 d. money demand curve will shift to the left.

Answer: b

> I tell my students that for this type of question they should draw a diagram to find the correct answer.

53. If Federal Reserve monetary policy sets an operating target for the money stock, then

   a. the money supply curve is horizontal.
   b. the money demand curve is vertical.
   c. the money supply curve is vertical.
   d. the money demand curve is horizontal.

Answer: c

I tell my students that for this type of question they should draw a diagram to find the correct answer.

54. If Federal Reserve monetary policy sets an operating target for interest rates, then the U.S. money supply will vary

   a. positively with the interest rate.
   b. negatively with the interest rate.
   c. positively with the demand for money.
   d. negatively with the demand for money.

Answer: c

I tell my students that for this type of question they should draw a diagram to find the correct answer.

55. The decision-making structure found in a country using the economic system of planned socialism is considered to be

   a. democratic.
   b. centralized.
   c. decentralized.
   d. utopian.

Answer: b

56. The Harrod-Domar growth model links _____ to the rate of economic growth.

   a. savings and investment
   b. imports and exports
   c. population growth rates
   d. government spending

Answer: a

57. The "vicious cycle of poverty theory" argues that Third World poverty is the result of

   a. developed countries.

b. rapid population growth.

c. a low saving rate.

d. primitive technology.

Answer: c

58. In less-developed countries, which sector of the economy provides the majority of the population with employment?

a. Manufacturing

b. Services

c. Industry

d. Agriculture

Answer: d

59. The Soviet leader who implemented the world's first centrally planned economy was

a. Vladimir Lenin.

b. Karl Marx.

c. Joseph Stalin.

d. Mikhail Gorbachev.

Answer: c

60. Which Soviet leader is considered the father of the Russian Revolution? This man also established the Communist Party.

a. Vladimir Lenin

b. Karl Marx

c. Joseph Stalin

d. Mikhail Gorbachev

Answer: a

PART FOUR

FOR YOUR REFERENCE

CHAPTER 30

A GLOSSARY OF ECONOMICS

Absolute advantage The ability of one country or entity to produce a good using fewer resources per unit than its trading partners.

Aggregate demand schedule A schedule relating aggregate demand to various price levels.

Aggregate supply schedule A schedule relating aggregate supply to various price levels.

Average propensity to consume (APC) The ratio of consumption expenditures to disposable income.

Average propensity to save (APS) The ratio of personal saving to disposable income.

Average total cost (AC) The mean cost per unit of output (total cost divided by total output).

Balance of payments An account recording a nation's international transactions.

Business cycle The pattern of rises and declines in national output.

Ceteris paribus Latin for "all else being equal"; a fundamental simplification (assumption) in many economic models.

Circular flow A model of the movement of resources, goods, and services among broad sectors of the economy.

Comparative advantage The ability to produce a given good at a lower opportunity cost.

Demand The quantity of a good that consumers are prepared to purchase at a given time and under given circumstances.

Demand curve A graphic plot of the quantities of a good demanded at each possible price.

Elasticity The ratio of the percent change in quantity supplied/demanded to the percent change in the price of the good.

Equilibrium The state in which no market forces operate to cause a firm to change its output, a household to change its consumption pattern, or a market to bring about changes in price or quantity supplied.

Financial intermediaries Institutions (such as banks) that borrow funds from savers and loan them to other individuals or institutions.

Fiscal policy The use of taxes and spending by a government to achieve desired economic goals.

Fixed cost (FC) The costs that a firm incurs irrespective of output quantity.

Full employment Employment of 93 or 96 percent of the labor force.

Giffen good A good whose demand decreases when price goes down. Contrast *normal good*.

Gross national product (GNP) The total value (in money) of all final goods produced by an economy during a year.

Indifference curve A curve showing the combinations of goods that yield the household the same total utility, so that the household is indifferent to distinctions among the combinations.

Indifference map A graphic representation of all the indifference curves (each representing a different level of total utility) of a household.

Inferior good A good for which quantity demanded falls as household income increases or as its price increases. Households substitute a more desirable (and more expensive) good for an inferior good.

Inflation An increase in the general level of prices.

Inputs Land, labor, capital, and raw materials that firms purchase to produce output. These are also the factors of production.

Keynesian theory The assumption that prices are rigid and that real output adjusts to changes in expenditures.

Law of demand A law stating that as the price of a normal good falls, quantity demanded increases, and vice versa.

Law of supply A law stating that as the price of a normal good falls, quantity supplied decreases, and vice versa.

Long run The time period during which all costs become variable costs.

Macroeconomics The study of the economy as a whole.

Marginal cost (MC) The costs a firm incurs in producing one additional unit of output.

Marginal efficiency of capital (NEC) The annual rate of return on each additional investment dollar.

Marginal factor cost (MFC) The additional cost to a firm of using one additional unit of an input.

Marginal physical product (MRP) The output obtained by using one additional unit of an input.

Marginal propensity to consume (MPC) The additional quantity consumed given one additional dollar of disposable income.

Marginal propensity to save (MPS) The change in saving for a one-dollar change in disposable income.

Marginal revenue The revenue received from the sale of one additional unit of output.

Marginal revenue product (MRP) The revenue received from selling the additional output produced by using a marginal unit of an input.

Marginal utility (MU) The utility the consumer receives as a result of consuming one additional unit of a good.

Market The entity in which goods are exchanged and equilibrium prices and quantities supplied are determined.

Microeconomics The study of the interaction of individual elements in the economy, such as firms and households.

Model A simplified representation of a real-world phenomenon.

Monetary policy A policy to manage the rate of growth of a nation's money supply to achieve desired economic goals.

Money A generally accepted medium of exchange.

Monopolistic competition A market with many firms, a differentiated product, and easy entry.

Monopoly A market in which a single firm produces all of the quantity supplied and the entry of new firms is impossible.

Net national product (NNP) The net money value of final goods and services produced in the economy during a year.

Normal good A good for which consumer demand increases as consumer income increases.

Oligopoly A market with few firms, dominated by a single or few large firms; product differentiation may or may not exist.

Opportunity cost The value of one alternative that is given up in choosing another alternative.

Output The quantity of a good that a firm makes that is put on the market.

Perfect competition A market with many firms, none of which alone is large enough to affect the market. Product is undifferentiated, perfect knowledge exists, entry and exit are easy, and MR = P.

Phillips curve A graphic representation of the trade-off between inflation and unemployment.

Price The value (in money) that must be exchanged to acquire a unit of a good.

Price leadership A market with few firms in which firms follow the pricing behavior of a dominant firm.

Production possibilities frontier (PPF) A curve representing the various combinations of goods that a society is capable of producing at any given time given fixed technology and resources, the resources being fully and efficiently employed.

Profit maximization The objective of the firm; the point at which MR = MC.

Public good A good supplied to all consumers, regardless of who pays or fails to pay for it. A public good is not diminished by consumption.

Quantity demanded The quantity of a good that consumers will buy at a given price.

Quantity supplied The quantity of a good that firms will produce at a given price.

Recession A decline in GNP for at least two consecutive quarters.

Scarcity The fundamental assumption of economics, which holds that resources are insufficient to satisfy all wants, needs, and desires.

Short run The span of time during which at least one input is fixed.

Stagflation A combination of inflation and recession.

Supply The willingness and ability of firms to produce and sell goods.

Supply-side economics An economic approach aimed at achieving efficiency by using government policies to stimulate production.

Total cost (TC) The sum of fixed and variable costs.

Total revenue (TR) The total amount of money, at a given price, spent by consumers on a given good and received by firms.

Total utility (TU) The sum of the utility a household receives from all goods on which it spends its income.

Utility The usefulness (satisfaction) derived from consuming goods.

Utility maximization The objective of the household's decisions regarding consumption.

Variable cost (VC) Cost to the firm of inputs that vary with output.

CHAPTER 31

RECOMMENDED READING

Bruchey, Stuart. *Enterprise: The Dynamic Economy of a Free People.* Cambridge, Mass.: Harvard University Press, 1990.

Carnes, W. Stansbury, and Stephen D. Slifer. *The Atlas of Economic Indicators.* New York: HarperCollins Publishers, 1991.

Casler, Stephen D. *Introduction to Economics.* New York: HarperCollins Publishers, 1992.

Cranford, John. *Budgeting for America.* Washington, D.C.. Congressional Quarterly, 1989.

Friedman, Milton. *Episodes in Monetary History: Money Mischief.* New York: Harcourt Brace Jovanovich, 1992.

Greider, William. *Secrets of the Temple: How the Federal Reserve Runs the Country.* New York: Simon and Schuster, 1987.

Griswold, Erwin N. *Federal Taxation: Cases and Materials.* Brooklyn, N.Y.: The Foundation Press, Inc., 1966.

Hamermesh, Daniel S., and Albert Rees. *The Economics of Work and Play.* New York: HarperCollins, 1993.

Heilbroner, Robert. *Debt and Deficit.* New York: W. W. Norton, 1989.

Hughes, Jonathan. *American Economic History.* New York: HarperCollins, 1990.

Krugman, Paul. *The Age of Diminished Expectations: U.S. Economic Policy in the 1990s.* Cambridge, Mass.: MIT Press, 1990.

Lebergott, Stanley. *Wealth and Want.* Princeton, N.J.: Princeton University Press, 1975.

Myers, Margaret G. *A Financial History of the United States.* New York: Columbia University Press, 1970.

Okun, Arthur. *Equality and Efficiency: The Big Tradeoff.* Washington, D.C.: The Brookings Institution, 1975.

Petersen, H. Craig. *Business and Government.* New York: HarperCollins, 1993.

Phillips, Kevin. *The Politics of Rich and Poor: Wealth and the American Electorate in the Reagan Aftermath.* New York: Random House, 1990.

Porter, Michael E. *The Competitive Advantage of Nations.* New York: The Free Press, 1990.

Russell, Cheryl, and Margaret Ambry. *The Official Guide to American Incomes.* Ithaca, N.Y.: New Strategist, 1993.

_____ *The Official Guide to the American Marketplace.* Ithaca, N.Y.: New Strategist, 1992.

Schwartz, E. L. *Longman's Economics: Our American Economy.* White Plains, N.Y.: Longman, 1994.

Somers, Albert T., with Lucie R. Blau. *The U.S. Economy Demystified.* New York: Lexington Books/Macmillan, 1993.

Walton, Gary M., and Hugh Rockoff. *History of the American Economy.* Fort Worth: The Dryden Press, 1994.

Wessels, Walter J. *Economics*, 2d ed. Hauppauge, N.Y.: Barron's Educational Series, 1993.

Wildavsky, Aaron. *The New Politics of the Budgetary Process.* New York: HarperCollins, 1992.

Note: This index covers Part One: Preparing Yourself and Part Two: Study Guide, pages vii-127 of the text. Material in the sample exams, pages 130-318, is not indexed.